The Great Good Place

The Great Good Place

The Country House and English Literature

MALCOLM KELSALL

Columbia University Press

New York

Columbia University Press
New York
Copyright © 1993 Columbia University Press
All rights reserved.

Library of Congress Cataloging-in-Publication Data

Kelsall, M. M. (Malcolm Miles). 1938–
  The great good place : the country house and English literature /
Malcolm Kelsall.
    p. cm.
  Includes bibliographical references and index.
  ISBN 0–231–08146–4
  1. English literature – History and criticism. 2. Country homes –
Great Britain – Historiography. 3. Country life – Great Britain –
Historiography. 4. Literature and society – Great Britain.
5. Historic buildings – Great Britain. 6. Literary landmarks – Great
Britain. 7. Country homes in literature. 8. Country life in
literature. 9. Dwellings in literature. 10. Manors in literature.
I. Title.
PR408.C65K45   1993
820.9′355—dc20   92–29879
                                                           CIP

Printed and bound in Great Britain

c   10 9 8 7 6 5 4 3 2 1

Contents

Plates

Acknowledgements

THE AUTHOR gratefully acknowledges permission to reproduce the following plates: 1, 26, 35, copyright The National Trust; 3, Barratt Developments plc; 4, private owner; 13, Mrs J. Loudon; 15, Pitkin Publications; 16, London Borough of Richmond upon Thames; 17, Devonshire Collection, Chatsworth. Reproduced by permission of the Chatsworth Settlement Trustees; 25, 27, 28, 36, *Country Life*; 30, The British Architectural Library, RIBA, London; 34, courtesy of Cardiff City Council.

Prologue
'To Penshurst'

THOU ART not, Penshurst, built to envious show,
Of touch, or marble; nor canst boast a row
Of polish'd pillars, or a roof of gold:
Thou hast no lantern, whereof tales are told;
Or stair, or courts; but stand'st an ancient pile,
And these grudg'd at, art reverenc'd the while.
Thou joy'st in better marks, of soil, of air,
Of wood, of water: therein thou art fair.
Thou hast thy walks for health, as well as sport:
Thy Mount, to which the Dryads do resort,
Where Pan, and Bacchus their high feasts have made,
Beneath the broad beech, and the chestnut shade;
That taller tree, which of a nut was set,
At his great birth, where all the Muses met.
There, in the writhed bark, are cut the names
Of many a Sylvane, taken with his flames.
And thence, the ruddy Satyrs oft provoke
The lighter Fauns, to reach thy lady's oak.
Thy copse, too, nam'd of Gamage, thou hast there,
That never fails to serve thee season'd deer,
When thou would'st feast, or exercise thy friends.
The lower land, that to the river bends,
Thy sheep, thy bullocks, kine, and calves do feed:
The middle ground thy mares, and horses breed.
Each bank doth yield thee conies; and the tops
Fertile of wood, Ashore, and Sydney's copse,
To crown thy open table, doth provide
The purpled pheasant, with the speckled side:
The painted partridge lies in every field,
And, for thy mess, is willing to be kill'd.
And if the high-swoll'n Medway fail thy dish,
Thou hast thy ponds, that pay thee tribute fish,
Fat, aged carps, that run into thy net.

And pikes, now weary their own kind to eat,
As loth, the second draught, or cast to stay,
Officiously, at first, themselves betray.
Bright eels, that emulate them, and leap on land,
Before the fisher, or into his hand.
Then hath thy orchard fruit, thy garden flowers,
Fresh as the air, and new as are the hours.
The early cherry, with the later plum,
Fig, grape, and quince, each in his time doth come:
The blushing apricot, and woolly peach
Hang on thy walls, that every child may reach.
And though thy walls be of the country stone,
They're rear'd with no mans ruin, no mans groan,
There's none, that dwell about them, wish them down;
But all come in, the farmer and the clown:
And no one empty-handed, to salute
Thy lord, and lady, though they have no suit.
Some bring a capon, some a rural cake,
Some nuts, some apples; some that think they make
The better cheeses, bring 'em; or else send
By their ripe daughters, whom they would commend
This way to husbands; and whose baskets bear
An emblem of themselves, in plum, or pear.
But what can this (more than express their love)
Add to thy free provisions, far above
The need of such? whose liberal board doth flow,
With all, that hospitality doth know!
Where comes no guest, but is allow'd to eat,
Without his fear, and of thy lord's own meat:
Where the same beer, and bread, and self-same wine,
That is his lordship's, shall be also mine.
And I not fain to sit (as some, this day,
At great mens tables) and yet dine away.
Here no man tells my cups; nor, standing by,
A waiter, doth my gluttony envy:
But gives me what I call, and lets me eat,
He knows, below, he shall find plenty of meat,
Thy tables hoard not up for the next day,
Nor, when I take my lodging, need I pray
For fire, or lights, or livery: all is there;
As if thou, then, wert mine, or I reign'd here:
There's nothing I can wish, for which I stay.
That found King James, when hunting late, this way,
With his brave son, the Prince, they saw thy fires
Shine bright on every hearth as the desires

Of thy Penates had been set on flame,
To entertain them; or the country came,
With all their zeal, to warm their welcome here.
What (great, I will not say, but) sudden cheer
Did'st thou, then, make 'em! and what praise was heap'd
On thy good lady, then! who, therein, reap'd
The just reward of her high huswifery;
To have her linen, plate, and all things nigh,
When she was far: and not a room, but dress'd,
As if it had expected such a guest!
These, Penshurst, are thy praise, and yet not all.
Thy lady's noble, fruitful, chaste withal.
His children thy great lord may call his own:
A fortune, in this age, but rarely known.
They are, and have been taught religion: thence
Their gentler spirits have suck'd innocence.
Each morn, and even, they are taught to pray,
With the whole household, and may, every day,
Read, in their virtuous parents' noble parts,
The mysteries of manners, arms, and arts.
Now, Penshurst, they that will proportion thee
With other edifices, when they see
Those proud, ambitious heaps, and nothing else,
May say, their lords have built, but thy lord dwells.
(BEN JONSON, 1572/3–1637)

PART ONE

Building

CHAPTER ONE

The English country house
National Trust and national symbol

THE GREAT HOUSE at Uppark was destroyed by fire late in the 1980s. That has been the fate of other country houses. But Uppark has a special destiny, for it is the property of one of England's wealthiest charities. The National Trust will restore it. One of the great hurricanes of the twentieth century has savaged that restoration. With Roman pertinacity the National Trust will return to its work. Brick by brick at Uppark 'the romance of its history' – so the Trust calls it – will re-emerge perfected by craftsmanship. That seems to be right, to be the English way. Abroad, in France, Jacobinical mobs once plundered the country houses of a hated aristocracy. But Uppark, on the contrary, was formerly chosen as a potential gift by the English nation to the Duke of Wellington, whose armies had extirpated the scourge of Jacobinism from Europe. In the general's native Ireland, within living memory, national indignation has set fire to the homes of an exploitative Ascendancy class. But in England the loss of a great house would be a tragedy. Its restoration is an act of piety, for it is in trust to the nation.

The socialist son of a servant at Uppark earlier this century perceived the signification of this conservatism. In the symbolic language of a novel he changed the name Uppark to Bladesover, recalling in that name both the chivalry of old, and the decay of the ancient aristocracy. This great house (Pl. 1), he wrote, 'illuminates' the condition of England:

I find in Bladesover the clue to all England. There have been no revolutions or abandonments of opinion in England since the days of the fine gentry, since 1688 or thereabouts, the days when Bladesover was built; there have been changes, dissolving forces, replacing forces, if you will; but then it was that the broad lines of the English system set firmly. (*Tono-Bungay*, II, 1)

That 'English system' was not merely the vestige of the old order still visibly written on the face of the countryside in great house and church, dependent farm and village. It embraced the whole nation, and, spreading from the country house might be read even in the architectural language of the city. The parks and museums, the great houses of London, were the most obvious signs of Bladesover. But the class structure of the middle-class suburbs, or the very upstairs-downstairs design of tenement houses, suggested the influence of the country house. The lower classes imitated the rich. The upwardly mobile 'hero' of this novel, inflated from keeper of a chemist's shop to millionaire, can express himself in no better way than by the purchase of an old 'stately home', Lady Grove, then in the construction of his own gargantuan folly, Crest Hill. That is the English way.

H. G. Wells was writing socialist satire. But his novel is itself permeated with deep nostalgia for that very Bladesover system from which the servile child escaped to become a writer.[1] There is about the English country house something more than the hierarchical snobbery of an exhausted social order. In the library the working-class child acquired a liberal education; in the park he learnt something of the sense of beauty.

Bladesover, in absorbing the whole country-side, had not altogether missed greatness. The Bladesover system has at least done one good thing for England, it has abolished the peasant habit of mind. If many of us still live and breathe pantry and housekeeper's room, we are quit of the dream of living and economizing parasitically on hens and pigs. . . . About that park there were some elements of a liberal education; there was a great space of greensward not given over to manure and food grubbing; there was mystery, there was matter for the imagination. (I, 5)

In becoming a writer, Wells had absorbed, inevitably, something of Bladesover. It was a carrier of culture. Though the obsolete house was now rented out to vulgar money, in the mind of the artist there remained a sense of something far more deeply interfused: 'there was mystery, there was matter for the imagination.'

It is a general feeling. Every English summer some hundreds of Bladesovers, survivors of time's decay and taxation's depredations, open their doors to a migratory horde of visitors. The great view of Longleat from Heaven's Gate above is now dominated by a visitors' car park besides which the palace of glass floats like an exhalation. Country house visiting is a national pastime. An observer from a foreign planet might wonder at the cause of the migration. The crowds are not impelled by mere idleness. It is not an obvious amusement to file in a ritual line through state rooms. An effort of the intelligence and the aesthetic imagination is needed to come to terms with the extraordinary visual display. Some hunger of the imagination, so Wells might claim, compels the eye to feed upon these signs from the past. Or is this a ritual act of folk memory performed by the tribe without knowing why, but because this ritual defines the tribe? The English people long since lost the uniqueness of their island language in the *lingua franca* of the world, and have lost their imperial role too like the Romans before them. It is necessary, therefore, that certain signs should define identity, and those signs are essentially conservative, the preservation of the landmarks of the past, peculiar to the history of this tribe in this place.

This is mere speculation – as if the country house were the national equivalent now of a place of pilgrimage (or even, to change the context, England's answer to Lenin's tomb). But conservative writing about the English country house this century has often turned to a national theme. One of its early historians, Hermann Muthesius, saw the love for such houses as an essential sign of the race.[2] He admired the whole of England as a great landscaped garden embellished with houses, each a sign of the self-sufficiency and independence of their owners. There was in the English, he thought, an inborn love of the beauty of the countryside, and an instinct to create 'a permanent dwelling place' expressive of the artistic culture of the people and their deep affinity with Nature. Set in contradistinction to the nomadic life of the city, the country house was the essential expression of England.

Muthesius, writing in the first decade of this century, was responding to the work of William Morris and to that vernacular architectural tradition which was to reach its apogee in the work of Sir Edwin Lutyens. The National Trust had already been founded, and *Country Life* had commenced publication. The sense that the country house was an essential expressive sign of England was already widespread. It runs on through the century. For Sackville-West, writing in the 1920s, a great palace like Knole was to stand as an emblem of the community, for the English, she believed, were at heart a rural folk, still tied together by their love of the countryside.

Knole was no mere excrescence, no alien fabrication, no startling stranger set between the beeches and the oaks. No other country but England could have produced it, and into no other country would it settle with such harmony and such quiet. . . . From the top of a tower one looks down upon the acreage of roofs, and the effect is less that of a palace than of a jumbled village upon the hillside.[3]

The great house is harmonised with the natural countryside. It is like a village, a sign of a people living together, not a palace, expressive of the grandeur and remoteness of power.

So also at Chatsworth today (one of the most popular places of contemporary pilgrimage) the visitor is told by its owner that this is 'not a palace, not a castle, not a museum', but a house loved and served by generations of Dukes of Devonshire as 'stewards and housekeepers', as though they kept their house in trust for all the nation (Pl. 2).

The house looks permanent; as permanent as if it had been there, not for a few hundred years, but for ever. It fits its landscape exactly. . . . The stone from which the house is built comes out of the ground nearby, and so it is the proper colour. . . .

5

All there is to be seen appears to have arrived by nature as though it fell into place without effort, and the ease and pleasure with which the eye takes it in underlines this feeling of accident rather than design. The highest compliment which can be paid about any new work done in the house, garden or park is to say it looks as if it had always been there.[4]

The great country house, it is claimed, is a natural excrescence. It has not been built so much as grown by organic process from the English soil. It is not a social phenomenon, but gives the impression of being out of time, 'as if it had always been there'. Thus, it is as much part of England as the rocks and stones and trees.

There is nothing eccentric about this view. It is not merely the apologia of an owner of great riches and an archaic property. *The Independent* newspaper recently carried a promotional article on the 'Devonshire', a four bedroomed house of the Barratt Premier Collection. The name 'Devonshire' alludes both to the county, and to the title of the owners of Chatsworth. Aggrieved builders had found that the English were not enamoured of the theory of the modern movement, and the article records that 'People are looking for a sense of place, to have a community feel . . . people want something they can feel comfortable in and can understand how it functions.'[5] Two detached houses in a rural setting illustrated the theme (Pl. 3). One, like the ancestral home of the Dukes of Devonshire, appears to be built from natural stone (in fact, stone-cladding), as if it 'comes out of the ground nearby'. A prominent chimney stack is expressive of hearth and home (though the house is centrally heated), and the visitor to the domestic hearth is welcomed at a gabled 'Tudor' entrance. But the porch before the door is neoclassically 'Georgian', and above it is the central section of a 'Palladian' window – for the architecture of neoclassicism is expressive of taste and style. The assemblage of the vernacular, both Tudor and Georgian, incorporates in its melange the whole history of the English country house, as if, to repeat the words in praise of Chatsworth, 'the highest compliment which can be paid about any new work . . . is to say it looks as if it had always been there.'

The other 'Devonshire' house is equally traditional. It is photographed against a screen of trees across a symbolic drawbridge crossing a miniaturised lake cum moat defensive. The house, hip roofed, tile hung, seen in this way is part castle (an Englishman's home is his castle), part vernacular cottage, blending with the natural world of the landscape, or landscaped park. The half-timbered gabled structure above the doorway is remarkable. The style of this bay is popularly known as 'stock-broker Tudor', a phrase expressive of new money going into old property. It is derived from the nineteenth-century arts and crafts movement, and deliberately recalls a vernacular cruck house. But any student of the eighteenth century will see too the same form as Marc-Antoine Laugier delineated then as the classic and original primitive hut, the first home of the human race, and which directly originated from nature and the trees of the forest.[6] It was believed that this original house too was formed from a timber gable upon a rectilinear timber frame. This was the natural way mankind first built – so it was claimed. There is, thus, a direct link between the Barratt Premier Collection, the palace of Chatsworth and primitive mankind. It takes us back to Adam and Eve themselves embowered in Paradise: 'the house looks permanent; as if it had been there, not for a few hundred years, but for ever.'

These historical links are there in the English house as intrinsically as the motions of the blood in the body retain immemorially the flux of the primeval oceans responsive to the phases of the moon. When socialist Wells wrote that Bladesover is England, and conservative Sackville-West saw Knole as 'a natural growth' of English soil, both were responding to an historical continuity so much part of the inherited culture that it is inescapable in the very doorknockers and windowpanes of suburbia: 'people are looking for a sense of place, to have a community feel. . . .' These things have been there as an inherited language from generation to generation.

What follows is an attempt to narrate how this has come to be. Like all histories it tells a story, and this is a story of fictions, of the way the country house has been represented to English people, how the leaves of the tree relate to its roots, of how and why we are as we are. It is a conservative history. The concern is with the idealisation of what Henry James called 'the great good place': the country house as the affectionate mind would wish it to be. That wish was often at variance with social and economic reality – to put it mildly. That is self-evident historically. The divide may still be seen in contemporary writing about the country house. The shelves of National Trust bookshops glitter with sumptuous picture books of stately homes; in the severer ambience of university libraries the reader is more likely to find the hostile analysis of theoretical Marxism. Since the year of revolutions – 1989 – that divide looks sharper still. But two ways of looking at things are implicit even in the most imaginatively beautiful transformatory writing about the great good place. The chapters which follow are merely a chronicle of an ideal representation, but an ideal often self-aware of its own fragility and imaginative status.

The emphasis is upon literature, for literature has been pre-eminently both the carrier of values from generation to generation between the writers and readers of books, and the creator of their values. But houses too may be 'read'. They are icons. Written sign and architectural sign reflect one another. Writers interpret what they see, and the way in which things are seen is conditioned by how they are described. There is no firm division between the visual arts and literature. Nor is there a clear divide between what might be called 'high culture' and the everyday. Great houses, like Penshurst or Stowe, have been made famous by writers, but even the domestic stoves at Kedleston, designed by Robert Adam, have resonances which carry the reader back to classical antiquity, for they appear to be antique urns. A novel and a great landscape garden, a National Trust guidebook and the design of a dormer window, all form part of an imaginative spectrum of meaning. Images beget images, and human beings are creatures of the imagination as much as of reason.

Two genetic codes of representation combine to give birth to this story.[7] Both are clearly written on the face of the Barratt home. One comes from classical antiquity, the other from the Gothic world. The classic world is the parent of much in the Gothic tradition, for the Goths read and creatively responded to the literature of the ancient world. Admittedly, the genetic image, like all metaphors, is imperfect for the very word 'code' is suggestive of a precision of form and motif which history does not supply. But certain elements will be seen endlessly to repeat themselves, to form, as it were, a grammar of expression, and yet, in infinite permutation, in ever changing context, to defy the pretence of scientific reduction.

Inevitably, the chapters that follow are selective in their examples. The concern is with the significant works that carry the conservative ideal. This is not a gazetteer of country house references, nor a record of what can be said against the idea of the great good place. Selectivity is easier from classical antiquity for only a limited body of writing survives. In English literature this is a more problematical matter, but there seem three major phases of transmission. There is firstly a genre of country house poetry in the seventeenth and eighteenth centuries which extends from Ben Jonson to Pope before diffusing itself in a plethora of second-rate poems in praise of estates. In the lifetime of Pope the country house ideal 'colonises' the new fictional form of the novel. Fielding's Paradise Hall, Richardson's Grandison Hall, establish a tradition in prose of which the most significant heir is Jane Austen. Ultimately, at the end of the nineteenth century, a later phase of the tradition emerges in the fiction of Henry James and his followers in the twentieth-century novel. There is a period between Austen and James, however, when the conservative ideal may be seen as progressively tattered or irrelevant in an industrialised society. What is remarkable is the way that it survives even at opposite political poles, both in the Young England writing of the future conservative Prime Minister, Benjamin Disraeli, and in the revolutionary socialism of William Morris.

The modern part of this story is, inevitably, the more familiar and easiest of access. The classical culture which first shapes the ideal is now as remote as the waters of the moon, yet it is the well-spring of modern culture, inescapably still with us. Even the world of the Renaissance has to be recuperated. But the comprehension of the present involves understanding how things came to be as they are, and the progress of this story is cumulative. Each repetition of the elements confirms and develops. As one comes to the familiar things of the present they change their shape in their new, yet ancient, tradition.

CHAPTER TWO

The Roman villa

IT IS APPROPRIATE to begin with an image (Pl. 4). It is a painting in oil by the British artist Richard Wilson, the date *c.* 1769–70. The image is mysterious. The richly wooded landscape and the foaming stream, the mountain in the background, which marries with the great swell of heavenly cloud, might suggest romantic Wales or Arcadian Lake District. A country house stands across the stream. The classical portico and four-square simplicity indicates a villa in the Palladian style, although the stepped upper storey, a kind of belvedere, is unusual. Perhaps the owner enjoyed the vista over what may be a landscaped park to the left, suitably decorated with 'pastoral' kine, and beyond to the spectacularly picturesque scenery. It could be any gentleman's seat of Wilson's time, except for the three figures in the foreground, for they are clad in classical togas. Two appear in solemn thought and procession, like figures from a frieze, the third is gesturing towards the ancient, circumambient trees.

Literature supplies the necessary gloss. The picture was known as 'Cicero'. The subject is drawn from the second book of the statesman's *De Legibus* (*Of the Laws*). There Cicero's brother Atticus describes just such a scene, as he and Cicero and their friend Quintus met at the statesman's villa at Arpinum to discuss high principles of State and of Justice. It is an ideal image derived from an ideal text, flattering to the owner of any English country house who might purchase it, for it suggests an affinity between his own residence and Arpinum, between an English patrician and the greatest statesman, orator and philosopher of republican Rome. At home, in one's own house on one's own land, true friendship and true thought might responsibly grow together, and one might too 'illustrate one's dignity by the splendour of one's life'. So Middleton, the biographer of Cicero, wrote.

The painting is suffused in a gentle but radiant light which, like the paintings of Claude or of Poussin, translates an already distant past into a dream-like vision. There is too an elegiac quality in that vision. It would remind the cultured man of the passing of a great civilisation, at this very moment becoming unhinged. For Cicero was murdered (43 BC) in the

10

bloody proscriptions of the civil wars which followed the assassination of Julius Caesar. The purity of the republic was soon to be debauched by the luxury and corruption of a declining empire. The image might serve, thus, both as a recollection of an ideal, familiarised in a British landscape, suffused with the radiance of a dream; and also as a *memento mori*, a reminder that civilisation is fragile, subject to decay, and that this ancient villa was now no more than a few ruined stones reabsorbed by the forces of Nature. To spread these ideas more widely, the image was promulgated downwards through the social hierarchy. The painting was 'popularised' by William Woollett's engraving of 1778, dedicated to Sir John Smith (a probable purchaser of the original).

This image of the classic villa represents one of the great motifs of the country house tradition, taken up by the English imagination from the writings of antiquity.[1] As Rome, so England. But it was already archaic and conservative by the time of Cicero himself. The statesman's philosophical idealisation of life in the rural villa owes much to the myth of the origins of the Roman people. That story told how a primitive farming folk of old, whose hardy virtue sprang from the soil, colonised Italy, and then the whole of the Mediterranean world. The founding patriarch, Romulus, had lived in a simple thatched hut like a poor countryman; it was reverentially preserved on the Capitoline Hill. Agriculture is next to wisdom, claimed Cicero himself. Though he was no farmer, farmers were of especial esteem. The literature of the country house in the Roman world has its roots in the myth of the original virtuous yeomanry. That literature is written, however, by the citizens of a sophisticated, metropolitan centred, empire.

The ancient warrior farmers of Rome are as much creatures of the imagination as the knights of Malory in English literature. They are especially the creation of the historian Livy (59 BC–AD 17), and by the time they stalked across the early pages of his *History of Rome*, it was believed that the 'last of the Romans' of that ilk were dead at Philippi (42 BC). It was many centuries since Cincinnatus the farmer had been summoned from his 'four acres' of ploughland to become dictator, defeat the enemy and within sixteen days lay down his office and return to the plough. The thatched hut of Romulus belonged to an even mistier past. It suggests affinities with the lost Golden Age. One of the fundamental myths of Mediterranean culture is that of a time when the earth brought forth its fruits of its own volition (*sponte sua*) and the human race lived in perfect harmony with Nature before the coming of war or law or commerce. As Hesiod wrote in *Works and Days*: 'remote and free from evil and grief men had all good things, for the fruitful earth unforced bore them fruit abundantly and without stint.' It followed that their houses were such as Nature itself might supply, natural in form, created without

11

the interpolation of an architect. Seneca, the Stoic philosopher (5/4 BC–AD 65), went so far as to claim that the fortunate first folk slept happy and secure in the open air.

There hung no fretted or panelled ceilings over them; but the stars quietly glided above them as they lay beneath the open sky, and the noble pageant of the night, the firmament, swept swiftly by, in silence conducting the mighty work. (*Epistles* XC. 42)

He wrote in the first century of the Christian era, and Christian tradition later reconciled itself with the classical ideal. So Milton, deeply embued with Stoicism, was to praise the bower of Adam and Eve, woven with flowers, where the great parents of mankind slept side by side like the very beasts on their grassy couch, or like birds in their nest:

> Sleep on,
> Blest pair; and O yet happiest if ye seek
> No happier state, and know no more to know.
> (*Paradise Lost*, IV, 773–5)

It is a motif English garden ornament will recreate in sylvan hermit's grotto or Gothic cottage, an Edenic ideal recalled too in English literature. So Fielding's Squire Allworthy lives at Paradise Hall, and Maria Fairfax, the restorer of Appleton House to an unfallen world, will be heralded by Marvell as 'paradise's only map'. Origins are holy.

The tougher reality which Seneca or Cicero knew was the Roman farmstead, that basic agricultural unit which rural industry dictates, working buildings grouped about a dwelling, the choice of site dictated by the necessities of produce and cattle. It is described in detail by the writers on rural economy, Cato, Varro and Columella. But for Varro, writing in the first century BC, the countryside was already suffering from gentrification. The rich build for ostentation, not for use, he complained. They aspire to the luxury of a Lucullus, that glutton known for the variety of his dining halls and the artifice of his pleasure grounds.

For Columella, a century later, that process of gentrification was already complete. The country house (*villa urbana*) was separated from storehouse (*villa fructuaria*) or working farm (*villa rustica*). One sees already in being that tripartite division which will be reproduced again in the villas of Andrea Palladio built, on the Roman model, for the Venetian gentry of the sixteenth cenury. So too Palladio's imitators in England will separate the 'home farm' (or *ferme ornée*) from the country house of the gentleman, but remembering old tradition may decorate the urbane villa with agricultural motifs – rakes painted on the wall of Dawley Farm (the home of Pope's 'guide, philosopher and friend', Lord Bolingbroke) or that most charming, of garden ornaments, Repton's working dairy at Uppark.

That phrase *villa urbana* provides another link across the centuries, for

12

a typical Roman country gentleman is a commuter to the city (the *urbs*). But the city is not his true home. On the contrary, he longs for the virtue of a country life, and the city is repeatedly the subject of satire. In this, English country house writers, like Fielding and Smollett, follow the example of a Horace or a Juvenal. No reader in this tradition would be surprised to hear of the humiliations of attending great men in town, of the corruptions of commerce or the law, of the idle pursuits of the rich. 'If good men are to avoid this kind of thing, there is only one way of increasing the substance of his family which is fitting for a gentleman, and that is the cultivation of a country estate.' So Columella wrote (I. 10). Yet politics is a necessary concern for many of the gentry, and since 'political ambition keeps most of us away from our estates, it is best to have an estate near town, so that we can visit it every day.' Do not be an absentee landlord, Columella insists – it is a theme echoed by Jonson in the poem which originates the tradition of English country house verse – 'To Penshurst' – as well as by Pope, Edgeworth, even Trollope. The resident master supervises the bailiff, and the bailiff looks to the tenants born on the soil, and thus attached to hearth and home. A huge kitchen feeds the *servi*; the country house itself will be handsome, though not ostentatious in its architecture. This is, however, a practical, not a poetic, ideal. Those *servi* are not servants, but slaves, some of whom sleep chained. The wise man will work his estate with small units of labour; that way he runs less risk of being murdered in a slave revolt. The disappearance of this idea in later writers is noticeable. It will re-emerge in England with a vengeance in the time of the French Revolution.

But as the 'luxury' (*luxuria*) imported from the empire increased (it was a common theme of moralists), the emphasis of leisured writers falls less and less upon the villa as a place of work, and more on the country house as a natural place for the 'good' life, or, unashamedly, the life of pleasure. In vain Seneca recalled Scipio's rough stone, fortified manor of old, whose unwashed owner smelled of war, of work, of manliness (*Epistles* LXXXVI. 12). Like Virgil's advice in the *Georgics* to the emperor Augustus to plough and to sow naked, such appeals to the virtues of primitive ancestors were more rhetorical than real (like the later, Victorian, invocation of St George – a farmer saint – and merry England). Horace (65–8 BC) addressed a verse epistle to his bailiff, but it was a poem on the virtue of cultivating a contented mind, not on the tillage of the estate. Pliny the Younger (61–*c*. 114) enjoyed inspecting the work carried out on his lands and acting as a charitable 'patron' (in so far as his 'modest' means permitted) – a kind of Allworthy figure – but the main tenor of his writing about his country houses is the pleasure of humane learning, and the recreation of the body. It is an ideal given classic status in later architectural history. Palladio in his *Four Books of*

Architecture (1570) writes that the 'ancient sages' used to retire to their villas, where

the body will the more easily preserve its strength and health; and . . . where the mind, fatigued by the agitations of the city, will be greatly restor'd and comforted, and be able to attend the studies of letters, and contemplation.

Here, being attended by virtuous friends and relations, by cultivating their house, their garden and their virtue, the ancients 'could easily attain to as much happiness as can be attained here below' (II.xii).

Palladio's idealisation is a summation of the writings of classical antiquity and was a channel through which they influenced the English Renaissance. For the gentry, Pliny, who describes in detail two of his great villas, and Cicero, who owned eighteen according to Middleton, might well be the most attactive authors. Among the Roman poets, Horace and Martial (40–c.104) seem closer to Jonson and Pope (and to a succession of younger sons become clergymen). The poets inhabit a smaller world. Horace compares his little place in the country (his Sabine farm) with the 'regal piles' of ostentatious men, whose ponds are as large as lakes and who have built pleasure grounds over the ploughland of Italy. Martial (a poor man) repeats Horace's themes.

Yet Horace owed his little Sabine farm to the great. It was a reward for his support of the new regime of the emperor Augustus. He was dependent in status and Pope was to criticise him for this. The Roman poet makes virtue of the gift in the praise of his little domain in its south-facing valley with its 'stream of clear water, and a wood of a few acres, and the unfailing promise of my cornfield'. Yet independence is better still. *Beatus ille*, he wrote, happy the man:

> Like the first mortals blest is he,
> From debts, and mortgages, and business free,
> With his own team who plows the soil,
> Which grateful once confess'd his father's toil.
> The sounds of war nor break his sleep
> Nor the rough storm that harrows up the deep;
> He shuns the courtier's haughty doors,
> And the loud scene of the Bar abjures.

That phrase, *Beatus ille*, gave birth to a wide tradition, but, as Horace wryly observed, few follow the ideal, and it does not describe his own condition. His were no paternal acres (and his father had been a slave). Hence the more imaginative appeal to the Golden Age of the first mortals, and the philosophic appeal to Nature. To recreate something of that happy time, he extends the hand of friendship in his verses to those who will join him at his domestic board in 'the feast of reason and the flow of

14

soul' (Pope's interpretation), and like any latter-day commuter oppressed by the work, the noise, the smoke of the great city, when in Rome his mind constantly turns to his place in the country. *O rus, quando ego te aspiciam?*

> O! when again
> Shall I behold the rural plain?
> And when with books of sages deep,
> Sequester'd ease, and gentle sleep,
> In sweet oblivion, blissful balm,
> The busy cares of life becalm;
> O! when shall Pythagoric beans,
> With wholesome juice enrich my veins?
> And bacon-ham and sav'ry pottage
> Be serv'd beneath my simple cottage?
> O nights, that furnish such a feast
> As even Gods themselves might taste!
> Thus fare my friends, and feed my slaves,
> Alert on what their master leaves.

It is Dr Dunkin, the eighteenth-century translator, who introduces the 'simple cottage' into this Arcadian image of the organic community,[3] and he seems to find a slightly tongue in cheek quality here. The passage occurs in a tale of a town and a country mouse, and if the country cousin is preferred to the urban sophisticate, who dwells in a great house, it seems as if the rural dweller is something of an unworldly and naïve philosopher. Though Horace is the celebrant of a modest life in the country, he is not really a country house poet. The 'mouse' afraid of what might befall him is not an inappropriate image for his relation to those great men of state who set him up on his farm.

In Martial we come closer to the villas of the ancients. He formally praises the houses of his friends, stringing together old commonplaces with memorable and elegant brevity. Here again the hateful business of the town is compared with the healthful ease of the small country estate; the organic community feeding off its simple domestic produce is contrasted with the luxurious and frigidly hierarchical banquets of the great in their 'gaudy and chill stone halls'.[4] His celebration of his friend Faustinus's villa at Baiae (III.s8) seems to have been known in large measure by heart by Jonson. Here is a useful farm, not a useless formal garden, the soil tilled by home-born slaves who cheerfully obey the bailiff and delight in their work (compare Columella's prosaic fears!). Visitors from the surrounding countryside bring voluntary gifts, and the buxom daughters of honest yeomen carry presents from their mothers in their wicker baskets. So the domestic and neighbourly hearth burns before the household gods.

Elsewhere the idea of the spontaneously happy community reaches back again to the idea of a Golden Age. He writes to a friend (I.50):

The neighbouring wood shall descend to your very own hearth which is ringed with the lowly children of your slaves

and at rural Formiae the very fish attract the line of the fisherman and offer themselves to be eaten. In its happy plenitude all things in the country willingly serve the master of the villa. It is an image of a Paradise created for Man. 'All things serve them . . .', wrote Wordsworth later of his Arcadian lakelanders.

In more realistic mode in 'De Rusticatione' Martial was thought to describe a typical day in the life of a country gentleman.

At break of day I say my prayers; then I go the round of my servants and the estate assigning my staff their duties; next I read and compose some poetry; then I rub myself with oil and take moderate exercise in the gym, happy to tone up my body and happy in my mind too (for I have no mortgage). Then, lunch. I have a drop to drink, sing and play, take a bath, have dinner, go to bed. Provided that my small lamp consumes only a little fuel, the night provides lucubrations like these to the nocturnal Muses.

Clearly the house is no longer thought of primarily as a working farm. It is a cocoon in which the pleasures of art may be cultivated by the owner of literary tastes. Self-evidently this representation of the country house life survives only because literary. Writers privilege their own activities as ideal. The money to support all this comes from elsewhere. It is something of an affectation to despise the world of affairs which is sloughed off like a dirty skin at the threshold of the villa. But it is also a reflection of a political reality. When the villas of the ancients are celebrated as the abode of leisure, part of the price to be paid by many owners was that real power resided elsewhere, in the capital of the empire, or in the court of the emperor.

The case of Pliny is particularly interesting in this respect, for he was a lawyer who survived under the tyrant Domitian, and became an important public servant. His *Letters* are a carefully constructed image of the fully rounded good man, and proleptic of Pope's manipulated *persona*. In the construction of this ideal self, his suburban and rural villas have an important part to play. The descriptions are the first 'guidebooks' to country houses to be written, but the very fact that such a guide should be composed is indicative that the houses themselves are intended as the outward signs of the inner values of their owner. The moral tradition and the architectural are intrinsically one. Translated by Robert Castell in 1728 as *The Villas of the Ancients Illustrated*, Pliny's descriptive letters become one of the major sources for the English recreation of the Roman villa.

The Laurentine house lay only seventeen miles from Rome, thus in the home counties (Pl. 5). The formal complexity of the lay-out suggests that the unbuttoned hospitality, which it was morally right for the owner to offer his friends, existed within a highly regulated domestic hierarchy. The house is axially arranged along a series of three halls (or courts), the first of which Pliny described (modestly, of course) as 'plain, though not mean'. From thence, via an oval colonnade, through a third area 'small but pleasant', there is a direct line of approach to the hub of the whole design, the seat of the master in his principal dining room (welcoming his guests). Looking out from there, the visitor perceived on the one hand the sea, on the other a vista back through the approach to 'the Woods and distant Mountains'. The house spectacularly links inner and outer, architecture and landscape, the pivot provided by the dining room, where, as Horace had written, one might enjoy philosophic banquets fit for the gods.

Castell's detailed (and highly imaginative) plans extend through three floors. To the south extended a suite of centrally heated family rooms, culminating in a large bay fitted with a library of favourite books. To the north was a matching suite such as a privileged house guest might use. (Something of the symmetry and the formality of an English palace like Marlborough's Blenheim seems to have shaped Castell's conception.) There are even matching gymnasia, a domestic one, and a major one connected with the bathing quarters. The house offers also no less than three further dining areas besides the room approached on the first formal axis: one on the second storey commended by Pliny for its panoramic vistas of the seashore and the surrounding villas of the gentry; another 'elsewhere' chosen because looking inward onto the owner's estate; and the pleasure garden.

The kitchen gardens lay another way, but the guest is not taken there, nor to that area which the antebellum country house in America would rightly call the slave quarters, and which hearth and home sentiment in England names the 'domestic' offices. Pliny's letter rather describes the family grounds to the north, planted with mulberries and figs and a pergola of vines, laid out by Castell with the same rigid symmetry as the house (the more freely conceived area of woodland to the west with temples, mounds and serpentine paths is Castell's English landscape invention). Pliny's long covered arcade, 'for largeness comparable to public buildings', leads along a terrace to another dwelling, part belvedere, built for himself, and his particular favourite. There are a couple of bedrooms and a tiny 'den'. Here is seclusion even from the country house itself, a cocoon within a cocoon. Sometimes the press of festive visitors at home drove him alone to this private retreat.

The second, Tuscan, villa was some hundred and fifty miles from Rome on the upper reaches of the Roman Thames (the Tiber). This dwelling is carefully landscaped in its presentation, the aim being now to praise not the conveniency of the suburbs to the city (hence all those noisy dinner parties), but rather the tastefulness of the owner's picturesque conception of the rural scene, and the skill with which the surrounding beauties of Nature are gradually brought under the control of art within the garden, the foil to the formality of a house enparked.

Imagine to yourself a vast amphitheatre, which only the hand of Nature herself could form: being a wide extended plain surrounded with mountains; whose tops are covered with lofty ancient woods; which give opportunity to frequent and various sorts of hunting. From thence the under-woods descend with the mountains: intermixt with these are small hills, of a strong fat soil . . . which for fruitfulness do not yield to the most level fields. . . . Under these hills the vineyards extend themselves on every side, and together form one long spacious view: their extremities and bottoms, are bounded as it were by a border of shrubs: below these are meadows and fields. . . . The meadows are flowery and budding, producing the Trefoil, and other herbs, fresh and as it were always springing; as being nourished by ever-flowing rivulets . . . whatever water [the land] receives, and does not imbibe, it throws into the Tiber.   (1728 edn, 80–1)

This is one of the first great descriptive settings for the country house. Many others follow in subsequent literature. This landscape is part relished as 'an exquisite painting', part invoked as a moral norm. Those sublime mountains testify to the creative power of Nature herself who alone could form them: *quale sola Rerum Natura possit effingere*. That phrase, *Rerum Natura*, links landscape both to natural religion and to poetry, for it recalls Lucretius's scientific and Epicurean epic celebrating the fertility of things, *De Rerum Natura* (*On the Nature of Things*). Those 'lofty ancient woods' are an immemorial sign too, quasi-religious, and will recur endlessly as a motif in country house tradition. Then, as one descends from the sublime to the beautiful, fecundity is brought within the service of civilisation. The soil is fat and fruitful, yet utility combines with beauty (as Socrates observed), for the delighted eye picks out the flowers budding in the meadows, and even the workaday occupation of farming tends towards pleasure, for the vineyards are 'bounded as it were by a border of shrubs'. The whole is composed into an image of continuous and ordered stability, for just as the mountains and woods are ancient, so too, the letter emphasises, are the dwellers on this fortunate soil:

[here] you see several old men grandsires, and great grandsires to adult persons; and hear the old stories, and sentences of their forefathers: so that when you come there, you would think you had yourself been born in another age.   (1728 edn, 80)

Since this is prose, not poetry, Pliny does not directly invoke the Golden Age, but one feels that the roots of these folk are still in that soil, just as one sees remote shadows of the *Urvolk*, the first dwellers on the site of Rome. Castell's reader too might recall the poet Claudian's praise of the old country man, happy because he never left his native clime of Verona. In such a countryside as this, so the myth went, the goddess Justice lingered longest before she quit this world, and is it not appropriate that a great scion of the Law like Pliny should establish his summer retreat in this temperately benign clime?

Pass through the 'old-fashioned' entrance hall (again the emphasis is on traditional virtues), and through the shady courtyards with their fountains which charm the ear with their plashing and their frescoes of birds in the trees (so Art brings Nature out of the meadows into the house), and the visitor sees to the north the great vista of the riding grounds, more beautiful even than the villa, Pliny comments. Here grow ivy and box and laurel. Choose sun or shade, serpentine alley or the straight path, the informality of Nature, or admire the name of Pliny picked out in vegetable lettering in the garden. If you choose to repose at the furthest extremity from the house, in a favoured place for a picnic, a summer house invites your siesta, a grotto with an underground fountain refreshes with its coolness, and a marble seat, if you sit upon it, causes a fountain to play. So, safe from the weather, or from intrusive neighbours, you may retire, as into a wood, in pleasurable quiet. (Marvell would understand Pliny's longings a millennium and a half later at Appleton House.)

So, finally, comes the usual praise of the healthy mind in the healthy body, and of a peaceful and honourable life.[5] Here in Tuscany, in a country house and park,

I . . . enjoy a perfect health of mind and body, for I exercise my mind with study, and my body with hunting. My domestics also want not their health: as yet (pardon the expression) I have not lost one of them I brought with me. May the Gods for the time to come preserve this pleasure to me and reputation to the place. Farewell.

(1728 edn, 93)

The life of the country house is part aesthetic, part moralised, but only remotely, even symbolically, agricultural. The tour of house and grounds has not involved kitchen or farmyard. The country people are distanced as vestigial types of the virtuous folk of old. The servants are cared for by their owner, who is glad not to have lost one. The 'neighbours' are the surrounding gentry in their villas, and share Pliny's tastes. Those tastes, the descriptive tour repeatedly makes clear, are those of the most sophisticated urban civilisation: books for the library, fine pictures, statuary and bronzes. The owner of the house is a man of great wealth and a collector from the finest sources of supply that the imperial position of

Rome can command. His country house needs to be large, not only to welcome visitors, but also because it is a repository for all the artefacts that a complex, acquisitive civilisation produces. Yet somehow this is untainted by getting and spending in the hateful world of business by being carried off and established in the purity of the countryside. Nothing more clearly indicates the separation of the country house in this phase from the self-sufficient farmhouse 'organically' related to its estate than Pliny's recommendation of his suburban villa that it is close to good shops in Ostia. The moralists said that everything was to be had in degenerate Rome for a price. But Pliny buys in what he needs. That was not degenerate because, as the great ridge of the Apennines at a distance indicated, all things might be related to Nature. What is Natural is healthy and good.

Pliny's letters represent the apogee of the villa life of the efflorescent empire. They speak to the literary imagination of subsequent generations, although the visual, architectural signs of the classic country house had disappeared long before the English gentry came to Italy on the Grand Tour seeking their predecessors on revered ground. Speculation might associate here and there some vestigial remains with some great name, and brood upon the countryside of the Campania or Naples, but for substantial buildings remaining above ground the eye would have to turn to temple and bath, arena and aqueduct. The idea of what Pliny's house might look like would be assembled from a composite body of the five orders of columniation, and from arch, attic, pediment and dome, the whole drawn together by a sense of symmetry and proportion derived from analogies with music and the harmony of the human body. The buildings of Renaissance Italy would indicate one possible form of reconstruction from the antique, authoritative because nearest the source; the treatises of Renaissance architects would form a library of pattern books. Any visitor to the Italian villas of the 'moderns' would see the similarities to Pliny's descriptions in parterre and terrace, fountain and grotto, courtyard and fresco, fertile vineyard and distant mountain, and rightly so, for the Italian drew upon the classic texts. In formal garden at Wilton, grotto at Stourhead, woodland ride at Cirencester, something of the same ideal might be recreated, adapted to the English scene.

This is a familiar architectural story. But it is not just architectural history. The classic house represents its owner. Pliny or Cicero, Horace or Juvenal, Varro or Columella moralise the villa. It is a significant focus for them and their society. If republican farm and imperial villa are icons of the rise and efflorescence of Rome, then decline and fall are written there too. The extraordinary richness of the Roman experience for English culture is that it provided a complete paradigm for the appearance of a civilisation from primitive stock through to the destruction of the entire tree. It is a pattern not fully apparent in the history of the country house until English experience itself has seemingly run through an analogous process. *Decline and Fall* is the title not only of Gibbon's eighteenth-century history of Rome, but also of a work by a twentieth-century English country house novelist (Evelyn Waugh). It is tempting to stay on the heights with Pliny, as many did. But the paradigm must be worked through. Statius and Sidonius were never classical poets popularly read, but in this story they will now acquire a new signification.

A complex development may be simplified by considering the changes in the connotation of a word familiar in the jargon of any modern estate agent: 'luxury'. 'Welcome home' to Tadworth Park, wrote George Wimpey in a recent advertisement. In 'picturesque rural surroundings' a 'luxurious' development of country houses was now for sale 'within 15 miles of Piccadilly Circus'. Any Roman gentleman would understand. But that word 'luxury' had once been an evil sign.[6] The old Romans, those who died fighting for the republic at Philippi, had been men of plain living and high thinking – not luxurious. The simple self-sufficient farmer folk of old gave all for the state, required nothing for themselves. Shakespeare's Brutus is their last heir. The American republic of George Washington cultivated the same ideal. Then, with the empire, came the lust for riches which corrupts. Private wealth, public squalor. The American example suggests a similar analogy again. But it is clear, even from this cursory survey of the houses of a Cicero or Pliny, Horace or Martial, that one man's simple living is another's luxury. Horace's claim to live off Pythagorean beans was just a joke. The moralising owner of a great villa liked to claim the virtues of old, but the claim is a ritual, if necessary, gesture. Then, the very pretence is dropped.

The traveller to the Bay of Naples may still see the ruins of the villa of Pollio Felix (Pollio the fortunate) at what was the fishing village of Puolo (before the hyperborean hordes of German tourists fell upon Italy). Statius, in the second half of the first century, addressed a panegyric to the owner of the house, celebrated as under the protection of Neptune and Hercules, god of civic virtue, to whom Pollio, caught out in a storm, had built a temple to shelter his retinue. But neither god, nor Nature, is now the real patron of the place, but the master (*dominus*) himself, who has built here works as vast as a city (*urbis opus*).

Here are spots that Nature has favoured, here she has surrendered to you and learnt unaccustomed gentleness. This level ground was once a hill; these halls were once wild countryside. There was not even soil where the tall groves grow. Pollio has made tame the plain, shaped and conquered the rocks, the earth gladly surrendered to him. The cliff learns to bear the yoke, the villa forces entry and the mountain is commanded to withdraw. . . . It is you who move the rocks, it is you whom the lofty rocks obey.

21

Inside, the ceilings glitter with gilded coffering, and the walls shine with marble. Here is gathered the richest repository of painting, sculpture, bronze, and the portraits of the great men of the past who serve as examples, 'countenances of chieftains and prophets and sages of old time, whom you carefully follow and whose influence permeates you'. But in what way now, one wonders? Each Kalends of December the old gesture is made to the organic community by the owners of such villas. The whole household is gathered together for the Roman Christmas. Strange luxuries (*novos luxus*) now grace the feast. There are boxing dwarfs, women gladiators, virgin prostitutes. Statius is not writing satire of the rich. 'For all things serve them. . . .'

Long may you live, richer than Midas and Croesus, more blessed than the monarchs of Persia or Troy. You are never troubled by the fickleness of power or the mob, by law or war. Your great heart is sublimely above all desires, hope or fear, beyond the will of fate, beyond the enmity of Fortune. Your final day will not find you lost in the maze of the world, but sated with life, ready to leave.

It was panegyrics like these[7] which stirred Pope's imagination to create a Timon, or bring all Alma Tadema or Cecil B. De Mille to mind. The combination of unashamed sumptiousness and transparent hypocrisy is astonishing. Nature is the servant of this lord, not a moral norm. The city is now reconstructed in the countryside. Here are riches beyond those of Midas, whose touch turned all to gold. Even the ceilings are gilded, a custom which had outraged severer moralists like Seneca.[8] That temple to Hercules in the grounds is not a place of worship, but a kind of picnic house. Pollio himself is god, a being unmoved by anything happening in the world outside. In Pliny one might sense still some balance between the old Rome, however ritually recalled, and the new imperial civilisation. In Statius one may perceive why moralists saw the decadence of Rome springing from that luxury which corrupted a sybaritic gentry. But, in England, if one were to walk through the great country houses of Syon or Osterley with Statius in hand, and study the decorative motifs of a Robert Adam, derived from the discoveries of imperial Pompeii or Herculaneum, or consider the labour which went into the creation of the great parks at Blenheim or Stowe, one may perceive why later moralists too saw the cult of Roman luxury as a warning as well as an inspiration.

One last house closes the imperial pageant: the castle of Pontius Leontius, described by Sidonius, the time the fifth century. ('Burgus Ponteii Leontii'.) The wheel has now come full circle, back to the fortress villa of a Scipio, and those republican generals whom, Middleton tells, built on hills for security. The Goths have come. 'No siege engine, nor ramp, nor catapult-shot, nor scaling ladder can shake your walls.' The stark fact is that the house is built on a hill top between the Dordogne and the Garonne not to enjoy the amenities of picturesque scenery alone, but as a refuge. The stately towers are both pompous and a safeguard (*pompa vel auxilium*). The pretence of panegyric is that Dionysius (the vine) and Phoebus (the arts) chose this site for Pontius. It would have been appropriate to add Mars.

Yet, once we have passed safely through the fortified gatehouse, the tour highlights the familiar features, long colonnades and lofty suites for summer and warm rooms for winter, elaborate baths, walls faced with marble and ceilings coated 'fittingly' with yellow gold: 'for the rich prosperity of this house allows no secrecy, and shows its wealth when it conceals the roof.' One can see what the Goths were after, and why the uneasy owner chose pictures of Mithridates and Lucullus to hang on his walls. Mithridates was the cruellest and most powerful of Rome's vanquished enemies, Lucullus a man notorious once for his luxury, but now seen as a general bringing aid to the besieged. One thinks of the Marlborough tapestries at Blenheim, or of the Marquess of Bute in Cardiff Castle whose gilded ceilings are concealed from vulgar eyes by Norman walls raised on a Roman encampment.

Two gestures are made to pristine simplicity. In the winter suite weaving chambers are included. They are grand, of course, built in a style to vie with the temples of Pallas, but here the lady of the castle 'strips the Syrian distaff and twists the silken strands along the light reeds and spins the pliant metal, making the spindle swell with the thread of gold'. Way back in memory is the image of the chaste Roman spinster of the republic at her domestic hearth, although the silk and gold this lady spins is now for ornament not utility. Again the castle seems to stand at a hinge of history, for if one thinks of the new Gothic order to come, there are other ladies in other castles at their tapestry, and the old tradition runs on in the girls at their needlework in Mansfield Park, and (most astonishing of all) in the statuette of Queen Victoria at Hughenden sitting at her spinning wheel.

The other ritual genuflection is to Nature and the world of the old countryfolk. Within the castle stands a secluded garden, private now, for the estate is on the defensive, not spreading into landscaped park. Here rises a spring, a military necessity, but described in Latin verse:

Where Nature bestows beauty there is no need of embellishment. There is nothing here counterfeit, nothing of artificial splendour. This is good. These are not stones dressed by sounding hammers; the tufa, worn by the weather, will not be replaced by marble. This is better than the Castalian fountain. You [my lord] may have everything else to make you rich; the hills may tremble before your power; here set your captives free, and may their loosed chains be transformed into happy vineyards on the hilly slope of this castle.

All things serve the fortunate master, both the panegyric of the poet and the slaves whose chains are metamorphosed into the trailing tendrils of the vines which joyfully surround the castle walls, not like a beseiging army, but as an image of the natural fecundity of the countryside which celebrates its lord *sponte sua*: of its own volition. This is an act of Nature, simple, unembellished. The garden is not only a foil to the house, though the contrast is aesthetically pleasing, it is also a justification of the sophistication, riches and power of the country gentleman and his dwelling. The more obvious the expression of power in fortifications and slaves, the more elaborate the mythological transformation of the whole as part of the natural order confirmed in and by the happy countryside itself.

This is a long way from the early Edenic folk of Seneca who slept secure on the naked earth while the pageant of the heavens wheeled above them, or even simple Cincinnatus, or the farmerfolk of Varro whose homestead centred on the farmyard. Yet the poor poet by his natural spring, the housewife at her spinning, the vineyards which cover the happy hillside, have these naïve traditions bred into their flesh and bone. But we are at a point too which is looking forward as well as backward, for this castle belongs as much to the Gothic world which is to come as to the Campania of suburban villas. What is remarkable is that the Roman paradigm will still fit the English experience. The English country house originated from the fortresses of the Goths, domesticated itself in Nature after the example of the villas of the Romans, and, in the nineteenth century, like Pontius Leontius, retreated again (if only in symbolic form).

CHAPTER THREE

The Gothic heritage

THE ROMAN TRADITION was rooted in the republican farm; its efflorescence was the luxury of the villa, an epicurean country retreat. The
Gothic inheritance was written in a different architectural language. It
may be seen in the great rock dominating the city of Durham: castle and
cathedral. They are the visible signs of the Norman Conquest. The land
was seized; a chain of military encampments thrown across occupied
territory. The first country houses were fortresses. As J. A. Gotch wrote,
'Everybody knows that an Englishman's house is his castle, but it should
also be remembered that in early times an Englishman's castle was his
house.'[1] For generations fortified households stood not as a symbol of the
virtuous life, nor as an expression of sophisticated connoisseurship, but as
a practical means for the control and administration of the surrounding
land. They are 'power houses', and the modern country house, so Gotch
claimed, is a direct descendant.

The termination of the Wars of the Roses and the establishment of the
peace of the Tudors is the watershed which divides the countryside of
fortified houses from that of the country house. 'Peace' and 'plenty' were
the gifts that came from Bosworth field, Shakespeare wrote at the end of
Richard III, and the peace of the Tudors culminated in Elizabeth:

> In her days every man shall eat in safety
> Under his own vine what he plants; and sing
> The merry songs of peace to all his neighbours,
> God shall be truly known; and those about her
> From her shall read the perfect ways of honour,
> And by those claim their greatness, not by blood.
> Nor shall this peace sleep with her.
>
> (*Henry VIII*, V.v.34–40)

The manor house had already crept out of its fortifications, and
Thornbury in Gloucestershire, begun in 1511, 'the last of the old-
style "castles"' was already an 'anachronism'.[2] Now at Burghley and
Hardwick, Holdenby and Longleat, Theobalds and Wollaton, the great
house sprang forth like an exhalation upon the peaceful fields. Hardwick
and Longleat shimmer with glass. At the Queen's reception at Kenilworth

25

in 1575, the house was described as 'transparent through the lightsome windows, as it were the Egyptian Pharos relucent unto all the Alexandrian coast'.[3] The vitreous surface of what have been called 'prodigy' houses emphasises the thinness and fragility of the walls (the very opposite of a castle). If these are also 'power' houses, it is power secured by law, not by keep and curtain wall. England is at peace. As Bacon wrote in his *Praise of Queen Elizabeth*, she 'received a realm of cottages, and hath made it a realm of palaces'.

Consider a traditional image of that Tudor peace, though not a palace. Stanway House (Pl. 6) stands a few miles southwest of Broadway in the Cotswolds, and has recently been opened to the public. James Neidpath, in an admirable guidebook, describes Stanway as

a typical squire's manor house, a gradual and organic accumulation of buildings, furniture and pictures, intimately related to the surrounding villages, woods and parkland, an harmonious product of vernacular craftsmanship and landscape rather than of metropolitan or cosmopolitan tastes and ideas.

That cluster of mellow honied stone buildings is exquisitely expressive of guidebook England. To the left of the gateway is the tithe barn formerly of the Abbots of Tewkesbury, a memento of the dissolution of the monasteries and of the agricultural importance of the country house. Visitors surrender their tickets in the audit room of the house, reminded that the estate has resisted the temptation to sell off its cottages lest such sale should 'diminish the visual harmony of its villages'. The 'organic accumulation' of buildings is thus expressive of an equally organic relationship between Lord Neidpath and his tenants, who has a ready ear to their 'complaints'.

Between tithe barn and gateway stands the church. Beyond, the driveway leads to the principal entrance to the house (not used by the paying visitor) and the great hall, 'the centre of the life of the manor where manorial justice was administered – the last manorial court was held here ca. 1800 – and where communal meals were eaten'. The 'harmony' of inter-relation is maintained. and the emphasis of the guidebook upon 'community' reinforces what the 'accumulation' of buildings in the manor self-evidently seems to show. This is local, rural and English, 'vernacular', not 'metropolitan', or, even worse, 'cosmopolitan'. This is the English equivalent of the *Urvolk* of classical tradition. You can hear the very peacefulness in the silence of the English countryside.

Probe a little more sceptically, however, and strange ripples appear on this tranquil surface. The gateway may serve as illustration (Pl. 7). It is later than the hall, *c.* 1630 rather than 1580–1600, and a clear manifestation of ostentation and importance in symbolic form, for its defensive capability is slight. It is loaded with emblems which, rather than

uniting the house organically with the village community, parade the old
world of the castle and feudal power. The vertically linked bay windows
echo the fortified towers of a medieval gatehouse between which would
have been portcullis and drawbridge. The three shells on the skyline,
seemingly innocent motifs, are the badge of St James of Compostella,
patron saint of pilgrims. They are there because Sir William de Tracy – the
ancestor of the builder of the house – was one of the murderers of Thomas
à Becket, and voyaged to Jerusalem to purge his soul (so the story goes).
As late as the eighteenth century another de Tracy carved a coat of arms
above the entrance as another memento of feudalism. But most remarkable is the entrance itself, for it is a Renaissance variant of a Roman
triumphal arch. In this, at least, the guidebook is false in denying the
cosmopolitan. The imposition of a triumphal arch as a motif in a gateway
is an apt link with the medieval coat of arms above. Classic and Gothic
signs of conquest are united. But one might compare Pliny. It is unlikely
that in welcoming friends to his villa he would have wished to remind
them of the tramp of legionaries back from the latest imperial victory.
Gothic Stanway, on the other hand, flourishes its arms in the face of the
outside world.

It is a common motif, and modest here compared with Oxburgh Hall
or Layer Marney. One of the most percipient writers on the English
country house refers to Oxburgh as an instance of 'the gatehouse as a
showpiece, as the favourite vehicle for the romantic and pompous display
which marks the emergence of the country seat as a work of art', and
immediately joins with the word 'romantic' another favoured expression,
'picturesque'.[4] It is well known that such motifs are part and parcel of the
Elizabethan cult of chivalry, and that castellated forms are used in the
devices of house or tournament.[5] In literature one thinks of Malory and
Spenser, and the rise of historiography in the work of Camden and Hall,
Holinshed and Stowe. As a work of art the English country house is
self-consciously and historically romantic in its inception, reluctant to
abandon the traditions of the past, seeking to incorporate into its form
memories of an older order, whether that be to avoid rash innovation, or,
as at Stanway, to record in stone the history of the family idealised (the
pilgrim's shell, not the assassin's knife), linking the history of Britain to
that of Rome. The picturesque gateway, only symbolically defensive,
celebrates the progressive nature of society, the old wars remembered (for
the race should not forget its history), but now replaced by times of peace
and plenty.

Yet every emblem on the gateway is a sign of power and bloodshed, and
words like 'romantic', 'picturesque', 'work of art' displace towards a
vague aestheticism what are precise statements of force and pomp. These
militant motifs are not repeated *inside* the gate, but directed outward to

villager or visitor. They are reminders that possession of the land was established by arms, and are a form of intimidation, even though made with a certain tact in architectural form. The date of the gateway, 1630, places it on the verge of a civil war; the design was said to be by Inigo Jones. He was the architect of the Stuart court. This is more than picturesque architecture. In context it is provocative.

Stanway gateway asks to be 'read', therefore, but how it is read depends where you stand, even, literally, whether within or without. The castle motif in the English country house is both symbolic and real. For the peace of the Tudors had not been as unbroken as panegyric had claimed, and under the Stuarts anachronistic castles found their outmoded function once more tragically revived. Even if one goes on to 'the peace of the Augustans', as late as 1745 the feudal chieftains of Highland Scotland poured into England, not finally defeated until the triumph of capitalism over the old order at Culloden. In the nineteenth century a democratic 'mob' set fire to Nottingham Castle in pursuit of political reform; in the twentieth, the withdrawal of the colonial power of the Ascendancy in Ireland was marked by the burning of great country houses. It is little wonder, therefore, that the symbolic language of the Norman Conquest, written on the gateway at Stanway, remains a common motif in the history of great mansions. At Broughton Castle (besieged in the seventeenth century) the visitor will see suits of armour hanging in the great hall, a memento of the feudal retainers of old, who were replaced by the yeomanry cavalry of the eighteenth and nineteenth centuries. When the third earl of Carlisle, early in the eighteenth century, swept away the village of Henderskelfe to build a new house, he pulled down the old castle too, but he called the new mansion by an old name, Castle Howard. At Osterley Park in the 1760s Robert Adam incorporated classic armaments into the plaster work of his decorative scheme – lest we forget – and as one moves into the less secure era after the Revolution in France and the new peasants' revolts – Luddite or Chartist – the architecture of feudalism re-emerges almost as a mania in what has been called 'the return to Camelot'.[6] At Castell Coch William Burges minutely restored a fortalice for the Marquess of Bute, complete with romantic moat and drawbridge, picturesque portcullis and dungeon. The castle stands where the Normans planted it, where the Welsh valley debouches into the Anglicised plain. The fierce mountain men are still controlled by the owner of the keep.

This is an obvious visual language of conquest. As Sir Henry Wotton wrote in 1624, 'there is a lordship of the eye which being a ranging, and imperious, and (I might say) an usurping sense, can indite no narrow circumscription.'[7] That word 'usurping' is provocatively chosen. But it is more than a visual motif, of course. Look westward from the Radcliffe

Camera in Oxford to Brasenose College (Pl. 8). One faces an embattled four storey gate tower in a grim crenellated wall. Within is a typical Tudor country house quadrangle with great hall, kitchens and suites of lodgings. Hardy's Jude the Obscure in nineteenth-century Oxford experienced, as well as saw, these structures of power and exclusion. But those admitted to fellowship within the walls of Brasenose College still act out the rituals of feudalism each evening of term as the retainers and servants of the house gather to serve the 'common' meal in hall, divided by the hierarchy of high and low table, of fellow and student and servant, of wine and choicest food on high, and beer and common fare on low. It is a jealously guarded ancient ritual of rank and power in which an old order selects and incorporates men (and women now), preserving muliplicity of con-nection with the estates of power in the realm (the head of this house is still a Lord), inspired by the images of great ancestors in portraiture on the walls. It is an especially privileged life, in which the continuance of the rituals of that privilege encourage claims to long continued superiority, and fosters an endless fascination in those excluded by that embattled gate.

A language of feudal conquest pervades the expressive forms of the English country house, therefore, long after the ostensible demise of feudalism, clinging in image, name or custom. But another massive act of expropriation has been in large measure suppressed. The great creative surge in building which marks the peace of the Tudors was enabled by the dissolution of the monasteries. Before the emergence of the country house as the dominant architectural sign upon the face of countryside, the two major forms were castle and religious settlement. The monastic settlements were expressive of an ideal antithetical to the materialistic powers of this world. Whatever the failures in practice, here were com-munities committed in principle to charity, to the care of the poor and the sick, to hospitality to the wayfarer – a welfare state within the state. These were also houses of learning and culture as well as piety, where retreat from the evils of Court and City was found among the beauties of Nature.

These houses and estates were privatised by the State, often sold cheap to buy support, and sold on for profit. The study of the country house as a work of art would not begin with the Tudors if the Tudors had not destroyed this antithetical order with a determination to annihilate which may serve as a reminder that the term 'Gothic' in one sense is linked with the word 'Vandal'. It is clear why it was necessary for the new country house owners to destroy the old signs, but it is still difficult to disentangle fact from the inherited prejudices of fiction, for so much of the subsequent history of England has been Protestant in origin, and written from the top down.

Stanway House again provides a clear example. The delightfully companionable guidebook tells the story of the dissolution of the monasteries of rural Gloucestershire thus:

Sir William Tracy . . . died in 1530, declaring in his will that he relied for his salvation on faith and not upon the prayers of monks, and when his body was subsequently exhumed and burnt by Chancellor Parker of Worcester, there was widespread revulsion shared, we may presume, by his younger son Richard Tracy, who in 1533 used his influence with Thomas Cromwell to obtain from Abbot Segar of Tewkesbury a lease of Stanway. Richard Tracy subsequently led the commission which dissolved the nearby Abbey of Hailes, and declared its phial of the Holy Blood to be duck's blood tinted with saffron.

The reader's own blood is supposed to boil at Catholic tyranny and superstition! But is this a disinterested witness? Of course not. It is written from the point of view of the owners of Stanway, whose house is built on monastic land from monastic stone. It is represented as an act of public service to take for oneself the land of these wicked monks. Chaucer and Shakespeare once told similar stories about the Jews.

Traces of the enormity of this social revolution may still be read in the names of many country houses: Forde Abbey, Lacock Abbey, Newstead Abbey, Woburn Abbey. After due passage of time the ruins of the old order might be subsumed into the new. At Studley Royal, built from the stone of the old monastic settlement, the remains of Fountains Abbey (Pl. 9) were eventually incorporated into the garden to become the most beautiful of all English landscape ornaments. The Gothic church, by a free running stream, counterpoints the classic temple of piety further down the valley, built on a formal lake. The owners of Studley Royal thus combine the best of both classic civic virtue and Christian piety. It is a powerful, comprehensive symbolism, and much needed. John Aislabie, the first begetter of these gardens, had retired to his country house from no free choice. He had been Chancellor of the Exchequer at the time of the South Sea Bubble. Not even Sir Robert Walpole, the longest serving Prime Minister of the eighteenth century, could 'screen' a Chancellor so involved with City corruption.

It is not until after Catholic emancipation in the nineteenth century, however, and the rise of Anglo-Catholicism, that the old ecclesiastical order reasserts itself in the architectural symbolism of the Gothic revival. There is, for example, the assertive Christianity expressed by Arundel and Cardiff castles, where the old imagery of Church and State is re-incorporated for pious or social ends. In the pre-eminent literary text of the revival, Pugin's *Contrasts* (1836), the praise of Gothic architecture involves an idealised portrayal of the good society of the middle ages compared with the acquisitive paganism of later capitalism. But most significant at this time is the rise of the nineteenth-century socialist ethic. For the old monastic order and the caring, communistic community have much in common. Thus, in the imagination of William Morris, the new Utopia of *News from Nowhere* inherits an idealised vision of the middle ages.

Even the university community becomes involved with the same revisionist vision. The aspiring Gothic of a great civic university like Glasgow speaks of a spiritual community of learning. Some shreds and tatters of that idea still exist. I think of that apocalyptic passage at the end of Professor David Lodge's *Nice Work* in which the tattered, battered, almost dissolved campus of Rummidge University becomes a Utopian community in which all classes join hands in the love of learning, and care, each for each. The idea survives even the abysmal redbrick architecture.

CHAPTER FOUR

Penshurst Place and the country house poem

THE COUNTRY HOUSE enters English literature at a specific place and time. Early in the seventeenth century Ben Jonson visited Penshurst Place, the home of the Sidneys, in Kent. He celebrated the occasion in panegyric verse. It is represented as an event something like a 'gaudy' at an Oxbridge college, a time to feast the extended 'family' of the house in hall. The verses are one of those notable examples which serve, as it were, as a lightning conductor, a focus for the discharge of accumulated energy. The whole classical literary tradition comes together here.[1] But the house belongs, architecturally, to the Gothic world. Jonson's success in fusing the classic and the Gothic stimulated many imitators, most notably Carew's 'To Saxham' and 'To My Friend G. N. from Wrest', Herrick's 'Panegyrick to Sir Lewis Pemberton' (of Rushden house), Marvell's 'Upon Appleton House' and the celebration of Chatsworth in Charles Cotton's *The Wonders of the Peak*, and then, cumulatively, in the next century, the whole tradition infuses the poetry of Pope.

The house which Jonson saw still exists (Pl. 10). It was nearly three centuries since the London merchant and financier Sir John de Pulteney had built the manor house (1338–49), fortified later that century by Sir John Devereux. It is centred upon a great hall (the focus also of Jonson's poem), whose roof still dominates the complex of buildings. It stands close by the local church, in the middle of a working estate. The house has been repeatedly extended, especially after passing into the hands of the Sidneys by gift of Edward VI in 1552. This process of 'organic' accretion fundamentally distinguishes Penshurst from the new 'prodigy' architecture of a Longleat, or of a Hardwick created as a whole 'on the instant'. The house discreetly ties together changes in the Gothic vernacular with hints of the new classicism of the Renaissance. Thus the Roman 'triumphal arch' in the celebratory entrance through the King's Tower is directly centred upon the Gothic doorway of the Sidneys' great hall. In the private rooms of the family, beyond the hall, the latest formalities of Renaissance style are incorporated in symmetrical decorative motifs, and the private courtyard includes one of the earliest classical loggias in England. But outwardly the house overall sustains a contrived casualness as diverse styles are tied together by the extended crenellation.[2]

The short guide entitled *What You Can See at Penshurst Place* gives an appropriate gloss:

A great walled garden with terraces and yew hedged walks surrounds the house. The house and garden together convey a strong feeling of unity in design formed over the centuries by successive owners. . . . It is fitting that the visitor should get his first glimpse of the house from the garden. The distant view of towers rising above battlemented roofs conveys the illusion of a medieval fortress. But on closer approach this impression yields to a much stronger feeling of a peaceful, unwarlike family abode which indeed it has been from the beginning.

The guide takes the visitor at once into the noble 'domestic hall' (Pl. 11), described as 'the heart of a peaceful manor house rather than contrived as the centre of a defended castle', and then, in a charming sally of the imagination, brings the men and women of the past alive again in reference to 'the ten life-sized figures which look down [in the hall], lively reminders of the men and women who worked on the lord's lands six hundred years ago'. There is little need to elaborate the way this description naturalises the city merchant's house in its rural garden and draws architecture and people together. Though the house appears to be a castle, it is the centre of a peaceful organic community. In this the guide is the late heir of Jonson's poem.

Jonson's 'To Penshurst' is an Arcadian praise of house and estate.[3] So much flows from this poem that it is given in its entirety as the Prologue to this book. It is a celebration of the fertility of the soil which gives its riches seemingly without labour to its lord and the happy husbandmen of the estate. The very birds and fishes offer themselves to be eaten; Pan, Bacchus, gods and the elements bend to the service of Man. Jonson, having praised Nature, then comes to the house. At the centre stands the ancient hall where the whole community is united in a feast, and linked by reciprocal giving and taking of gifts, from each according to their ability, to each according to their need. The lord, thus, gives more than do his tenants (as God to Adam). At Penshurst

> all come in, the farmer and the clown:
> And no one empty-handed, to salute
> Thy lord, and lady, though they have no suit.
> Some .... send
> By their ripe daughters, whom they would commend
> This way to husbands; and whose baskets bear
> An emblem of themselves, in plum, or pear.
> But what can this (more than express their love)
> Add to thy free provisions, far above

The need of such? whose liberal board doth flow,
With all, that hospitality doth know!

Such a community, linked in reciprocal harmony, might be seen as the Golden Age restored, or even as a second Eden. Although in Paradise there had grown that forbidden tree whose 'mortal taste brought death into the world, and all our woe', here, at Penshurst, this is replaced by another tree

which of a nut was set,
At his great birth, where all the Muses met.

This is a literal tree planted on the estate to celebrate the birth of Sir Philip Sidney – writer and warrior – but it is also the family tree of the house which has created this happy world. In a pendant poem of 'To Penshurst', in the lines 'To Sir Robert Wroth', Jonson spelled out the paradisiacal archetype. 'The rout of rural folk' who throng about the hospitable lord recall,

that age, of old,
Which boasts t'have had the head of gold.

It is an idealisation which combines classic with Christian literature. It was Virgil in the *Georgics* who hailed his native soil as the country of Saturn, a land where the Golden Age was restored. In the country house poetry of Martial there were, before Jonson, happy workers bearing gifts, happy animals offering themselves as willing sacrifice. The banquet as a sign of hospitality was a motif inherited by Rome from the Greeks before them. Thus, the Gothic hall at Penshurst incorporates the rural homestead of Italy of old, and the villas of the ancients, just as architecturally it blends vernacular and Renaissance motifs. The local reality is understood through an inherited poetic and panegyric tradition already two millennia old. As Sir Philip Sidney himself had written in the *Apologie for Poetrie*, in such writing the desires of the mind transform things as they are. Such verse is exemplary. It shows how the ideal country house would be, the ideal landlord, the ideal tenantry. You cannot accuse poets of lying, wrote Sidney, for they do not claim to tell the literal truth.

This is a vision of Penshurst which suppresses, therefore, all darker aspects of the scene: the harshness of labour, or poverty, or, even, exploitation. This turning away from the 'dark side' of the landscape has brought down the indignation of Marxist criticism on Jonson and his followers for, it is claimed, their panegyric 'mystifies' the day-to-day realities of rural life.[4] Such adverse criticism, indeed, points to what is not in the verse. On the other hand, all visions of an ideal society are open to the same objection (not least Marxist Utopianism judged by the Stakhanovite reality of Eastern Europe). Should one want to argue about 'realities' behind poetic panegyric, it might also be claimed on Jonson's behalf that there were good contemporary arguments for celebrating the great country house. The kind of behaviour Jonson describes, the Gothic 'old English hospitality', is well documented,[5] and, as contemporary witnesses like Bacon and Harrison wrote, great houses signified great prosperity.[6] The application of capital in building and servicing a house was a major boost to the economy of any rural area; the use of that capital in productive and ecologically sound farming released that super-abundant fertility which enabled the tenantry to enjoy the holiday and communal feast which Jonson records. This productivity can be seen in the very countryside we have inherited today.

But that is to turn away from a poetic vision of an ideal society to debate issues of economic history. The major strength of Jonson's panegyric, and of the tradition it initiates, is that this poetic conservatism is not mere blind idealism. On the contrary, Jonson is always aware of an alternative, a dark face of what he describes. It is written into the history of the tradition, for the classic villa had always two manifestations, the country house of pristine simplicity and true culture, and the house of *luxuria*, of ostentatious show. Or, as Spenser Christianised the alternatives in *The Faerie Queene*, there is a 'House of Holiness' and a 'House of Pride'. The panegyric of 'To Penshurst' begins and ends by comparing the ideal country house with its alternative – a House of Pride:

> Thou art not, Penshurst, built to envious show,
> Of touch, or marble; nor can boast a row
> Of polish'd pillars, or a roof of gold:
> Thou hast no lantern, whereof tales are told;
> Or stair, or courts; but stand'st an ancient pile,
> And these grudg'd at, art reverenc'd the while.

> Now, Penshurst, they that will proportion thee
> With other edifices, when they see
> Those proud, ambitious heaps, and nothing else,
> May say, their lords have built, but thy lord dwells.

It is striking that the country house tradition enters English literature with a negative phrase: 'Thou art not', which carries with it a sense of 'Thou shalt not', as if the house were a Biblical commandment reified. Again classic and Gothic blend in the description, for these other houses, unnamed, are compounded of ancient motifs and present examples. That 'roof of gold' has been described before, but not on English soil. It aroused the anger of Roman moralists concerned at the loss of virtuous ancient simplicity, and in the lines 'To Sir Robert Wroth', Jonson specifically imitated Virgil in an attack on 'proud porches, or their gilded roofs'.[7] That row of 'polish'd pillars' too suggests a classic portico. The reference to marble may recall the well known praise of Augustan architecture, that the emperor found Rome brick and left it marble – words we have already seen imitated by Bacon describing Elizabeth. Jonson's followers certainly saw the connection between the ancients and the moderns. Thus Herrick writes in his praise of Rushden house that 'No widow's tenement was rack'd to gild/ Or fret thy ceiling':

> or to build
> A sweating closet, to annoint the silk-
> Soft-skin, or bath in ass's milk:
> No orphan's pittance, left him, serv'd to set
> The pillars up of lasting jet.

Here again are roofs fretted with gold. Those sweating closets are (presumably) Roman, and one may search in vain through seventeenth-century England for baths swimming in ass's milk.

The contemporary social reality is expressed in the great 'prodigy' houses of the age. If no widow's tenement was rackrented to pay for the *good* country house, *elsewhere* this was not the case. So Jonson writes that Penshurst was raised on 'No mans ruin, no mans groan', carrying, thus, contrary implication for the House of Pride, namely that it is 'grudg'd at'. There is some speculation as to which specific houses Jonson had in mind, and Theobalds, where the proletarian poet was insulted by Lord Salisbury, has been a favourite candidate. Or did he think of the great staircase of Knole in comparison with the humbler stone treads of Penshurst, or the lantern of Wollaton, or the marble hall of Hatfield? Or had he a literary text in mind, building his House of Pride from the ideal palace of Bacon's essay 'On Building' with its 'great and stately tower', its pillared galleries, many courts and belvederes? But Jonson's criticism is deliberately unspecific. It seems as if it were a general social phenomenon he had in mind. Thus 'a thousand' might 'sweat' under the implication of the verse (as Pope was to learn in his satire of Timon's villa).

One example may illustrate the social reality. Wollaton (Pl. 12) is one of the most fantastic of Elizabethan prodigy houses, a veritable 'house of envious show'. The great lantern which soars above the walls is a symbolic, turreted keep within a keep buttressed by towers. Olive Cook has described it as a 'theatrical' castle, 'which despite the monumentality of its shape is all fantasy, semi-transparent, brittle and defenceless',[8] Classic combines here with Gothic, for the basic design is from a neoclassical villa of Serlio, the symmetrical design adorned with the classic orders and busts of Aristotle, Diana, Hercules, Plato, Virgil, eager to speak of virtues. But they are virtues separated from the community. For the Bugges, who abandoned the family name for Willoughby, abandoned too their old house in the village, close by the church, and climbed the hill to build anew in splendid isolation. Great matching suites of rooms provide separate accommodation for the lord and his lady, or Sir Francis and his monarch, should the Queen choose to visit. Like many great houses of the time, great expense was incurred lest 'Queen Elizabeth sleep here'. The whole is dominated by the Prospect Room, a giant lantern superimposed above the hall, with no function except to delight the lordship of the eye, and no hearth. No one could 'dwell' there (to use Jonson's word). It is a magnificent, but unhappy, house. The chance of history has left more than ample record of the violently troubled life of Sir Francis, his quarrels with the retainers of his quasi-feudal household and his family.[9] H. G. Wells would appreciate the irony that this house is now a museum, a fossil of the Bladesover system. Other prodigy houses vanished like bubbles. Nonesuch is no more.

By comparison with such 'proud, ambitious heaps' swiftly raised as status symbols, it can be seen why Jonson should praise Penshurst as an old English house of 'ancient reverence', no work of 'foreign architect' (and the very word 'architect' is both alien and new at this time). It is a necessary complimentary stratagem, for the Sidneys themselves were comparatively new at Penshurst. But it is the *old* building which consecrates the fresh owners as if by sympathetic magic (why else, even now, should old houses carry a premium in price?). There is too, as so often in Renaissance panegyric, a hortatory element in the praise, for that word 'envious' in the praise of Penshurst – 'Thou art not built to envious show' – might, *sotto voce*, apply to the Sidneys themselves, unable to build a great, new house, and therefore envious of the rich. But remember that Penshurst is sufficient for the true ends of hospitality, even to entertain the King, the poet writes. One day the great man dropped by unexpectedly (!) yet found the mistress of Penshurst had everything prepared. Good traditional customs are never found wanting.

> they saw thy fires
> Shine bright on every hearth as the desires
> Of thy Penates had been set on flame
> To entertain them.

The principle which Jonson suggests is spelled out by one of his imitators. Carew writes in 'To My Friend, G. N. from Wrest':

> Nor think, because our pyramids, and high
> Exalted turrets threaten not the sky,
> That therefore Wrest of narrowness complains
> Or streightened walls, for the more numerous trains
> Of noble guests daily receives, and those
> Can with far more convenience dispose,
> Than prouder piles, where the vain builder spent
> More cost in outward gay embellishment
> Than real use.

A house is for 'use', not for the embellishment of Titanic 'pride' which threatens heaven. That concept of utility is to be one of the great moving forces in the country house tradition. 'Houses are built to live in, and not to look on; therefore let use be preferred before uniformity', wrote Bacon, commencing his essay 'On Building'; so too Sir Henry Wotton in *The Elements of Architecture*, 'the place of every part, is to be determined by the Use' (7), and Evelyn repeatedly in his *Parallel of the Ancient Architecture with the Modern*. In the architectural writers this is part of a debate between Gothic organicism and classic symmetry, but in Jonson and Carew it is expressive of a moral norm. The house should be useful to the community. (In Pope the idea will become the centrepiece in his comparison between proud Timon's villa and the work of Lord Burlington.)

Thus, an essential difference between Wollaton and Penshurst lies in the hearthless Prospect Room which uselessly dominates one, and the communal great hall which is the focus of the other. That blazing fire that stands in the middle of Penshurst's hall is deified by Jonson as a sign of the household. He calls it the Penates, the god of the home. As a domestic symbol it relates to the function of the Sidneys as good householders, and good parents, pious before God as part and parcel of their *pietas* (in the classic sense) to the family. Round the communal hearth the children are raised religiously and in the 'Mysteries of manners, arms and arts'. (The word 'mystery' seems to relate both to the courtly customs of a great house and to the mysteries of religion.) It is appropriate, therefore, that in this poem the lady of the house, Barbara née Gamage, has a role as keeper of Penshurst at least as significant as that of her husband. (The comparison with the violent quarrels, well documented, at Wollaton may not be entirely coincidental.)[10] So the visitor to Penshurst may still see, in the family apartments, Gheeraerts's fine portrait of Lady Barbara Sidney and her six children, the mother's hand resting protectively on the shoulders of a young boy, next in line, the girls in the picture either mirroring their mother's posture, or more intimately hand in hand, learning already their maternal and domestic function. It is an image as much matriarchal as patriarchal, and, in this story of the country house, proleptic. More and more the woman will become the spirit of the house.

Jonson, the celebratory poet, rejoices that he too is part of this extended family. Yet, just as the ideal character of the house is defined by a negative, 'Thou art not', so too the communal gathering round the Penates of the hearth at Penshurst carries with it clear recognition that other houses have other customs. We are never permitted to forget the House of Pride. Witness the praise of Sir Robert Sidney,

> whose liberal board doth flow
> With all, that hospitality doth know!
> Where comes no guest, but is allow'd to eat,
> Without his fear, and of thy lord's own meat:
> Where the same beer, and bread, and self-same wine,
> That is his lordship's, shall be also mine.
> And I not fain to sit (as some, this day,
> At great mens tables) and yet dine away.

Jonson well remembered the insult Lord Salisbury had rendered him at Theobalds by offering him inferior food. The classical poets Martial and Juvenal had recorded similar treatment. But here does Jonson protest the opposite too much? There would be no need to go on at such great length about bread and beer and wine if this guest were not conscious (acutely conscious?) of inferior status, of being an outsider who *on this occasion* is made to feel at home. If you were at home all the time, you would not think to remark upon it. One might put this down to Jonson's own prickly pride, were it not that Carew and Herrick both pick up the issue. At Saxham (whose very name recalls 'ancient honesty') Carew remarks,

> Thou hast no porter at the door
> T'examine, or keep back the poor;
> Nor locks, nor bolts

and Herrick (at Rushden) has a passage remarkable in its graphic vigour:

> For thou no porter keep'st who strikes.
> No comer to thy roof his guest-rite wants;
> Or staying there, is scourg'd with taunts
> Of some rough groom, who (irk'd with corns) says, Sir,
> Y'ave dipt too long i' the vinegar;
> And with our broth and bread, and bits; Sir, friend
> Y'ave far'd well, pray make an end;
> Two days y'ave larded here, a third, ye know,
> Makes guests and fish smell strong; pray go
> You to some other chimney . . .
>   No, no
> Thy house, well fed and taught, can show
> No such crab'd vizard: thou hast learnt thy trains,
> With heart and hand to entertain.

Herrick's ear catches the false accents of politeness in that reiterated 'Sir', dropped soon for the familiarity of one servant to another, 'friend', or to be replaced even with the blows of a superior servant to an inferior. Those 'bits' and 'broth', and the dipping in the vinegar have a graphic quality of Dotheboys Hall which Dickens would appreciate. No, *no*, Rushden is not like that, but the reiterated negative seems as if necessary, for the old feudal top down hierarchy is still clearly in place. Rushden's household is not based upon social equality, for the word Herrick uses to describe the master's dependants is 'train'. So too, at Wrest, Carew tells that the distinction between commoners and those of 'wealth, parts, office' is expressed in the distinction of the well-ordered hall. Where Jonson sat at Penshurst in the feudal pecking order is not recorded, only that all were feasted alike.

These panegyrics, then, are written by outsiders, poets invited in, welcomed, but always aware that their privileged status is flattering, and, indeed, demands (as proper payment) due commendation. These poems are, in a way, among the most eloquent 'thank you' letters in English, though they are far more. In this respect, though classical in their representation, they are a long way from the letters of Cicero or Pliny, or even parts of Horace's verse epistles. These Romans built, or owned, villas. But the English country house tradition is originated by, and belongs to, outsiders. It is a paradox (a Marxist might write 'contradiction') that the ideal signification of what an American visitor, Henry James, was to call 'the great good place' is created and sustained by those who do not belong to the patrician order.

It is inevitable, therefore, that Jonson's panegyric never explores much of the architectural iconography of Penshurst, long gallery, private parlour or garden. It would imply an intimacy he did not have, or, quite simply, a knowledge of the house he did not possess. He stays in the hall. It can be facile to read through the gaps in a poem into this kind of invisible territory, for everything that is not within is without, and any world you wish can be constructed in contradiction to the actually written. Yet it is not inappropriate to take the guide *What You Can See at Penshurst Place* as a 'control', as it were, and record how much Jonson leaves out. One element in particular relates back to Wollaton, Penshurst's great alternative. It is the military motif, the country house as symbolic castle. Jonson, by merely passing through the gate, cannot have avoided seeing triumphal arch and battlements there.

What You Can See, in the lines already cited, is at pains to emphasise the peacefulness of Penshurst despite the obvious outer fortifications. 'The distant view of towers rising above battlemented roofs' conveys only the 'illusion' of a fortress; this is a manor house rather than a 'defended castle'. So too Jonson's celebration is of a world at peace. Yet it is something of a 'contradiction' that the guidebook (1988) also tells that the then owner served in the Grenadiers (with great distinction), that he married first the daughter of Field Marshal Viscount Gort, and then the daughter of General T. H. Shoubridge. Likewise Jonson, by the very mention of Sir Philip Sidney, is praising that flower of chivalry who deliberately sought the field of battle and whose helmet is still preserved at Penshurst as a memorial to his tragic death. The traditions of war are never far from the English house.

Jonson's allusions to these things are remote. The children are brought up to follow their parents in 'arms and arts', but even the great archetype, Sir Philip Sidney, is thought of as poet, not man of war. That suppression is appropriate to the Arcadian and paradisiacal end. Yet the entire architectural structure and history of the house is dominated by Sir John Devereux's fortifications, still plain to see. Even in the peaceful centre of the house, the great hall, the motif of military crenellation is continued in the screen, and in the arms of the Sidneys, above the door, the simple 'W' of William Sidney has been turned into an heraldic phaeon, an arrow-head. The military motif is something that needs accommodation in the celebration of the country house since it is intrinsic to the building.

Jonson's imitators are, in a way, his most sympathetic critics. They tell us what his contemporaries responded to in his verse. It is Carew who is the first to seek to come to terms with images of war in his description of peaceful Wrest. He was a cavalier, and, like Horace, received an estate from his monarch. He died on the eve of civil war. The celebration of Wrest is, in date, and in its military motifs, an equivalent of the gateway at Stanway, for Carew's poem is an attempt to reconcile the old feudal language of conquest to a Stuart peace, and yet is aware, in a time of increasing social stress, of the significance of images of force. The poet writes that Wrest is 'an island mansion'. Thus he makes it a type of the island of Britain moated by the sea. But in so doing he emphasises too that this is a fortified manor house. Then, in a remarkable 'conceit', he seeks to transform into an image of Golden Age fertility the signs of war and of a house fearful of 'envy' (again that Jonsonian word) behind a double moat.

> This island mansion, which i' th' centre plac'd,
> Is with a double crystal heaven embrac'd,
> In which our watery constellations float,
> Our Fishes, Swans, our Water-man and Boat,
> Envy'd by those above, which wish to slake
> Their star-burnt limbs, in our refreshing lake,
> But they stick fast nail'd to the barren sphere,
> Whilst our increase in fertile waters here
> Disport, and wander freely where they please
> Within the circuit of our narrow seas.

This moat, it is said, has no military function. Instead its circular form mimics in the microcosm the heavenly crystalline spheres of the macro-cosm. Just as Man and the world were planted at the centre of God's universe, so too Wrest is planted by divine correspondence in the centre of its waters. Above is the sign Pisces; below fishes swim. That word 'embrac'd' indicates how much Heaven loves and protects Wrest, like a parent. But then the conceit is stretched further, for the 'star-burnt' spheres 'envy' the moat for they are almost crucified above (it comes close to blasphemy). That extraordinary exaggeration may be a sign of unease, for by transferring envy to the divine spheres above, Carew suppresses allusion to any kind of social envy from below – from those, for instance, who do not possess riches and estate. The text is emphatic in its insistence on communal possession in its reiterated 'our' – the house belongs to all of us – and the implication is that Wrest, like Penshurst, is an open house. At Penshurst the Sidneys offered 'free provisions', here 'we wander freely where [we] please'. But that 'we' may mean only the household guests. One may recollect a similar strained emancipation motif in the castle of Pontius Leontius where the poet called to the house 'set free your captives, and may their loosened chains be transformed into happy vineyards'. The fortified home, which is a sign both of power and of the need for fearful security, is transmuted by poetry into a happy image of 'our' freedom which is celebrated by Nature, or by Nature's God. But the remarkable effort required to effect the transformation both in Sidonius and in Carew is unfortunately related to the real contemporary need for defence both in the Roman empire and in seventeenth-century England at a time of coming civil war.

Just as with the gate at Stanway, therefore, how 'we' view this depends on where we stand – inside or out. Interpretation, too, depends on how significant the context of the historical moment seems. Seen retrospectively, after the passing of many years, the kind of transmutation Carew achieves has been extraordinarily effective. Removed from contemporary stress, filtered through picturesque tradition, it produces, for example, three hundred years later this beautifully evocative passage on the fortified house of Ightham Mote with which Olive Cook begins her history of the English house:

it awakens thoughts of Tennyson's 'lonely moated grange', for there are the 'marish mosses' creeping down on the edge of the dark water, there is the silver-green poplar and looking down through the latticed windows from the higher ground beyond the moat, there is the thick-moted sunbeam so loathed by Mariana slanting across a dim chamber. For this island dwelling is essentially romantic. It merely toys with the idea of defence. Enveloped in silence, which in the present age is itself a thing to wonder at, it wears the semblance of a dream, annihilating time.

By way of literature the house has become soft, misty, remote. How much harder Carew had to work at his theme to blunt envy and change that 'toy' of defence into a conceit. Its very toy-like nature is part of the problem for his age. Faced with armies of Levellers and levelling artillery, many a cavalier gentleman found his castle's defences only too symbolic, and, in Olive Cook's word, 'romantic'. At that historical moment another symbol also changed its significance. For the conservative, and the cavalier, the banqueting hall at Penshurst, Rushden, Saxham, Wrest, had been the sign of the harmonious community, to which 'all' could 'come in' without let to enjoy 'our' 'free provisions'. But on the notorious January day of 1649 when the King ascended the executioner's scaffold in Whitehall, he stepped out to his death from an uncompleted great house, a palace which would be seen by those without as a House of Pride. The heart of the house, as was appropriate, had already been constructed. The King went to his death from a banqueting hall. It is not an accidental choice. It is an ironic, revolutionary comment on the idealism, the ideology, of that country house tradition which 'To Penshurst' originates.

CHAPTER FIVE

The old manor house and the new

HOW FAR IS the conservative idealism of Jonson, Herrick, Carew, affected by the sense of the gathering storm of civil war: *aprés nous le déluge*? The old manor house they celebrate had already been separated from the centres of power. Jonson would not have needed to emphasise so much that 'thy lord dwells' at Penshurst, had not events (in fact) so often drawn Sir Robert away to court.[1] The houses built 'to envious show', whose 'pyramids, and high exalted turrets' threaten the sky, manifestly threaten also the social influence of modest Penshurst, Rushden, Saxham, Wrest. They are clear indications of the massive concentration of wealth and power elsewhere, and the accusation made by conservative poets is that new owners have betrayed their obligations to the community. They do not accept the responsibilities of charity and hospitality, nor do they possess the love of their people.

Myths of the Golden Age always look back to a lost past. By the time Jonson was writing the great hall was already an archaic symbol. The flight had long since begun from the hugger-mugger stench of communal living into the comfortable tranquillity of private apartments. Langland had lamented this in the fourteenth century.[2] But it was said of the age of gold that it lingered longest and last among old country folk. The communal parish feast in the old manor house is a sign of the vestiges of a valued tradition, the last active and visible bond of community. Perhaps this is merely an empty ritual (disguising the realities of power and property), but it may equally be said that rituals are the sacramental signs of those inexpressible emotions by which human societies seek to express their relationship. It would be unwise to underestimate the strength of the feudal bond.[3]

The power of the idea may be illustrated by an image (Pl. 13). It represents an act of public charity at Tichborne house. *The Tichborne Dole* (1670) was shown in the exhibition 'The Treasure Houses of Britain' in Washington, 1985–6. It was part of a sumptuous collection of paraphernalia representative of 'five hundred years of private patronage and art collecting', as mouth-watering to auctioneers (Jackson-Stops edited the catalogue) as the sight of the disintegrating Roman empire must have been to Alaric. It is remarkable that *The Tichborne Dole* should now be given this consumerist context, for the painting is an icon of the kind of society which might have comprised the estate at Penshurst. The folk are gathered in a forecourt, for the hall cannot hold them (in any case, it is desired to show the house), and they are arranged by the artist in hierarchical order. A miracle like that of the loaves and fishes is actualised here. The family of the house are about to give to the larger family of the estate.

One recognises that it is an old manor house. The traditional 'U' plan is dominated by the great hall, entered by a simple porchway (no great turreted gateway), and surmounted by a lantern which would have served as a vent for the central fire beneath. On one side will be the kitchen, on the other the parlour and private apartments. The communal hall is what ties them together architecturally and symbolically. Though the monasteries were dissolved, Sir Henry Tichborne acts the part of a religious father of his people (and the girl who carries the loaves of charity in her apron became a Benedictine nun). The family, as supporters of the old order of things, were loyal adherents of the Stuarts. Their unfortunate choice, or destiny, may be one reason why the old manor house, now in 1670 markedly anachronistic, is unmodernised. It is a very solemn picture. The whole is frozen into a ritual, performed once only in the year on Lady Day, and still 'enacted' (so the catalogue tells us). There is no merrymaking here. It is part religious, part deferential. It is a very problematic image. An old idea of spontaneous liberality has now been turned into a memorial icon. It is out of date, like the great hall in the house, and therefore needs to be placed on record.

Compare another image (Pl. 14). This is what the visitor sees on entering Hardwick, one of the great Elizabethan show houses. The old screens passage of the traditional vernacular house has been replaced by a row of Doric columns supporting a gallery above. The hall itself has been turned on its axis by 90 degrees, and has become a vestibule rather than a room for the whole household. It draws the visitor on and up a splendid flight of stone steps to a great chamber on the first floor, the lodgings of Bess of Hardwick and Arabella Stuart (pretender to the throne of England), and still on and upward to the great gallery and the main great chamber on the floor above. The ground floor hall cum vestibule is overwhelmed by a colossal fireplace on which two stags rampant support the coat of arms of the only begetter of this house. Above, in the gallery, Justice and Mercy, in effigy, stand above the mantle, and in the Green Velvet Room a stone Charity surmounts the fireplace. Most striking of all, in the High Great Chamber, the Royal Arms, emblazoned above the fire, incorporate Bess's initials, E. S., and on the plasterwork frieze the

story of the virgin goddess Diana is told, for the mistress of Hardwick
had aspirations to match that other Bess – Elizabeth, the virgin queen
– who never visited this house. Here, upon a dais, under a canopy of
state, the great lady would receive visitors who had climbed so high to
meet her, and preside over masques made for her entertainment as she
dined. This great symmetrical, 'architect' designed house[4] expresses in
its form the hierarchy and order of a society very different from that
of Penshurst, or that revealed in the Tichborne dole. It is an expression
not of community, but of power and state. The visitor to Hardwick
will see today the old manor house standing opposite. It is in ruins.
Bess kept it in repair, however, as a kind of hotel for a train of ceremonial
visitors.

At Coleshill (begun 1649), the old style great hall has gone entirely.
This simple, gentleman's house, by Pratt after Serlio and Palladio, seems
now so typically English, acclimatised in park and woodland, that an
effort of the imagination is needed to relate the revolution in its architecture to the social revolutions of the age. But cross the threshold and one
would have entered the atrium of such a Roman villa as Pliny might have
conceived had he been an Englishman and lived then. It is a square
hallway rising through two storeys. The principal staircase branches to
right and left, breaking at a half landing, then ascending to a gallery
above. The walls are decorated with classical busts, wreathed; the
doorways surmounted by broken pediments, the principal entrance (to
the dining room on the first floor) dominated by another bust. It is a kind
of mausoleum to the great men of classical antiquity. You pass through
classic ground to dine above. Balancing the hall on the entrance floor was
a parlour, below your feet were the kitchen and pantry in a half cellar. The
servants' hall was tucked away in a south-west corner. This is a house
divided 'upstairs/downstairs', serviced by servants' staircases rising, out
of sight, from subterranean regions.[5] 'All come in, the farmer and the
clown', wrote Jonson of Penshurst, but now it is inconceivable to imagine
this staircase (heavy with swags of artificial fruit and masks of lions)
thronged with the ripe daughters of peasants carrying real plums and
cakes. This is rather a house which a housekeeper might show to visiting
gentlefolk.

Coleshill was destroyed by fire in 1953. At one time its architect was
presumed to be Inigo Jones. The house is approximately contemporaneous with the most luxurious work of the architect of the Stuart court.
His redesign of Wilton House reaches its climax in the double cube
room (Pl. 15). The litany of the guidebook expresses something of the
ceremony, and the difficulty, of approach to a great man like the Earl
of Pembroke, through the little ante-room, and corner room, and the
colonnade room, and the great ante-room. How far you might get within,

how far the Earl might go forth to meet you, were the formally contrived signs of rank and wealth.

Once within, here is the 'gilded roof' of *luxuria*, heavy with the golden fruit of a Hesperidean paradise, which spills from the allegorical painting on the ceiling down the walls, echoed again in the golden frames of family portraits and golden figures on the overmantle offering homage to the family, in the family coat of arms, the family motto of feudal fealty – 'One will I serve' – and then, still glistering gold, even the very door handles glow, until the whole profusion falls, not to earth, but to the scroll feet of William Kent's vast, unwieldy, immobile furniture (of the next generation) which is posed in magnificent discomfort around the marble mantle, itself encrusted with inedible fruit.

The function of this room is to flaunt wealth unashamedly. It is the English equivalent of the villa of a Pollio or Pontius Leontius. One wall is entirely filled with Van Dyck's largest family group, flanked by portraits of Charles I, who loved Wilton, but whom the family deserted, and his queen. Philip, fourth Earl of Pembroke, is seated in Van Dyck's painting with his second wife, the Countess of Dorset, beside him. They are clad in the discreet sobriety of black, which serves to heighten the glorious, glowing cavalier costumes of the spreading dynasty around them. Dormer, Earl of Carnarvon, has joined daughter Sophia on the Earl's left, wearing his bride on his right hand and his sword on his left. Lady Mary Villiers, daughter of the first Duke of Buckingham, is ascending a shallow flight of steps on the right to join her spouse, Charles, Lord Herbert. Behind him is the exquisite, shimmering, almost angelic beauty of Philip, the fifth earl to be, and beyond him more sons; while already gathered into the Court of Heaven (as it were) are deceased children in the forms of angelic putti, lifted on clouds above, gesturing towards the Father below. Even the angels are guardians of the family. It is a great secular altar piece celebrating not the Virgin birth (a mother with only one child), but the fecundity of the dynasty, the family connections through the 'accrements of marriages', and its ostentatious, unashamed and armed wealth. 'One will I serve', says the golden motto. That 'one' to be served might be God, or King, but considering the history of a family that so successfully weathered the civil war, on the evidence of this portrait, the motto meant 'put yourself first'.

Jones, the architect of the setting – or should one write 'set', thinking of his palatial designs for court masques? – worked several variants upon this room. At Wilton again there is the single cube room, dominated now by portraits of the Stuart Restoration (for the family changed sides successfully once more). In Greenwich there is the atrium of the Queen's House, a vestibule as at Coleshill, not a hall for communal feast. And at Whitehall there is the great room used for court masque

47

and pageantry. It is the banqueting hall. It was Jones who had designed the room from which his royal patron, Charles I, stepped to
his death.

CHAPTER SIX

Appleton House
In time of war

THE OWNER OF Appleton House, General Fairfax, was one of the greatest of Cromwell's marshals, but had broken with the regicides on a matter of 'conscience' at the time of the invasion of Scotland, and had retired to his property in Yorkshire. He waited upon events, to re-emerge at the Restoration. Meantime he chose Andrew Marvell as tutor for his only daughter, Maria. The poet has often been praised for his paradoxical wit and ironic stance. This is not unrelated to his suspenseful and ambiguous position at Appleton House, in terms of both the wider political scene, and his own role as a writer within, and yet without, a great man's establishment.[1]

If the country house tradition were constructed merely from *topoi*, repeated themes and conventions strung out on a literary thread like glass beads in a necklace, then they might be numbered in sequence in Marvell's 'Upon Appleton House'. Here again is the praise of the House of Holiness in comparison with the House of Pride, of the fertility of the land and the family, of the charity of the owner of the house and the happiness of his estate, of the incorporation of old-time war in images of peace, and of the restoration of paradise. Though the house Marvell knew no longer exists, imagination has reconstructed it in the style of the old manor house depicted in *The Tichborne Dole*.[2] Poem and house are utterly traditional. But the execution of the King has fundamentally changed the context. Old things in new times alter their meaning.

Marvell begins his poem with the usual contrast of the House of Pride with that of modest goodness. He praises the 'sober frame' of Appleton compared with that foreign architecture of conspicuous waste which distinguished cavalier prelate or aristocrat:

> Why should of all things Man unrul'd
> Such unproportion'd dwellings build?

Better was what Marvell called[3] the 'unenvy'd greatness' of Fairfax, picking up a key word of Jonson's. He compares with Fairfax the man of pride who,

49

> superfluously spread,
> Demands more room alive than dead,
> And in his hollow palace goes
> Where winds as he themselves may lose.
> What need of all this marble crust
> T'impark the wanton mote of dust,
> That thinks by breadth the world t'unite
> Though the first builders fail'd in height.

The moral allusion is to the Tower of Babel, that pride which aspired to reach Heaven. One might think of the ascent to Bess of Hardwick's great chamber; more specifically Marvell refers to the great façades of show houses. The builders of such places have 'imparked' themselves, separating house from estate with unproductive pleasure grounds, encrusting it with luxurious marble, their very cultivation of architectural symmetry a sign (paradoxically) of the lack of proportion in their minds. Such criticism is fundamentally within the tradition of the country house poem.

But there is now a new threat to the moral order. It is that of republican egalitarianism among the Cromwellian revolutionaries. It is one thing to define the good house by comparison with the perversion of excess; it is another to find the very country house order challenged. The overthrow of the aspiring pride of the Stuart aristocracy was not an act which merely redressed an imbalance in the social hierarchy. It had brought in question the very existence of that hierarchy. There was a demand from extreme republicans to 'level' all social distinctions. When Marvell, alone, walks round Appleton, the mown meadows of the estate acquire an especial significance. Traditionally they would have been images of fertility. Now they call to mind those forces in the State as much opposed to Appleton House itself as to the Court. Level fields suggest the Levellers. The allusion is oblique, but undoubtedly there when he writes of the meadowland as

> this naked equal flat,
> Which Levellers take pattern at.

There is something disturbing in those words 'naked', 'equal', 'flat'. Then, in a pun on the word 'rase' (destroy), he sees worse troubles to follow:

> The villagers in common chase
> Their cattle, which it closer rase.

This kind of community is now too 'common'. It is potentially destructive. Shortly afterwards, when the river overwhelms the water meadows, 'the Flood' is called to mind, and with that Biblical punishment come images of disordered hierarchy and predatory threat:

> Here salmons trespassing are found
> And pikes are taken in the pound.

50

1   View of Uppark from the south-east

2   Chatsworth, from Llewellyn Jewitt and S. C. Hall, *The Stately Homes of England* (1874)

3   Two Barratt houses from the Premier Collection

4 Richard Wilson's painting of Cicero at his villa at Arpinum (c.1769–70)

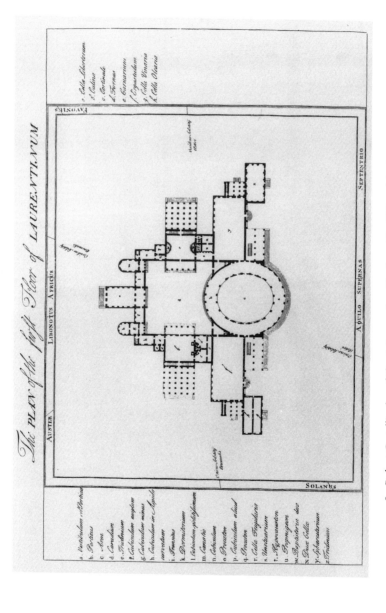

5 Robert Castell's plan of Pliny's Laurentine villa, from *The Villas of the Ancients* (1728)

6   Stanway House

7   The gateway of
Stanway House;
visitors are directed
by the notice to a
back entrance

8 Brasenose College, 'preserving' and 'building'

9   Fountains Abbey

View from the Garden.

10   Penshurst Place, from Llewellyn Jewitt and S. C. Hall, *The Stately Homes of England* (1874)

11 Penshurst Place, the great hall, from Llewellyn Jewitt and S. C. Hall, *The Stately Homes of England* (1874)

The poet, in such circumstances, retreats to an 'Ark' of security upon the estate of Appleton. Or, to vary the allusion, to avoid a flood, you take a stand on high ground.

These motifs are lightly touched, playfully treated. They have to be teased from the text of a poet who calls himself an 'easy philosopher'. It is an obvious defensive strategy not to take the threat from the Levellers too seriously. But theirs is a different order of values against which to measure the rightness of the house. It is a challenge which the usual *topoi* of the good estate seemingly allow Marvell easily to accommodate. The process of levelling is incorporated into the praise of the fertility of Appleton. The mowers 'level' the fields, but it is to gather a crop of hay, and it is the cattle which rase (crop) the grass yet closer to grow fat. The potentially subversive social image dissolves into a literal description of agricultural process. So too the disorder of the allegorical Flood that follows is once more subsumed into the generosity of Nature. Meadows need inundation for their growth, and those trespassing salmon and predatory pike turn out, after all, to be once more those fish celebrated by Martial and by Jonson, who offer themselves to their owner to be eaten. Eventually, as the poet will claim, through the Fairfax family, paradise will be regained on the estate, and in the State. The political message is clearly spelled out in the pendant poem to Appleton House, 'Upon the Hill and Grove at Bill-borow', when Marvell speaks of the emblematic 'hill' (which is Fairfax) raising others to its height. You 'level' upwards.

> Not for itself the height does gain
> But only strives to raise the plain.

Of course there is an element of sleight of hand about this. By making it a playsome image you duck the social issue. The poet's problem is that he has to face two ways. On the one hand, tradition required that modesty be compared with *luxuria*; on the other hand Fairfax must be represented as a truly great man, thus justified against the levellers in his possession of house and estate. His classical inheritance gave the poet the *topoi* for the praise of modesty; he has to find his own way to reconcile this with greatness. A continuing stress is created in the poem in the process, which, aesthetically, one might call 'paradox', or, politically, an ideological 'contradiction'.

Consider the problem Marvell has, accordingly, in establishing the proper magnitude of Fairfax's greatness. It is part of the social standing of Fairfax that he had, in fact, several country houses besides Appleton, and, if not as many as Cicero possessed, there are a number Marvell might have selected for praise:

> Him Bishop's-Hill, or Denton may,
> Or Bilborough, better hold . . .
> But Nature here hath been so free
> As if she said leave this to me.

These are larger houses than Appleton (it seems). But the longer the list, the more one wonders at the criticism of those proud men who are 'superfluously spread'. To justify Fairfax's choice of residence, therefore, Marvell adopts a familiar 'natural' archetype of modest size. Appleton, he writes, is 'Romulus his bee-like cell'. The hive of the bee is invoked as the sign of natural goodness. This is linked to the familiar symbol of the primitive hut, the *casa Romuli* preserved on the site of Rome. Marvell works his image of primitive simplicity hard. He recalls the classic tale, told by Virgil, of how the great Hercules and Aeneas, the mythic ancestor of Romulus, had themselves used such a hut.[4] Fairfax belongs in such an heroic age:

> When larger sized men did stoop
> To enter at a narrow loop;
> As practising, in doors so strait,
> To strain themselves through Heaven's gate.

This Christianises Virgil, and makes the modest dwelling of Appleton paradise again. Yet the text, once more, is strangely ambiguous. If Heaven's gate is Fairfax's estate, yet the other allusion is to the parable which tells that it is easier for a camel to pass through the eye of a needle, than for a rich man to enter the kingdom of Heaven.

More extraordinary yet is the image Marvell uses to describe his great man entering his modest house:

> Yet thus the laden house does sweat,
> And scarce endures the master great:
> But where he comes the swelling hall
> Stirs, and the square grows spherical;
> More by his magnitude distrest,
> Than he is by its straitness press'd:
> And too officiously it slights
> That in itself which him delights.

When this 'larger sized' man enters the 'narrow loop' of Appleton, the building blows up like a balloon in a desperate attempt to accommodate him. If one did not know there was a cupola above the hall at Appleton, it would be difficult to comprehend these lines which, in a Vitruvian conceit, inscribe the body of Fairfax within both a square and a circle, making his body the measure of architectural proportion.[5] This kind of thing has been rhetorically called 'metaphysical wit', but if one compares

Jonson, Carew, Herrick, the difference is not merely a stylistic matter. For them the function of the idealised hall was to focus the life of house and estate in a communal ritual of hospitality and charity. At Appleton the function of the hall is to express Fairfax's *magnitude*, and Marvell goes on to apologise that this hall is a 'low thing', even 'clownish' (a Jonsonian word again, but in different context, for at Penshurst the 'clown' entered, and was welcome).

Of course, the usual moral argument is then advanced. Since this is not a House of Pride, even this low dwelling, in which Fairfax delights, has its use:

> A stately frontispiece of poor
> Adorns without the open door:
> Nor less the rooms within commend
> Daily new furniture of friends.
> The house was built upon the place
> Only as for a mark of grace;
> And for an inn to entertain
> Its lord a while, but not remain.

The emphasis on charity to the poor, who gather at the door, is in the tradition of the Tichborne dole, and within are the friends of the house. The imagery still seems ambivalent, however. It was the praise of Wrest that it did not show people in statuary, but thronged the hall with real men and women. Marvell's words fulfil an opposite function. The poor 'without' (the word has a double sense) are transformed into 'a stately frontispiece'. They are a kind of ornamental porch, declaring Fairfax's state; while even his friends undergo metamorphosis into 'new furniture'. ('Old' friends, presumably, would imply the shabbiness of 'old' furniture.) There is ambiguity too even about the Christian image of Appleton as an 'inn'. In this we know that Marvell was complimenting Fairfax on his pious declaration that the house was an inn – a temporary stopping place – on the way to eternal rest. But it had been the praise of Penshurst that 'thy lord dwells' permanently. What Marvell celebrates as piety would be satire in Jonson. But, then, Fairfax had been driven against his will to reside at Appleton – but only until more propitious times. It is too small a place for such a great man. In a proleptic image, Marvell imagines how future times will judge the house:

> And surely when an after age
> Shall hither come in pilgrimage,
> These sacred places to adore,
> By Vere and Fairfax trod before,
> Men will dispute how their extent
> Within such dwarfish confines went.

The tension between the greatness of the family and the smallness of the house remains. At Wilton, Van Dyck has, perhaps, added a few inches to the Pembroke clan in the magniloquence of his painting; Marvell, following in the tradition of the house not built for envious show, has gone over the top by turning Fairfax and his wife (née Vere) into the giant race before the Flood.

These lines introduce also one of the major themes of the poem. Appleton House, like so many other country estates, is founded upon the dissolution of a religious settlement. That is why the allusion to pilgrims is appropriate. It is both praise of the family, and yet another apologia. The real function of the former nunnery is now fulfilled by the country house. So Tichborne. Marvell, however, seems obsessed with the matter. The tale of the dissolution of the nunnery at Appleton begins in the eleventh stanza and continues until the thirty-fifth. There is a danger in explaining away too much.

> At the demolishing, this seat
> To Fairfax fell as by escheat.
> And what both nuns and founders will'd
> 'Tis likely better thus fulfill'd . . .
> Though many a nun there made her vow,
> 'Twas no religious house till now.

The sterile nuns had no daughters (but that is scarcely surprising!). The corrupt Roman Catholic church had forfeited its proper spiritual lease (but this is Protestant history). Sir Thomas Fairfax, of 'ancient house', in those times rightly repossessed the property by 'escheat'. That technical word concerns a 'fief' reverting to its lord when a tenant dies without leaving a successor fit to inherit the original grant. The argumentative strategy is clear; so clear, however, that one can see the potential lie behind it. The very rhyme seems to draw attention to it. The word 'seat' rhymes with 'cheat'. Perhaps we have here merely extreme Protestant insouciance before defeated Catholicism. But the lines seem to betray also an unease about the very act of possession. They explain the problem away, and yet draw attention to it. It is in a manner analogous to the iconography of the gatehouse at Stanway which both reminds of the murder of Thomas à Becket and sublimates it in the symbols of pilgrimage.

A similar sublimation occurs with the images of war with which Marvell's poem abounds. The political situation requires 'Upon Appleton House' to be a celebration of retirement to a country house in an age of violence, and to praise a great warrior who has chosen peace. This virtuous choice is justified especially by comparison with the supine self-indulgence of the corrupt Catholic order which once possessed this property. Yet the poem is full of tensions between the inner and outer worlds, war and peace. How could it be otherwise when the owner of the house is in enforced retreat? This is especially clear when Marvell comes to describe the formal garden which separates the house from the outer world. He tells of Fairfax how

> when retired here to peace,
> His warlike studies could not cease;
> But laid these gardens out in sport
> In the just figure of a fort;
> And with five bastions it did fence,
> As aiming one for ev'ry sense.
>
> When in the east the morning ray
> Hangs out the colours of the day,
> The bee through these known allies hums,
> Beating the Dian with its drums.
> Then flow'rs their drowsy eyelids raise,
> Their silken ensigns each displays,
> And drives its pan yet dank with dew,
> And fills its flask with odours new.

The interlude continues for more than thirty lines on the theme that out of the strong comes forth sweetness, and ends with an invocation to

> that dear and happy isle
> The garden of the world ere while
> Thou paradise of four seas.

Will we 'never know' a time when only gardens had towers, and only roses stood in arms? Thus it is that an estate, seized originally by force, and owned by a man of arms, incorporates in its iconography all the images of war, and yet Marvell claims for the country house that it stands as a sign of that peace for which the whole nation longs. So too, at Fairfax's other house at 'Bill-borow', the aged trees (which give 'sacred shade') transform into 'other groves' the pikes among which Fairfax had fought. Nature itself heals the wounds of civil war.

It is the theme of the Golden Age restored, of the house as 'Paradise Hall' (to adopt Fielding's fictional name). Here, in the estate or the garden of a country house, if anywhere, is 'Heaven's gate'. Are Hesperidean fables true? asked Milton. If true, here only. The poetic ear tells one that it is only a kind of imaginative play, the poet cannot be too serious about the fiction. But what pity that only in the garden of retreat can paradise be regained in all its peaceful, innocent sensuality. In this garden General Fairfax is alone with his virtue. Yet Fairfax did not wish to be alone here. His place should not be at Appleton but in the wider garden of the State. The poem moves one way, then another, seeking resolution.

> And yet there walks one [Fairfax] on the sod
> Who, had it pleased him and God,
> Might once have made our gardens spring
> Fresh as his own and flourishing.

This rocking one way, then another, is complex. So too was the situation, fraught with difficulty, even danger. Real life is recalcitrant.

Poems, however, move to resolutions, the closure of their themes. The ending here is that, as it were, 'given' by the country house tradition. Paradise will be restored. But the chosen instrument for this happy end is not Cromwell's great general after all, but Maria Fairfax, Marvell's pupil, all the daughters of her father's house, and all its sons too. At the end of the poem we leave the general, and the suspenseful ambiguities of his position, and move to unqualified panegyric of Maria. She is both a 'virgin nymph', and yet an image of fecundity, the *genius loci* (the guardian spirit of the place) who resides in these gardens, meadows and woods, representative of the 'ancient stocks' of the venerable trees and the family. Ultimately, in the most grandiloquent compliment ever paid to a teenage child, she is 'paradise's only map'.

> 'Tis she that to these gardens gave
> That wond'rous beauty which they have;
> She straightness on the woods bestows;
> To her the meadow sweetness owes;
> Nothing could make the river be
> So crystal-pure but only she;
> She yet more pure, sweet, straight, and fair,
> Than gardens, woods, meads, rivers are.

The name Maria is a fit designation for a daughter dwelling in a former nunnery. This Virgin Mary will bear a child who will redeem the garden of England.

Panegyric could go no further. The imaginative leap submits the shows of things to the desires of the mind. If this resolution in a Golden Age is the expected *topos*, yet, on the other hand, it is like nothing that precedes it in the depiction of the country house. We have seen the chaste Roman matron at her spinning wheel, or Lady Barbara, the fertile mother of a prolific race, keeper of the domestic hearth. But Marvell here plunders Petrarchan love poetry, for Maria is Ma Donna, My Lady herself, and yet the generative goddess Venus, mother of Nature, but Christianised. It is a necessary fiction both to resolve the poem, and because the Fairfax family must make destiny their choice. Their future hangs by the slender thread of this one child only, and a girl. In making this resolution, however, Marvell makes the country house poem anew. Woman has emerged from the periphery to the centre of consciousness.

It may be that Marvell reflects here a changing social ambience. As the country house becomes more a place of retirement, forced or chosen, then the role of woman as the centre of the household grows.[6] How neat it would be if literature might be translated back like this into a few generalisations about material culture. The change, however, relates to highly specific circumstances. Compare the position of the Fairfax family at Appleton with the Pembrokes, celebrated by Van Dyck at Wilton in his great secular altar piece, and it is obvious how much generic convention, and particular circumstances, change the signification of what is shown, and how it is shown.

Yet this is a special moment in the story of the representation of the country house, as Marvell generates a symbolism of woman both as the *genius loci* of the land, and as a saviour. She has many successors: Sophia Western in Fielding, Fanny Price at Mansfield Park, Aurora Raby at Norman Abbey, the heroines of Virginia Woolf, Daphne du Maurier's nameless heroine in *Rebecca*. 'Upon Appleton House' is a proleptic poem, but such teleological history always falsifies origins by turning works of art into precursors of things the artist can never have foreseen. The creator is always aware of the patterns that the past can yield; the way the work of art itself becomes part of a new pattern belongs to the unforeseeable future.

If Maria Fairfax is a sign of the new femininity of the country house, she is also, in relation to earlier writing, an intensely isolated figure. She is never seen in relation to her father or mother, nor as part of an extended family group like the Pembrokes at Wilton. There is something strange about this loneliness which is not necessarily part of her symbolic function. It relates to the isolation of the poet himself. Marvell cannot address General Fairfax as friend, nor is he seen sitting at the communal hearth eating the same food as his host. The household tutor is an employee, and 'Upon Appleton House' is primarily set outside the household, in grounds where the writer wanders communing with his own imagination, turning compliments to a great man. It is as if the inside/ outside division at Appleton mirrors the upstairs/downstairs divide of Coleshill. If this is so, then the writer turns ultimately to celebrate a woman in the house because her position, in some measure, reflects his own separated, sensitive, role.

One final point. Maria's destiny lies outside the closure of the poem, yet, by a strange coincidence, links back again to poetry, and to the family portrait at Wilton. The woman ascending the steps in Van Dyck's picture is Lady Mary Villiers, daughter of the first Duke of Buckingham. Maria

Fairfax married the notorious second Duke, George Villiers. It is an object lesson in the capacity of country house dynasties to survive by political marriage. Maria's husband built Cliveden, 'a delightful place on the banks of the Thames', a later poet wrote, but called it also 'The bow'r of wanton Shrewsbury and Love'. He does not name Maria, deserted by her husband for the Countess of Shrewsbury. The theme of the house as an 'inn', with which Marvell played, receives then a bitterer treatment:[7]

> In the worst inn's worst room, with mat half-hung,
> The floors of plaster, and the walls of dung,
> On once a flock-bed, but repair'd with straw,
> With tape-typ'd curtains, never meant to draw,
> The George and Garter dangling from that bed
> Where tawdry yellow strove with dirty red,
> Great Vill'ers lies – alas! how chang'd from him
> The life of pleasure, and that soul of whim!

It is a sign of Villiers's Satanic fall that he is not within the walls of his home at Cliveden, but without a proper dwelling in a little ale-house at Helmsley, without friends or wife, 'without meat or money, deserted of all his servants almost'. So the legend ran. The voice condemning Maria Fairfax's husband is that of Alexander Pope, the most powerful of those poets who chose the country house as their theme, and the lords of prodigy houses as the butt of their satire.

CHAPTER SEVEN

Pope and Timon's House of Pride

MARVELL IMAGINED Appleton House becoming a place of pilgrimage. Alexander Pope's villa fulfilled that ideal. It is one of the great familiar images of the eighteenth century; its iconographic signification spelled out both by Pope's poetry and by the 'Epistolary Description of the Late Mr Pope's House and Gardens at Twickenham' (1747), then repeatedly canonised by painting.[1] It is one among numerous houses of the time to achieve something of a mythic role. Stowe was celebrated both by Pope and by Thomson, and is the subject of a series of remarkable guides explaining the meaning of house and grounds; Shenstone's estate, The Leasowes, and Henry Hoare's Stourhead were constructed to elaborate iconographic programmes. Charles Cotton's attempt to establish Chatsworth late in the previous century as a magnet for the discerning visitor was only less successful because Cotton was a minor poet, and Derbyshire was remote.

Pope's villa at Twickenham is only a symbolic country house. His few acres of garden are only the sign of an estate; his box-like dwelling the suburban retreat of a man of letters, no house of 'ancient reverence' (Pl. 16). He earned the money to buy the place from the skilled marketing of his edition of Homer. The investiture of the villa with all the cultural panoply of the country house tradition is a sign both of the fundamental importance of that tradition, and of the way literature creates and transmits values. In particular Pope modelled himself on classic originals. In the 1730s a long series of 'imitations' of Horace make Twickenham the modern equivalent of the Roman poet's Sabine Farm, but it was Pope's boast that, unlike Horace, he was an 'independent' man, indebted to no prince or peer, and, with the epistolary and satiric verse of Horace, he liked to think he combined the republican fervour and philosophic principle of a Cicero, or some other hero of Rome when it was virtuous. I am, he claimed, the last of the Romans.

He is also. in many ways, the last of the cavalier country house poets, a late supporter of the dethroned Stuarts before Hanoverian triumphalism. Many of Pope's friends were either Catholic or Jacobite, or, if neither, at least isolated by opposition to the hegemony of the First Minister of State, Sir Robert Walpole. Hence, in many cases, withdrawal to their country houses, and the creation there of an iconography of opposition. In this context the cult of the Stuart architect Inigo Jones by Pope's circle unites aesthetic principle to ideological desire. His friend Lord Burlington's new villa at Chiswick, by celebrating an architectural line from Jones to Palladio to Vitruvian Rome, is imaginatively a centre for cultural Jacobitism.[2] Pope's projection of his own villa as part of this opposition is, thus, intensely conservative and reactionary. As such it is also strongly domestic. Neither his religion, his politics, nor his feeble health permitted the poet an active public life. Much of his time was spent in isolation, and in looking after his aged mother. Paradoxically, therefore, a poet whose conservativism expresses itself in the celebration of the manliness of classic public virtue possesses many of those qualities which, by contra-distinction, may be claimed as 'feminine'.

The struggle between Pope and the Walpole regime has been called the opposition of 'mighty opposites'.[3] Since part of that opposition is expressed by the symbolic signification of the country house, the traditional distinction between the House of Pride and the House of Holiness remains fundamental to the structure of Pope's imaginative creativity. On one hand is the 'house of envious show', as expressed in his verse by Timon's villa (in 'An Epistle to Burlington'), on the other the house of virtue whose true lord 'dwells': Pope's Twickenham. *Luxuria* or virtue. As Alberti, the Renaissance architect, had written: 'we ought to imitate the Modesty of Nature', but, he added, 'the World never commends a Moderation so much as it blames an extravagant Intemperance in Building.'[4] That 'modesty' of what is 'natural' was to be established as 'commendable' by Pope's verse in opposition to the 'extravagance' of Whig corruption, spelled out in the visible face of its architecture. In practice, as Alberti perceived, it was an end more easily accomplished by negation, by 'blaming' what should not be.

That negation is intrinsic in the tradition. 'Thou art not', Jonson had begun in praising Penshurst. So Pope's 'Epistle to Lord Burlington', and his right use of riches in his buildings, centres itself upon the great satiric depiction of Timon, who has built as one should not.

> At Timon's villa let us pass a day,
> Where all cry out, 'What sums are thrown away!'
> So proud, so grand, of that stupendous air,
> Soft and Agreeable come never there.
> Greatness, with Timon, dwells in such a draught
> As brings all Brobdignag before your thought.
> To compass this, his building is a town,

60

> His pond an ocean, his parterre a down:
> Who but must laugh, the master when he sees
> A puny insect, shiv'ring at a breeze!

The word 'pride' is placed in the forefront of the description. As a house Timon's villa recalls, for instance, the great works of Pollio Felix. Nature has been subject to an imperial colonisation. Even the ocean is merely a pond in the garden, and the city has been imposed upon the countryside. 'Inverted Nature' Pope calls it later, faced with

> Trees cut to statues, statues thick as trees.

One of the great faults of Timon's villa (and everything, except the master, is big) is that this is no longer the centre of a fertile estate. The land has been enparked, vastly enclosed, to create grotesque pleasure grounds, which give no pleasure and raise in the poet contempt rather than envy. In one of the most romantic images of his satire, Pope, contemplating a useless fountain in the park, creates the uncreativity of the place, both ridiculous and tragic at the same time:

> Un-water'd see the drooping sea-horse mourn,
> And swallows roost in Nilus' dusty urn.

This is like the world of Appleton House after the Flood, where everything is in the wrong place, but Marvell's strategy was always to link disorder with concepts of fertility and regeneration as the Natural order, expressed by the house, ultimately restores itself through the Fairfax family. But here the imperial villa is an 'empty cistern'. Even the colonised Nile has become a desert. There are no waters of regeneration.

The focus of the community of house and estate had been the great hall. If this were an anachronism even by the time Jonson wrote, it has become a grotesque parody here:

> But hark! the chiming clocks to dinner call;
> A hundred footsteps scrape the marble hall:
> The rich buffet well-colour'd serpents grace,
> And gaping Tritons spew to wash your face.
> Is this a dinner? this a genial room?
> No, 'tis a temple, and a hecatomb.
> A solemn sacrifice, perform'd in state,
> You drink by measure, and to minutes eat. . . .
> Between each Act the trembling salvers ring,
> From soup to sweet-wine, and God bless the King.
> In plenty starving, tantaliz'd in state,
> And complaisantly help'd to all I hate,
> Treated, caress'd and tir'd, I take my leave,

61

> Sick of his civil Pride from morn to eve;
> I curse such lavish cost, and little skill,
> And swear no day was ever past so ill.

Step by step we have seen the community vanish. At Penshurst they all came in; at Appleton House there was a stately frontispiece of poor at the door; here all one is aware of is the sound of a hundred footsteps scraping the marble hall, that marble itself one of the signifiers of 'Pride' (the word is reiterated), that 'scraping' carrying with it the sense of servility. But Jonson would have picked up the remarkable fact that Pope, a linen draper's son, is not insulted by a host emphasising rank by discrimination of diet – the usual complaint. On the contrary, the writer is 'complaisantly help'd', but to all he hates. He is 'treat'd' even 'caress'd', yet somehow 'tir'd'. And for all the infertility of the parkland, Timon's board is laden with food. Pope's complaint is merely that the meal is too ceremonial, too much ordered by the clock.

One might ask, therefore, what Pope is doing as an honoured guest at this meal in the first place? The answer is very different from that one might offer for Jonson or Marvell, and is given away in the first line of the fantastic description: 'At Timon's villa let us pass a day. . . ' The poet is here as a country house visitor. His writing belongs to the domain of the 'house party'. He is the kind of person the owners of country houses invited to stay, like Mr Yates in Jane Austen, for instance. The historical referent for this is obvious in Pope's real-life activities. The houses of his acquaintances were places he visited on his 'rambles', often staying for weeks, writing letters in prose and verse advising on architecture and gardening. Marvell called Appleton House an 'inn' (in a moral sense). For Pope the country house has become a kind of Grand Hotel, and he is giving Timon a one star rating. Do not stay here more than a day. There is about this even an element of snobbery (might one call it inverted pride?), for Timon goes out of his way to treat and caress him, but this visitor has the good sense, and the good taste, to mock his preposterous host.

The word 'taste' is crucial. The key to what is wrong with Timon is that his house embodies bad taste. Where bad taste ends, and bad morality begins, is a problematic issue. There is, for instance, even in this House of Pride, a chapel, and when Pope ridicules 'the Pride of pray'r', it is the ill taste of the painted sprawling 'saints of Verrio or Laguerre' on their gilded clouds which offends him as much as the soft Dean 'Who never mentions Hell to ears polite'. The 'Argument' to the poem had made the aesthetic point clearly at the beginning, reiterating it almost to excess. The aim was to give in Timon's villa

A description of the false Taste of magnificence; . . . [with] a word or two of false Taste in books, in music, in painting, even in preaching and prayer, and lastly in entertainments.

In general, Pope claims, this poem concerns 'The abuse of the word Taste'. Thus Timon is satirised not so much for enclosing his park against his tenants, but because 'Soft and Agreeable come never there'; not for denying access to his person (for he meets Pope at his study door) but for the false ceremonials of the approach:

> But soft – by regular approach – not yet –

not for the parsimony of his hospitality, but for 'such lavish cost, and little skill'. These abuses of taste would not have any relevance to Jonson or Marvell. It is not his host's taste in food which Jonson commends at Penshurst, nor his employer's connoisseurship in landscape gardening which Marvell commends at Appleton.

This epistle is part of a sequence by Pope to friends who were, like Timon, enormously rich: Burlington the builder of Chiswick villa, Bathurst the creator of the great landscape park at Cirencester, Cobham the owner of Stowe. The great country house is, as it were, a 'given' social fact. The poet has the delicate task in writing to Burlington to mock the abuse of wealth, and yet to accept its possession in superabundance. It is a necessary strategy that there should be a defence, therefore, which may be offered even of Timonesque riches:

> Yet hence the poor are cloath'd, the hungry fed;
> Health to himself, and to his infants bread,
> The lab'rer bears: what his hard heart denies,
> His charitable Vanity supplies.

Thus, wrote Pope, 'The *moral* of the whole' is shown, 'where PROVI-DENCE is justified in giving wealth to those who squander it in this manner', it being dispersed to 'the poor and laborious part of mankind'. It is what later economic theory has called the 'trickle down' effect. For Pope, it is God's will that 'private vices are public benefits'. Even the rich, like Timon, have their uses.

Pope's attempts to reconcile Divine Providence to the economics of greed may sometimes appear complacent. But the phrase 'private vices, public benefits' was a notorious paradox of the time. It is the central argument of Bernard Mandeville's *The Fable of the Bees* (1714). Though it is a view which fits uneasily with traditional Christian morality, there is a clear enough social reality behind Mandeville. As Cotton wrote of Chatsworth, great houses dispense great wealth, and the tradition of charitable giving operates even on Timon's pride.[5] If he gives for vanity, at least he gives charitably – if that is what Pope means, for the lines are ambiguous. There is an alternative interpretation. It is that 'A bad Taste employs more hands, and diffuses expense more than a good one', as Pope puts it, glossing his own lines. Hence those hundred footsteps scraping in the hall. The great country house is a major employer of labour. Thus it diffuses riches widely, and stimulates the economy. It is worth recalling the other part of Mandeville's paradox, which is sometimes suppressed. Communistic 'virtue', he claims, is an economic disaster. What one has is a choice of the lesser of two evils. Capitalism, at least, delivers the goods. Swift, Pope's friend, who understood paradox, knew what Mandeville meant. His communist Utopia in *Gulliver's Travels* is a land fit only for horses, who are virtuous but poor. Pope has to live in the real world of great landed families.

Yet Nature itself, as an instrument of Providence, will root out Timon. In lines suggestive of Marvell's resolution in 'Upon Appleton House' Pope writes:

> Another age shall see the golden ear
> Imbrown the slope, and nod on the parterre,
> Deep harvests bury all his Pride has plann'd
> And laughing Ceres re-assume the land.

'Providence' has it all ways. Timon's vanity does good; but the divine order operating through Nature will do better. A sceptical mind might suggest that it is not so much the goddess laughing Ceres (Virgil's *laetes segetes*) who reassumes the land, but another landlord. But that is Pope's point – if one wishes to turn visionary verse into social commentary. As a matter of fact, any estate where expenditure exceeded income would be taken in hand at some time, by trustees or another owner (Timon has no children). Income would be increased by more efficient farming, here by ploughing up the park. (Smollett, in *Humphrey Clinker*, describes a similar process.) In this way the social order corrects itself, whether one calls this 'the Market', or Nature, or Providence. It is not an easy process, but 'the perfection of Nature' belongs only in Swift's Houyhnhnmland, not in this world.

This is hard bottomed poetry. Pope is writing for friends who ran great estates. He is much closer to them than is Jonson below the high table at Penshurst, or Marvell as Maria Fairfax's tutor. Yet there is a problem in the historical referent. The poem fixes Timon's villa as a type of the House of Pride, but who exactly, in the real world, is Timon's antithesis? Who holds the land and plants the happy grain? It should be Pope's friends, of course, Bathurst or Richard Boyle (Lord Burlington). But as Pope moves to celebrate them, the poetry suddenly begins to elide so many things that

the very quickness of the hand, rather than deceiving the eye, is a sign
of uncertainty.

> Who then shall grace, or who improve the soil?
> Who plants like BATHURST, or who builds like BOYLE.
> 'Tis use alone that sanctifies expense,
> And splendour borrows all her rays from sense.

> His father's acres who enjoys in peace,
> Or makes his neighbours glad, if he increase;
> Whose cheerful tenants bless their yearly toil,
> Yet to their lord owe more than to the soil;
> Whose ample lawns are not asham'd to feed
> The milky heifer and deserving steed;
> Whose rising forests, not for pride or show,
> But future buildings, future navies grow:
> Let his plantations stretch from down to down,
> First shade a country, and then raise a town.

Read quickly, the implication here is that Bathurst and Boyle are happy
husbandmen, enjoying their father's acres in peace. Yet by the paragraph
division Pope separates the real persons from the mythical type. Boyle's
building, in fact, is his work in the style of Jones, Palladio and Vitruvius.
Chiswick Villa, and Burlington House in London, have nothing to do
with the country estate. Bathurst's 'planting' refers to the great rides of
Cirencester park; Brobdingnagian works Pope called them in his letters (a
word he used also of Timon). This was a gigantic exercise in landscape
gardening. Again, it is not the management of a 'useful' estate. The poem
has jumped from Timon to Providence, to Bathurst and Boyle, to an
unspecified lord, but not come to rest at any real country house. There is
no Penshurst Place, Saxham or Wrest.

That insecurity expresses itself in some odd ambiguities.[6] Thus the
double sense of the line about tenants:

> Yet to their lord owe more than to the soil.

The ideal origin of this lies in the 'old English hospitality' in which, as
Jonson wrote, the lord of the manor gives more in presents than he
receives. In the rather chillier world of Pope's country houses, the line
makes one ask who is taking from whom? Although Pope probably has in
mind productive and supportive investment by the landlord, the line
might just as well describe rackrenting (and Burlington owned extensive
Irish estates). One sense is that the tenants owe the landlord more in rent
than they can get out of their work on the land. It is an odd ambiguity
in a poet who is usually precise. There is too a problem for the lord's
neighbours. The panegyric had begun by describing the conservative

situation in which the lord enjoys his father's acres in peace, the old Rome of the Cincinnati as it were, but the word which rhymes with 'peace' is 'increase', and at the end of the passage great forests have driven not only 'laughing Ceres' from the land, but as the plantations march from down to down over a whole county, one may wonder what happened to the tenants who tilled the soil, and to the neighbours who held the land? An ancient, stable community of small farmers has given way to an England of great estates owned by great Lords (*latefundia* the Romans called them in their time). Though Timon was a type of the abuse of the old order, how exactly does he differ from a Bathurst (or Cobham), who put down thousands of acres to landscape park, or Burlington, who sold estates to raise capital to construct Palladian mansions? Except, of course, that these great men were Pope's friends.

CHAPTER EIGHT

The decay of the old manor house

WHAT WAS NOT available to Pope as a moral sign was the 'house of ancient reverence', as Jonson called it, or 'the old manor house', as the novelist Charlotte Smith rechristened it. If Penshurst was archaic when Jonson wrote, by the early eighteenth century such country seats were out of date in every way. As a structure to be lived in, they no longer fitted their current social functions;[1] as aesthetic objects they offended the 'taste' of the age. At Blenheim, where a great house was being built for the Duke of Marlborough at public expense, the old manor of Woodstock was totally destroyed, though Elizabeth herself had lived there; at Grimsthorpe the ancient hall was drowned beneath the waters of a lake. Moreover, the preservation of an old building might be read (in a competitive society) as a sign of social failure, even as evidence of social disaffection. A few years ago Mapledurham was open to the birds who nested in its crumbling ceilings, its garden a field of brambles and nettles. This had been the home of Pope's Catholic friends, the Blounts, and to such ends might the choice of the wrong religion bring families.

The sense of the passing of an old order is pervasive in Pope, but it has passed away so far that it never directly emerges even in the idealism of his poetry. It subsists more strongly in his carefully edited letters which are Pope's subtextual commentary on his poetic life. But only once does he move so far as to compose a formal panegyric on an old manor house, when he celebrates the former home of the Raleighs still preserved at Sherborne in a letter written, appropriately, from Mapledurham.

The present master of this place . . . will not disgrace [his forefathers] as most modern progeny do, by an unworthy degeneracy, of principle, or of practise. When I have been describing his agreeable seat, I cannot make the reflection I've often done upon contemplating the beautiful villas of other noblemen, raised upon the spoils of plundered nations, or aggrandized by the wealth of the public. I cannot ask myself the question, 'What else has this man to be liked? What else has he cultivated or improved? What good, or what desirable thing appears of him, without these walls?' I dare say his goodness and benevolence extend as far as his territories; that his tenants

live almost as happy and contented as himself; and that not one of his children wishes
to see his seat his own.   (22 June ?1724)

Here the old house is clearly compared with the villas of modern pride
(with a probable sneer at the detested Marlborough at Blenheim).
Sherborne is reared 'with no man's ruin, no man's groan', but descends
through a family line distinguished for that benevolent goodness which
ensures that the tenantry live 'almost as happy and contented'. Pope
records this goodness at work in the community in the 'noble monument'
erected in Sherborne Abbey, in a 'neat chapel' dedicated to the towns-
people; and he celebrates too the ancient honour of the family represented
by the ruins of the castle 'demolished in the Civil Wars after it was nobly
defended . . . in the cause of the King'. The castle has now become a
picturesque garden ornament naturalised among the 'inexpressibly awful
and solemn' trees of the estate in which Sir Walter Raleigh's old, turreted
house reposes.

   Yet, interwoven with this praise of ancient piety to Church, State and
family (which Nature itself is now witness to), another order of value
intrudes. In the language of the modern age, Sherborne is an 'agreeable
seat', one to be compared with the 'beautiful villas' of others. The moral
eye is also an up-to-date aesthetic eye, and when Pope writes of
'improving' the house and estate (another current word), he thinks at
once of architectural modernisation:

one of the flat sides toward the garden has the wings of a newer architecture with
beautiful Italian windowframes done by the first Earl of Bristol, which, if they were
joined in the middle by a portico covering the old building, would be a noble front.

The old building would be ennobled and made beautiful if it were
concealed by the new Italian style. A 'foreign architect' (to use Jonson's
pejorative term) is needed to cosmeticise the house. In so doing, the
emblematic signification of Sherborne changes.

   It is a sign of that change that the whole estate is conceived by Pope as
one picturesque garden, and it is one of the qualities of that picture that it
is empty of people. Pope 'dare say' that the owner's goodness extends
as far as his territories, that the tenantry are 'almost as happy and
contented', but that 'dare say' betrays that Pope has not met the tenants in
the fields, nor have they come in to the house to meet him. Pope's
particular concern is advising on the venerable and picturesque garden
(like Marvell, his place seems to be more outside than inside the house).
Here he would raise an obelisk to the family, there create paths up half-
tumbled walls from one view to another, on a neighbouring hill construct
a little temple, nearer at hand create gaming rooms in the castle ruins. But
this charming world of piety and pleasure belongs only to family and

friends. Though there is a constant appeal to Nature, only men and women of taste are properly appreciative.

Pope's description of what had happened to the old great hall at Stanton Harcourt (another ancient manor) shows how the old conception of ancient hospitality has now decayed.

The great hall is high and spacious, flanked with long tables (images of ancient hospitality) ornamented with monstrous horns, about 20 broken pikes, and a matchlock musket or two, which they say were used in the Civil Wars. . . . In this hall, in former days, have dined Gartered Knights and Courtly Dames, with ushers, sewers, and seneschals; and yet it was but t'other night that an owl flew in hither, and mistook it for a barn.   (?September 1718)

The Stanton Harcourt letter is among the funniest Pope ever wrote, and matches Swift's send-ups of Irish country houses.[2] It would be foolish to be too solemn about Pope's misfortunes in this rambling, leaking, smoking, creaking, mouldering, smelly hotch potch of a Gothic mansion inhabited only by a distressed poet, a crazy old steward, the ghost of Lady Frances, and grey-haired rats themselves so hungry that they are nibbling the few remaining books in the library. But Stanton Harcourt is, as it were, Sherborne unmodernised and unimproved, soon to 'fall to ruin'. It is a sign for Pope of the crazy design of the house that the entrance does not lead to a vestibule but to a brewery. It is a blunder in taste that he comes in via the domestic offices of the screens passageway. Compare the broken bottles bearing the family arms which litter the way with the generous fare of Penshurst, and the 'blazing Penates' there with the chimneys here green from disuse. The state of the kitchen says it all:

By the blackness of the walls, the circular fires, vast cauldrons, yawning mouths of ovens and furnaces, you would think it either the forge of Vulcan, the cave of Polypheme, or the temple of Moloch. The horror of this place has made such an impression on the country people, that they believe the witches keep their Sabbath here, and that once a year the Devil treats them with infernal venison, a roasted tiger stuffed with ten-penny nails.

This has all the playful 'horror' of eighteenth-century Gothic fantasy, but beyond the game it can be clearly seen that the kitchen has lost its former function in the house, as the house has lost its function for the estate.

Pope moralised the loss of charity, hospitality and responsibility in the description of Cotta's estate in the 'Epistle to Bathurst':

> Like some lone Chartreux stands the good old hall,
> Silence without, and fasts within the wall;
> No rafter'd roofs with dance and tabor sound,
> No noontide-bell invites the country round;
> Tenants with sighs the smokeless tow'rs survey,

And turn th'unwilling steeds another way:
Benighted wanderers, the forests o'er,
Curse the sav'd candle, and unop'ning door;
While the gaunt mastiff growling at the gate,
Affrights the beggar whom he longs to eat.

Cotta's old manor house stands as a sign of miserliness in this epistle, but the moat choked with cress and the courtyard filled with nettles, like Stanton Harcourt, is a sign too of architectural form decaying with lost function. (Charlotte Smith uses much the same device in *The Old Manor House*, 1793.) The alternatives are represented by Cotta's son, whose prodigality ruins the estate and family, and by the addressee of the poem, Lord Bathurst, celebrated by Pope for the magnificence of his landscape projects at Cirencester. But there is no old Tudor landlord, risen like Lazarus from the grave.

Even to hint at that ancient alternative (and its traces can still be found) promotes laughter in Pope, though mixed with Yuletide affection, or is it affectation?

They tell me at ----- certain antiquated charities, and obsolete devotions are yet subsisting: that a thing called *Christian* cheerfulness (not incompatible with *Christmas* Pies and plum-broth) whereof frequent is the mention in old sermons and almanacs, is really kept alive and in practice: that feeding the hungry, and giving alms to the poor, do yet make a part of good house-keeping, in a latitude not more remote from *London* than fourscore miles. (28 December 1724)

But Pope could never determine what house name to place into his blank space, and this fabricated letter was never written to anyone. In such news from nowhere we find a lost Christian, Christmassy, Merry England, charming, yet laughed at by the writer in the whimsicality of his own composition. So too the old Romans said that though virtue could no longer be found in the megapolis of Rome where everything could be had, for a price, yet among the old country folk the Golden Age had lingered longest, reluctant to depart. But where, now, were these old country people? What would replace the old virtue?

CHAPTER NINE

Pope's Palladian villa

POPE RESOLVED to create within the imaginative world of his villa at Twickenham a country house ideal difficult to find in the world outside (Pl. 16). A renovatory classicism was to be superimposed upon an archaic native tradition. It had its architectural sign. It was the Palladian portico Pope added to the river façade of his villa. But even the rhythm of his windows across the façade, 1:3:1, is a meaningful motif, endlessly varied in the new country houses of the time, for it too spoke Palladianism in its Renaissance numerology.[1] The very word 'villa' is so laden with associations that merely by linking it with his home Pope achieved a major iconographic aim. It united him both with Palladio, and with the great patron of the arts, Lord Burlington, whose villa at Chiswick the poet praised (in contradistinction to Timon's), and whom, in miniature, Pope followed. Burlington, superabundantly rich, did not need to content himself merely with a portico. He translated the whole design of Palladio's Villa Rotunda from Vicenza to Chiswick, linking it by a passageway to his old manor house. It is an iconographic act on the grandest scale.

The architectural history of English Palladianism is well known.[2] The cultural shorthand it embodies is implicit in the history of the Roman country house, whose form and values Palladio imaginatively recreated in *The Four Books of Architecture*, rendered into English between 1715 and 1720, and supported by translations of Pliny by Castell and Melmoth. The villas of the Veneto were the places of retreat from business for the rich of the great republican and commercial empire of Venice, a place where the owner might find his true self separated from the vices which commerce brings, or from the disappointments of politics. In a rural Elysium the arts might thrive and the cardinal virtues be cultivated by a soul at liberty. One branch of this philosophy derives from the dialogues of classical philosophy, and its aim of health of mind and body. Another branch springs from the ideals of the monastic life and the Christian humanism of Petrarch. Both are grounded in Nature. Palladio's villas are often closely tied to productive farms, practical homesteads, if not for the lumpen clod-breaker. They are secured ultimately by the fertility and self-sufficiency of the land.[3]

Strictly speaking by the Palladian canon, Pope's Twickenham and Burlington's Chiswick are suburban villas – *villa suburbana* – to be distinguished thus from the *casa di villa*, a country seat on an estate, or the *villa rustica*, a farmstead. But that distinction was not maintained when translated to England, whether Palladianism was written across the great face of a palace like Holkham Hall, or in the discreet domesticity of Marble Hill house. It is a moral programme, direct or implied, which the educated eye was supposed to read. Thus, at Twickenham, though the agricultural farm is self-evidently absent, symbolic Nature is present miniaturised in the garden; and though England was manifestly neither the Roman nor Venetian republic, it is one of the major pretences of the architectural expression of the age that it was.[4]

A visitor to Twickenham, arriving by the Thames, was to be met, so Pope planned, by a series of emblems which would locate his villa in the imagined classic tradition, Roman or Renaissance. His friend Joseph Spence tells in his *Anecdotes* (620) that the design was

to have a swan, as flying into the river, on each side of the landing-place, then the statues of two river gods reclined on the bank between them and the corner seats, or temples with

Hic placido fluit amne Meles

on one of the urns, and

Magnis ubi flexibus errat Mincius

on the other. Then two terms in the first niches in the grove-work on the sides with the busts of Homer and Virgil, and higher, two others with those of Marcus Aurelius and Cicero.

One would need to write much of the history of European culture to elaborate this programme. The use of great names is incantatory. Here is the classic villa of a great poet whose high calling derives from his epic predecessors. Here too is the home of a philosopher and statesman to whom a republican senator (Cicero) and a philosophical emperor (Marcus Aurelius) are, as it were, familiar visitors. Thus republic and empire, poetry, philosophy and politics, are all incorporated in the ceremony of welcome to the Palladianised villa behind, and set in the garden as if the presence of Nature were the means of reconciliation, or the guarantee of Truth. There is also a recondite aspect to the allusions which suggests a high cultural elitism. If an educated visitor might identify Pope's second Latin quotation as from the *Georgics* (identifying the Thames with the 'winding' river Mincius in the Veneto, by which Virgil was born), he might be forgiven for giving up on the first. It is from the

Renaissance poet Poliziano, whose 'Ambra' refers to another villa by a river – the 'placid' Meles – where Lorenzo the Magnificent and his circle met to discuss philosophy and cultivate the arts, Lorenzo himself being a pretender to poetry.

The approach to Pope's classic portico before a *piano nobile* is as emblematic as the processional route at Penshurst. This had led through the crenellated royal gate to the new owner's armigerous doorway before the great hall, and then to the private garden beyond. The 'Epistolary Description of the Late Mr Pope's House and Gardens' (1747), now the most famous of the accounts of the poet's intentions, orientates the visitor in a similar linear way. But two symbolic approaches are combined at Twickenham (clearly visible Pl. 16), one above (the portico) and one beneath. This lower entrance leads to Pope's celebrated grotto, which, descending beneath the house, bypasses it to emerge in the emblematic garden beyond. It was in this grotto, which he endlessly embellished, that Pope liked it to be imagined that he composed his poetry (Pl. 17). The 'Description' gives this account of the façade:

Over the front entrance into this grotto lies a balustraded platform, and serves the building both as a vestibule and portico; for a balcony projecting from the middle window of the second storey, and supported by pillars resting upon the platform, makes so much of it resemble a portico; but the platform extending without these pillars, becomes more a vestibule: add to this, the window opening into the balcony being crowned with a pediment, gives the several parts an air of one figure, or whole, and adds an inexpressible grace to the front.

This elaboration of Pope's embellishment shows the effectiveness of the motif. The visitor's eye is fixed upon it. Taste works upon sensibility to reveal how the diverse elements of the structure are harmonised in the design, and the symmetry creates an inexpressible feeling of grace. It is small wonder that Pope found it ridiculous at Stanton Harcourt to be precipitated into the kitchens. This is a far more regulated and graduated progress: 'But soft – by regular approach – not yet. . . .' The choice appears to be open between entrance within, by portico and vestibule, or passage beyond to the pleasure grounds by way of the grotto. The inner world of this country house or the miniaturised estate of the garden are both combined by upper or lower approaches, the first the product of classic architecture, the other suggesting the foundation of Nature. Pope might not have attacked Timon so much for *false* ceremony were he not aware how ceremonially formalised was his own iconographic programme. For his river façade is not really for 'use' at all. In fact, the practical front door is on the other side of the villa and merely abuts the road; it is never shown in the images of the house. The function of the river front is to make a programmatic statement.

The writer of the 'Epistolary Description' accordingly assembles a catena of quotations from Pope's verse which spell out his intentions. Here is hospitality, and the dignified ease of the philosopher statesman in retirement, and, less evident, but, implied *sotto voce*, republican idealism. Pope's is a dedicated house:

> To Virtue only and her friends a friend,
> The world besides may murmur or commend.
> Know, all the distant din that world can keep,
> Rolls o'er my grotto and but soothes my sleep.
> There my retreat, the best companions grace,
> Chiefs out of war, and statesmen out of place.
> There ST JOHN mingles with my friendly bowl,
> The feast of reason, and the flow of soul.

Just as the progressive sequence of entry to Penshurst was centred on the hall (the place of the communal meal), so too here a 'feast' is celebrated. But the feudal conception that 'all come in' has been replaced now with the select dinner party of a Horace or a Pliny, or a Socratic symposium. *Mihi et Amicis* was one motto Pope selected for his house, having no coat of arms to set before his gate: 'for myself and my friends' – such as Henry St John, Viscount Bolingbroke. No one else is permitted entry. His retirement, which suggests something of the monastic ideal, is exclusive. Or if one compares Cotta's old hall, here too at Twickenham one sees no 'tenants' or 'benighted wanderer'. Another motto he chose was *Libertati et Amicitiae* – 'to freedom and friendship'. Read in one sense that word 'freedom' suggests an Epicurean withdrawal from society. Pope has opted out from certain communal cares.

But 'freedom and friendship' has an especial political significance. Pope here is 'imitating' Horace, virtually translating the Roman poet, but with modern equivalents. Twickenham is an equivalent of Horace's Sabine Farm revived. The alert classical reader would know that at this point Horace was praising the great republicans of old who had retired to their country houses. He was thinking specifically of the warrior Scipio and the philosopher Laelius, and their patronage of poets. Pope's modern chief out of war is the discredited general Peterborough, his statesman out of place is the disgraced Jacobite Viscount Bolingbroke, philosopher as well as politician. The Palladian villa at Twickenham, modelled on the ancients, is a focus for that kind of public idealism which Rome showed when it was virtuous. But it is also a centre for the opposition to the government. Pope's retirement has been forced by political circumstance. So too has that of his friends Peterborough and Bolingbroke. If Pope could, he would make Twickenham a power house.

The antithetical house might well be Walpole's Houghton (Pl. 18), where, for a few weeks of the year, the First Minister of State descended with his political entourage to plan the next session's ministerial campaigns, and to play at huntin', shootin' and fishin' with the Norfolk gentry. In a way this is far more a contemporary equivalent to the old English feudal tradition than Pope's suburban life. Houghton is like a castle of old, uniting county and country about a veritable power house. But seen from Pope's hostile standpoint, Houghton would represent the House of Pride. Whereas Walpole's state rooms merely displayed the luxury of his acquisitions, especially displayed in his picture collection, Pope was studious to emphasise the virtuous simplicity of his villa, which he filled, not with expensive works for the connoisseur, but with the portraits of his friends, who take their place among images of Homer and Spenser, Shakespeare, Milton, Newton, Inigo Jones and Palladio: 'To Virtue only and her friends a friend.'

Pope especially wished to emphasise his political liberty in his choice of society. One sees in him the emerging conception that an Englishman's home is now his castle, his place of security against the State. He wrote:

> But thanks to Homer since I live and thrive,
> Indebted to no prince or peer alive.
> ('Imitations of Horace', Ep. II, ii, 68–9.)

and in so doing made both an economic and a moral statement. It was his translation of Homer which had been the source of that income which enabled him to establish himself as an independent writer at Twickenham. The translation is also imbued with the high ethical seriousness of Renaissance commentary upon the epic. His freedom from the patronage of the Court is that of a gentleman based upon property. It is also a moral and a republican liberty. Compare the dependence implied by the royal arms of the donor above the gate at Penshurst, or the relation of patron to poet in Jonson, Carew, Herrick or Marvell. Pope mocked Walpole for accepting from the Court the Order of the Garter (displayed among busts of Roman emperors at Houghton). At Twickenham, on the contrary, it is the poet who is free to patronise great men by inviting them to his dinner table.

There is about this something of a competition for symbolism. Houghton too was a Palladian villa, and thus part of the same iconographic tradition as Pope invokes. Any reader of the government writers of the age will find much the same ideological apparatus as at Twickenham, yet turned round *mutatis mutandis* for the purposes of the administration. But to follow that line would be to translate Pope's verse into mere ideology, whereas what the writer seeks to achieve is to turn the politics of the country house into poetry. Imaginatively conceived, Pope's Twickenham, as described by him, does not actually function as a dwelling but as a series of significant signs.

That is particularly noticeable in the lines on 'the feast of reason', quoted above. The place of this symposium is neither the 'hall' (as tradition would have it), nor the dining room. Instead the location is Pope's grotto, that mysterious entrance always shown in images of the house from the river, leading beneath the Palladian portico, yet supporting it. The 'Epistolary Description' quotes the 'Imitations of Horace' (Sat. II, i):

> There my retreat, the best companions grace,
> Chiefs out of war, and statesmen out of place.

In matter of fact host and guests would have sat in 'the great parlour' (so described in the inventory taken after Pope's death) at an oval table round which ten might have dined in comfort. Service would have been from two marble tables upon brackets, reflected in the large glass with a gold frame on the wall, where hung also portraits of Pope, his father, mother and aunts, landscapes and still lifes, and (inevitably) 'a drawing of Homer'. Afterwards the company would have withdrawn to 'the best room fronting the Thames', with its handsome walnut chairs and pink and silver settee upon a large French carpet. Or they might have browsed in the library. Did the poet's elderly mother join St John and Peterborough, or did she prefer a discreet retreat elsewhere (like the almost invisible servants), her portrait on the wall serving as sufficient recall of her presence?

Rather than describe how his house functioned, Pope prefers a poetic synecdoche (the grotto) – a part of the house stands for the whole (just as one might call an old manor house a 'hall'). He also describes the grotto as the place where, in reflective introspection, he creates poetry (he no more writes in his library than eats in his dining room). It is a sign of hermit-like withdrawal from society amongst what the philosopher Shaftesbury called the 'solemn representation of things natural'.[5] The house is a monastery undissolved, home of the last of the monks as well as the seat of the last of the Romans.

It is appropriate, therefore, that the writer of the 'Epistolary Description' of Twickenham, landed from the Thames, does not enter the house itself. That would have been irrelevant iconographically. Its exterior records sufficient message of the classic/Palladian tradition. Instead he enters the one open passage before him which leads, beneath the portico, directly into the grotto, a region, he records full of 'deception' and 'mirrors' reflecting the natural spring and the ores and minerals within, and giving glimpses of the world without between river and garden, so that 'by a fine taste and happy management of Nature, you are presented with an indistinguishable mixture of realities and imagery'.

The author 'holds the mirror up' to Pope's intentions, reflecting them in the language of the time. That balance between reality and imagination, between taste and nature, is exactly what this country house is about. The groundwork is the divine rationality of things, God as expressed through the creation and creativity of Nature. The rocks beneath the house, gathered lovingly by Pope and arranged as a natural history museum and as a cave of the Muse, are literally the foundations of the villa, which rises upon them like a restored ruin of Rome from the engravings of Piranesi or Domenico Cunego. Metaphorically this is also a Sybil's cave, a realm of poetic prophecy; or that grotto where the nymph Egeria was said by legend to have taught religion and policy to wise Numa, one of the first rulers of Rome. To appreciate this is a sign of 'taste'. Only the educated elite will generate this association of ideas. But it is not an affectation of scholarship. It reveals the order of things.

The visitor emerged from the grotto into the garden, first into the 'wilderness', the uncultivated original paradise, then, by way of a temple, to more cultivated realms beyond. The meaning of that needs no gloss. Pope chose to relate house to this natural world by one major sign. Within, in the dining parlour, hung the portrait of his mother; here, at a climactic point in the garden, upon a mound, surrounded by cypresses, he raised to her memory after she was dead a heaven-directed obelisk:

the plinth of the pillar bears this inscription on its four sides, beginning with that which faces the walk

AH EDITHA!

MATRUM OPTIMA.

MULIERUM AMANTISSIMA.

VALE.

One may compare Marlborough, self-gloriously on his column at Blenheim, the cynosure of his own eyes, in an estate where all the world is centred on his dining salon. Pope prefers, domestically, to pay the tribute of familial piety to his mother which Roman *pietas* and Christian reverence both enjoin.

Yet that tragic '*vale*' – farewell, Edith, best of mothers, most beloved of wives – speaks too of Pope's unique position in the inherited tradition. He is literally alone. Compare the fertility of a Barbara Gamage, which matches that of the country maids and the trees of her estate, or even the hope that Marvell reposed (in vain) in the generative and regenerative power of Maria Fairfax. For Pope there were no children to inherit even his small estate (even if the anti-Catholic laws had allowed), and though the family portraits hung upon the wall, as they should in the country house, this was not the family home. This house, in which the lord dwelt, was only an inn where he reposed as a passenger.

It is a condition which Pope repeatedly emphasises in his verse, and in it is one of several similarities which attracted him to Horace, childless on his Sabine farm. The 'Epistolary Description' ends with a series of passages from Pope on the transitoriness of estates:

> Let lands and houses have what lords they will
> Let us be fix'd, and our own masters still.

As Shaftesbury asked, 'what point of urns and obelisks in retir'd places' if there is nothing 'answerable to this in the mind of the possessors'? But Pope's mind is indeed 'answerable' as he provides the moral gloss on that destiny which he must make his choice. Let us be, in virtue, our own masters. Yet that morality also draws attention to how far his symbolic country house is separated from the old tradition which linked the home of ancient reverence to its estate handed down from father to son. Nowadays landlords treat houses as marketable commodities. So Pope wrote to his friend, Dean Swift:

> What's property? dear Swift! you see it alter
> From you to me, from me to Peter Walter.

The name Peter Walter is introduced with a sneer. He was a money lender, a land steward, and became a landowner and parliamentarian, dying worth £300,000, so Pope claimed. The short example of the meteoric rise of a new man encapsulates a substantial lesson in economic history. Capitalism has replaced feudalism. The country house, like everything else, is subject to the laws of the market. If that is not Pope's vocabulary, which is moralistic, it is the economic reality he perceived in his society.

There is another change in the order of things which was not yet so apparent. Twickenham provides the first major instance of the suburban-isation of the country house in England, the transfer of the ideals of the great estate to the small garden, the spread of what Wells called the 'Bladesover system' into the life style of the lower classes. Here is a private house close to good communications to the city with a few acres of lawn screened by trees. It enjoyed what the poet Thomson called 'elegant sufficiency' (*Spring*, 1161). There is a nominal kitchen garden, but, as Pope remarks in his verse, he can easily send out for what he needs.[6] A classical façade was placed upon the plain box of the building to add status, but, as the 'Epistolary Description' tells (perhaps recalling Timon), without 'the vastness of expense and magnificence'. This is the beginning of the cultural language of suburbia, *rus in urbe* – the countryside, and the country house, in the town. As architectural history tells, the villa style inundated London by the end of the century. If one may for a moment permit a certain play with motifs, Pope's grotto, which in fact is a passage under the mainroad which separates house and garden, is an early instance of an urban underpass. It divides the pedestrian from commuter traffic. And can it be that the last bastardised offspring of the Popeian grotto where 'a million diamonds shine' are the garden gnomes peering through the rockeries of present day Twickenham?[7] An age which has lost its cultural inheritance still has its mythology, if now drawn from Disneyland and not from classical antiquity.

CHAPTER TEN

The houses of Pope's Timonesque friends

POPE'S VILLA stands at an architectural crossroads. One path leads to suburbia, the other to the grandiloquent palaces of the eighteenth-century oligarchy. Colossal wealth multiplied 'modest' Palladian pavilions across a vast façade, seeking to justify great expenditure by the signs of republican simplicity, yet ostentatious of grandeur. Thomson in *The Seasons* called Hagley merely a 'Hall' where the old 'hospitable Genius lingers still', but the old black and white house was, in fact, demolished by Pope's friend, Lord Lyttelton, and the massively expensive Palladian country seat which replaced it is securely separated from its tenantry by a famous landscaped park. At Holkham too Lord Leicester cultivated the Palladian mode. Many years and vast expenditure went into the construction of the symbolic house and on enriching the interior, especially the great collection of books (Pl. 19). Outside the landscaped park rolled to the horizon. Lord Leicester, like Pope, achieved a contemplative solitude:

It is a melancholy thing to stand alone in one's own country. I look around, not a house to be seen but my own. I am Giant, of Giant Castle, and have ate up all my neighbours – my nearest neighbour is the King of Denmark.[1]

Among Pope's immediate circle, the most extraordinary example of image building is Bolingbroke's construction of Dawley Farm. When he returned from political exile in 1725 (he had been a Jacobite), a large part of his fortune was sunk in purchasing an estate to make a public and symbolic statement about classic and republican virtue. Like Munodi, the admirer of the ancients, in *Gulliver's Travels*, the aim was to follow 'the best rules of ancient architecture', and thus to adopt morally too 'the old forms . . . in every part of his life without innovation'. To achieve this end, paradoxically, the Manor of Dawley was new built, £200 alone being spent by Bolingbroke 'to paint his country-hall with trophies of rakes, spades, prongs, &c. and other ornaments merely to countenance his calling the place a farm'. Four hundred acres of parkland were turned to pasturage or planted as orchards without regard to economic cost. Thus the world would see him as a statesman of old. Swift, with rare flattery, rose to the bait, praising him as Cincinnatus, and asking when would Bolingbroke, philosopher statesman as well as farmer, arise 'like the Dictator from the plough?' Pope preferred the example of Laelius, to whom he alluded in his 'imitations' of Horace, a man 'celebrated for his statesmanship, his philosophical pursuits, and his friendship . . . delighting, in his retirement from public affairs, in the society of the poet Lucilius'.

> Here the proud trophies, and the spoils of war
> Yield to the scythe, the harrow and the car.

So the celebratory verses 'Dawley Farm' portray Bolingbroke.[2]

But the real-life Bolingbroke was quite unable to live up to his own exercise in image building. No one believed that the ambitious statesman had really become an old time farmer, nor that Dawley, rebuilt to be old, was anything but the smartest of modern country houses. 'Dawley Farm' remarks of Bolingbroke that 'what he built a palace calls a farm', and wishing to praise all things exclaims:

> See! Emblem of himself, his villa stand!
> Politely finish'd, regularly grand!

This 'grand palace' promptly ran Bolingbroke into serious financial trouble, the cost of the house and the income from the estate being out of balance. His attempt to rebuild not a house but a political career by the pretence of Roman virtue convinced no one in power, and by the 1730s he was desperate to part with Dawley at any price: the 'establishment' he had always contemplated at Dawley became 'useless' to him, 'none of the favorable contingencies that might have happened, did happen'. He retired to France, but neither he nor Pope was prepared to draw the obvious moral. Muses do not cultivate the soil, as 'Dawley Farm' had fancifully claimed, but ''Tis use alone that justifies expense', and this expense was so much poeticised waste.

The same financial problems struck Bathurst's projects at Cirencester and Burlington's at Chiswick. At Cirencester, Swift remarked on the 'two thousand five hundred acres of garden and not a codling to eat', and Pope's letters are full of comment on Bathurst's 'work in the Brobdingnag style': the plan to join Severn and Thames by a tunnel 'not above twelve or fifteen miles'; the fantasy for a pyramid a hundred feet square; the even greater fantasy of transporting Pope's own villa to become a garden ornament there with some 'three or four million of plants' out of the nursery to amuse him. One project completed was the construction of 'Alfred's castle' from the remains of the old demolished manor house of Sapperton. This was a temple to ancient British liberty, and here the tenantry were to be feasted, but only once a year. Old style hospitality and Timonesque reality are utterly at variance.³

Chiswick never pretended to be anything but a symbol (Pl. 20). As Lord Hervey observed, it was 'too little to live in, and too large to hang one's watch'. The villa was a temple to the arts, a repository for books, statuary and pictures, a restaurant for entertainment, a summer house for the garden. There was no surrounding estate. Duty, from time to time, drew the reluctant Burlington from London to Yorkshire to attend to his lands, his family and neighbours. His property in Ireland was beyond the pale. The purpose of the estates was to provide money for the passionate aestheticism of 'taste', and when the cost of this 'useless' expenditure proved too great, the Irish lands were sold.

It is difficult, therefore, to distinguish between Pope's fictional Timon and his real friends. The crucial case is Viscount Cobham's Stowe, a house and estate which has canonical status both for the poet and for his age, celebrated by Pope and by Thomson ('the fair majestic paradise of Stowe'), where Pope himself is commemorated in the Elysian Fields of the symbolic garden, and for which a series of laudatory guidebooks explained the key significance of the place for the perambulatory eighteenth-century visitor.

Yet there is no major structural or functional difference between an obviously Timonesque palace like Marlborough's showplace Blenheim – which Pope despised – and Stowe, the Palladianised sign of Cobham's patriot virtue (the architect Vanbrugh worked at both). Though there was no ancient manor (like Woodstock at Blenheim (Pl. 21)) to be demolished at Stowe, the simple 'Wren' house of 1680 was already, by Pope's time, out of keeping with the ambitions of Viscount Cobham, and the old was gulped down the maw of the new, first as part of a patched architectural mess of agglomerated pavilions, looking more like a 'street front' than a unified design, then gradually digested, until by the 1770s the last visible traces of the old manor house, except the door, were stuccoed over, provided with an attic, crowned with vases and lost in the unified neo-Palladian, neo-Adam building which we now see (Pl. 22).

As at Blenheim, the visitor would have entered by the vestibule of a great hall. The ceiling of the hall, by Burlington's protégé, William Kent, is still extant. Cobham was known as 'the greatest Whig in the army' of Marlborough, and Kent's ceiling shows the great man receiving a sword, not from his general, but from Mars himself. The Great Parlour beyond also recalls Blenheim, for it is hung with tapestries from the Art of War series from Lambert de Hindt's designs, decorated with the Viscount's coat of arms and crest. From the central Great Parlour there stretched the usual baroque enfilade of state rooms, ten in number, four hundred and fifty feet across the façade, mirroring each other: state dressing rooms, state bedrooms and beds, and a long gallery where a hundred might sit down to eat. Further tapestries, again ornamented with Cobham's arms, depicted the triumphs of Mars, of Bacchus and Neptune, Diana and 'laughing Ceres'. There were Siena marble chimney pieces, elaborately carved and bronzed allegorical reliefs, pompous ceilings of elaborate scrollwork on a mosaic ground. These were fit rooms in which to receive a king, and if this were to be long awaited, yet as leader of the opposition, Cobham several times entertained Frederick, Prince of Wales.

Pope's silence on the economy of this house is not the least of the evasions of his poetry, faced by the discrepancy between old ideal and new luxury. But it is the garden he particularly commends, and it was to the garden that the visitor's attention was especially directed by the long series of guidebooks, for here a moral was spelled out which justified possession of all this for 'envious' eyes. The ornaments and vistas of the natural scene are, in many ways, the visible recreation of the ideology of Popeian verse. Here many of the motifs of the country house tradition are preserved as if ritual totems. There is the fertility of the soil, commemorated in temples of Bacchus and Venus; hospitality in a Temple of Friendship; religion in the village church, now enparked as one of a number of Gothic ornaments in a classic scene. But above all is written here the greatness of the family, and the great events in which they had been involved, in Cobham Monument, Grenville Column, Temple of Concord and Victory, Queen Caroline's Monument and Queen's Temple. From these the assiduous visitor could reconstruct much of the history of the times. The function of the display, the opening of house and grounds to the public, the provision of a guidebook, justify the wealth and power of the family by showing that this estate is the proper foil for men and women of heroic stature. It is appropriate that eventually the great vista from the house should be closed by a triumphal arch beyond which nothing can be seen, so that those who own the house themselves might daily contemplate 'monuments of their own magnificence'.

It is extraordinarily beautiful. Here is the perfection of Nature in the English countryside, idealised in the interchange of venerable trees, reflective water and rich verdage. Looking out from selected points of view the eye perceives the park blending imperceptibly with the fertility of the surrounding farmland, the whole estate become a garden.[4] It is the landscape of Constable. Gazing inwards you see glimpses of classical antiquity, a temple, a bridge, a column part hidden, part revealed by the landscape. It is romantic, evocative, the world of Claude's great Arcadian paintings, or Keats's imagination. In the centre of all, the great house resides, at peace in its own land, its great library rich with the learning that will explain the scene, its great family the only begetters of the munificence of the display.

It is conceived on the grandest scale. The best part of a square mile is devoted to the house enparked. It is a spectacular example of the rejection of the doctrine of 'use'. It is a sign of the greatness of the family that so much can be devoted only to display. This is the superfluity of wealth; it overflows like a fountain, it is a theatre for magnificence. Severe morality might comment in the words of Dr Johnson (in *Rasselas*) upon the pyramids: he that has built for use till use is satisfied must begin to build for vanity. But Johnson, like Pope, was a conservative and a reactionary. There is a new morality expressed at Stowe.

The guidebooks of Seeley, Gilpin and Bickham deliver the message.[5] In Gilpin's *Dialogue Upon the Gardens at Stowe* (1748), one of the characters, Polyphon, expresses the old morality. He is concerned to see so much land taken out of the productive economy. But Calliphilus (whose name means lover of beauty) puts a superior case, part aesthetic, part moral and part economic: do not house, estate and the tourist industry generate substantial employment? 'Variety of trades, supports poor families and encourages Art and Industry.' But more important than this, since the garden (and later the house) is open to all, the spirits of all are refreshed by perceiving great works of art among the beauties of Nature. In Thomson's words, the visitor

> Will tread in thought the groves of Attic land;
> Will from thy standard taste refine her own.
> *(Autumn,* 1056–7)

Taste, ultimately, is moral, and the estate is a declaration of virtue's principles, literally inscribed in the mottoes of the emblematic garden buildings, which Gilpin and his fellow travellers assiduously record.

It would be a substantial task to describe the whole, but at the heart of the garden is a group of buildings which may illustrate the essential message. In the region known as the 'Elysian Fields' (Paradise's only map) there face one another, across a stream called the river Styx, the Temple of Ancient Virtue and the Shrine of British Worthies. The Styx, in classical mythology, divided the living from the dead, and the god Mercury presides above the Shrine ready to carry the souls of the Moderns to join the Ancients (Pl. 23). (Nearby the ruins of a Temple of Modern Virtue satirised the corruption of the Walpole regime.) The Ancients are Epaminondas, Homer, Lycurgus and Socrates, the greatest general, poet, statesman and philosopher of antiquity. The Moderns include Alfred, Elizabeth, William III, Drake, Raleigh, Hampden, Shakespeare, Milton, Pope, Newton, Locke and Inigo Jones. These are fit counterparts for the Ancients – 'a sacred band/ Of princes, patriots, bards and sages', Gilbert West described them in laudatory verse[6] – and each is celebrated by a suitable inscription. But this is a promiscuous trawl of modern England.

It is an extraordinary act of elision which unites Shakespeare, the panegyrist of Elizabethan chauvinism, with Milton, the regicide; Inigo Jones, the designer of fulsome flatteries for the Stuarts, with Hampden, who defied them; William III, the hammer of the Catholics, with Pope, a sentimental Jacobite. Yet the implied argument is that the country estate here (as at Appleton House) is capable of absorbing and reconciling the tensions within society, of harmonising them in imaginative structures, and by recreating order within Nature, it renews the present while preserving the past. The best of all these great men lives on in spirit at Stowe.

Nearby stands a remarkable Gothic structure. It is the Temple of Liberty (Pl. 24). It was the belief of the time that the ancient Saxons were the first builders in Gothic form, and the founders of the free British constitution. Thus, the architectural motif stands for that old, free England of which the Whigs claimed to be the guardians. In Gilpin's *Dialogue* this is joined also with ancient Roman republican freedom. The party politics of this need not concern us, nor the history. But here again is a variant upon the idea of the primitive house. There is an appeal to architectural origins as the guarantee of virtue, underwritten by the setting in the right order of Nature itself. Imperceptibly this is blended with a metaphoric recreation of the ancient country house. We have seen before irregular 'Gothic' forms tied together by an onrunning crenellation. Structurally abstracted it is the Penshurst motif. The tower clapped on one corner first recalls the form of a fortress, but on closer examination suggests rather a parish church with quatrefoil windows, bell loft and crocketed finials. The old manor house and the village church, always closely related, are here made one. The joining of Gothic fenestration to elongated classical orders provides yet another historical elision. The ancient Saxons and the first Romans were, after all, at one. Liberty is thus expressed by the creation of the sign of a house of ancient reverence normatively uniting two traditions, classic and Gothic.

Judged from a different historical perspective, it is easy enough to be critical of an ideology which claims that Nature and the Ancients, classic and Gothic, the Whig party and correct taste, are the same. The very necessity of expressing this merely in signs such as the Temple of Liberty may betray an unease at the obliteration of the old conservative country house tradition by the construction of a vast political power house and palace like Stowe. But the aim of the guides is to justify the signs as correspondent to reality, to promote the greatness of the house because it is correspondent to its virtue. As Seeley records of Lord Cobham's pillar, it celebrates one 'who hath imitated the virtues of L. Lucullus, a truly great man', whose greatness manifests itself in 'magnificently adorning' his country seat. Lucullus we have met before in late Roman panegyric.

His example may serve to remind us that this is the villa architecture of an idealised imperial people. Great power requires great houses to express it. That is the accepted decorum.

So the four quarters of the world, it is said, bring their gifts to Stowe, and it is a sign of the virtue of the family that they 'build their empire on their people's love'. It is a new variant on the old theme that 'all come in' bringing their affectionate tribute. The 'Bladesover system' has become the centre not only of England, but of the entire subject globe. The peaceful garden, like the house itself, is full of the emblems of imperial war (the very trees in Thomson's celebratory poetry stand like files of soldiers). Yet it is the purpose of imperial war to defend lawful peace. So Virgil had written in the *Aeneid*.[7] So here, at Stowe, the *pax Britannica* being assured throughout the world, 'From storms secure the peaceful hinds reside.' The house is the guarantee of this, as it is of agricultural and commercial plenty, of religion and of liberty.

There is no reason to deny that there are real grounds for this celebration. Improved agriculture generated real wealth, as did imperial commerce. If 'liberty', so often celebrated in Whig ideology, often means only the freedom of the great landed aristocracy, who appropriately saw their political role mirrored by a Scipio or Cicero of old, yet the discourse of civic freedom and responsibility was not without its effect on the way men and women acted. In its perfected form Stowe seeks to represent a moment of eternal equipoise in which enormous wealth flows in to the family (Hester's 'seven hundred children' commemorated in the Grenville room!) and equally great benefits, cultural, economic and political, flow forth.

Yet there is a point (but what point?) at which mere accumulation becomes offensive. The figure of Timon is never far away. Neither park nor house was let alone; the park constantly extending by hundreds of acres at a bound to incorporate ever more symbols, the house continually refurbished to keep pace with a rage of taste: library and music room and giant oval saloon as a Pantheon to the family, with a Roman triumphal procession on the frieze; and into these rooms poured pictures and furniture and *objets* of every kind as colossal wealth expressed itself in colossal acquisition:

everything is in the modern and most superb taste [wrote George Bickham on Cobham's death in 1750], gilded carvings, glasses and sconces, without number; fine wrought frames, well-painted ceilings, variety of pictures, on all subjects, by the ablest masters; marble busts, statues, curious chimneys, elegant tables, rich hangings and tapestry, gilded furniture.[8]

The key word for Bickham, as for Pope, is 'taste'. 'Use' has little place here. Such is the profusion of objects that they are already beyond number, and the superlative adjectives are expressive not of function but of a kind of auctioneer's admiring patter – superb, fine, elegant, rich. This gilded *luxuria* has been executed in every field by ablest masters. This is display for the sake of 'taste, expense, state and parade . . . in some of the finest rooms perhaps in *Europe*' – to employ Lord Hervey's words on Walpole's Houghton. It overwhelms, just as Cotton had been over-whelmed at Chatsworth the century before when his celebration of the house became merely a list:

> The rooms of state, stair-cases, galleries,
> Lodgings, apartments, closets, offices . . .
> The picture, sculpture, carving, graving, gilding . . .

If Timon's villa were Canons house, as is sometimes suggested,[9] Timon-esque plunder from the fall of Canons was carried to Stowe, supple-mented from the Ducal Palace at Venice, and from the sale of Fonthill in the early nineteenth century. After remorseless political campaigning came the Order of the Garter, and (as at Houghton) another space in the ceiling might be filled by elaborate plaster celebration. In 1820 and 1845 the vast anachronism of Borra's state bed was remodelled and re-furbished, Queen Victoria's state visit being the apogee of the houses's history, and the prelude to its financial smash in 1848. Timon had over-reached himself.

That moment, the hinge of fate, is recorded by the diary of a Victorian visitor, Elizabeth George. Like Bickham, she too found she could not number exactly. 'The profusion of rich and costly objects of Art and decoration at first astonished but soon absolutely wearies and perplexes the senses', she records. She 'walk'd freely about, at liberty' (she uses the key Whig terms) but with little more to do than 'gaze on the valuable and rare paintings, sculpture, etc. . . . Rembrandt Wouvermans Teniers etc. . . .' The et ceteras indicate the uselessness of cataloguing all this, 'a great portion being merely for show . . . inconvenient and uncomfort-able'. Less than half a day of this sort of sight-seeing was enough (and for most visitors still is).

We were quite tired in less than two hours and much as I appreciated the Duke's kindness in having invited us to go I felt quite a relief when we got back to our own homely but snug and comfortable home.[10]

Jonson had made the same distinction two hundred and fifty years before between the show house and that place where a family dwells, though the word 'snug' is expressive of a world of difference between Elizabeth George's 'home, sweet home' – 'be it ever so humble' – and the mysteries of manners, arms and arts which a great country house was to teach its children. But for her Stowe is now failing to teach even a lesson in art history. This visitor is overwhelmed with the cultural paraphernalia of what has become a great museum, a list of things, not a home.

But the capacity of the old house to renew itself remains inexhaustible in English culture. After the place was sold up, emptied of the Cobhams and their 'old heir-looms' (the phrase is that of the auctioneer's priced and annotated catalogue), the vacant space was filled with the rising generation. Stowe became a great public school, its celebrant one of the major teachers of English literature of our time, G. Wilson Knight, whose history *The Dynasty of Stowe*, published in the last year of the Second World War, proclaims its message on 'Public Schools and the Empire': 'Aristocracy of some sort there must be. A ruling group must exist.' That word 'public' carries with it the old message that 'all come in', though, in fact, public school means private – those with the wealth to enter. But with that proviso, the mysteries of manners, arms and arts are still taught to the ruling classes at Stowe. The country house still lives on in the 'houses' of the school.

PART TWO

Preserving

CHAPTER ELEVEN

The country house ethos and the Georgian novel

THE GEORGIAN NOVEL inherited the country house tradition as formed and given by poetry and translated it for a wider audience. The 'great good place' has central signification in the writing of Fielding, Richardson, Smollett, who create Paradise Hall, Grandison Hall, Bramble Hall; the very reiteration of the word 'hall' indicates a strongly conservative feeling. In a similar conservative vein Jane Austen conceives Donwell Abbey (Mr Knightley's ancient home), Pemberley (Mr Darcy's ancestral dwelling) or Mansfield Park, saved by the pious love of Fanny Price. In Scott, though English houses are rare, Willingham in *The Heart of Midlothian* and the anglicised Tully Veolan in *Waverley* have similar significant status. If the novel is a 'bourgeois' form (a word often bandied about), then the literate commercial classes (and especially the woman reader) wished to settle into the traditional order embodied by the rural estate.

This brief litany of names is of fictional places. Of course. One expects that in the novel. Yet the country house poem had centred upon real places, and continued to do so in some dozens of further examples well into the nineteenth century.[1] The one major exception in the early novel is Ralph Allen's new Palladian house, Prior Park, alluded to, though not named, in *Tom Jones*. But Fielding, in celebrating Allen's civic humanism and commercial virtue, his hospitality, piety, charity, adds this is but 'a single instance and I really know not such another'.[2] It is a remarkable statement from the creator of Squire Allworthy. It suggests an acute awareness of a gap between the historical referent – the actual great houses of the age – and the inherited motifs of the country house tradition. It is as if the conventions will not stand up to a closely naturalistic comparison with the outside world. Or, if such comparison were made, it would provoke a major tension, even crisis. It is a matter which the imaginative artist does not wish to explore. He needs the stable norm of an ancient tradition.

This conservativism is intrinsic. This is the story of something always archaic, indeed valued for that very reason, in the old farmer folk of pristine Rome, the old English hospitality, the 'old' classic portico clapped upon a contemporary building, in the very name *Paradise* Hall. It is not possible to go further back than that, though it is the nature of paradise always to be lost. The language of literature is not necessarily a reflection of the 'realities' of the times, but deliberately backward looking, carrying lovingly with itself the accumulated perceptions of the past, slow and reluctant to change. Not make it new, but make it old. If a Roman paradigm fits Georgian England, and the age continually sought to explain the present by the classic past, we find in the novelists the last vestigial celebration of a pristine morality seeking to sustain itself, by whatever mutations, before the overwhelming development of alien forces. It is the pressure from that 'other' which will now be our subject. But, first, the translation of the old myth into the new fiction.

Fielding's *locus classicus* merits extended quotation.

The Gothic style of building could produce nothing nobler than Mr. Allworthy's house. There was an air of grandeur in it that struck you with awe, and rivalled the beauties of the best Grecian architecture; and it was as commodious within as venerable without.

It stood on the south-east side of a hill, but nearer the bottom than the top of it, so as to be sheltered from the north-east by a grove of old oaks, which rose above it in a gradual ascent of near half a mile, and yet high enough to enjoy a most charming prospect of the valley beneath.

In the midst of the grove was a fine lawn, sloping down towards the house; near the summit of which rose a plentiful spring, gushing out of a rock covered with firs, and forming a constant cascade of about thirty feet, not carried down a regular flight of steps, but tumbling in a natural fall over the broken and mossy stones, till it came to the bottom of the rock; then running off in a pebbly channel, that with many lesser falls winded along, till it fell into a lake at the foot of the hill, about a quarter of a mile below the house on the south side, and which was seen from every room in the front. Out of this lake, which filled the centre of a very beautiful plain, embellished with groups of beeches and elms, and fed with sheep, issued a river, that for several miles was seen to meander through an amazing variety of meadows and woods, till it emptied itself into the sea; with a large arm of which, and an island beyond it, the prospect was closed.

On the right of this valley opened another of less extent, adorned with several villages, and terminated by one of the towers of an old ruined abbey, grown over with ivy, and part of the front of which remained still entire.

The left-hand scene presented the view of a very fine park, composed of very unequal ground, and agreeably varied with all the diversity that hills, lawns, wood, and water, laid out with admirable taste, but owing less to art than to what nature could give. Beyond this the country gradually rose into a ridge of wild mountains, the tops of which were above the clouds. (*Tom Jones*, I, 4)

The sun is just rising on this scene, and with the sun rises the owner of Paradise Hall, Mr Allworthy: 'a human being replete with benevolence, meditating in what manner he might render himself more acceptable to his Creator, by doing most good to His creatures'. The divine correspondence is striking; one of the oldest of conservative analogies adapted here to Whig society, for it is the independent gentleman not the king who now rules the kingdom of the country estate. Here are none of the negatives of Jonson's 'Thou art not', or Marvell's ambiguities, or the symbiosis of Pope's Timon with Bathurst or Burlington. Instead we see Paradise Hall from a great height, almost as if we were the Creator Himself contemplating His beneficent and natural creation. It is a viewpoint which inscribes the house in an historical setting for which age and continuity are symbols of value, what Burke was to describe as the wisdom of our ancestors.[3] This is an old manor house, 'venerable' like Penshurst, and implying thus the old values of charity, hospitality, care for the estate, which Allworthy will specifically show as the novel develops. Its 'Gothic' form, like the Temple of Liberty at Stowe, alludes to the 'ancient constitution' of the realm; and ancient religion is also recalled. '[T]he towers of an old ruined abbey' remind that Paradise Hall has been built from the very stones of the monastic settlement, and thus the country house has taken over the religious and charitable functions performed by the monks of yore. Protestant expropriation is suppressed by picturesque image; the passage of time has healed any wound by the translation of virtue from one House of Holiness to another.

The grove of old oaks confirms the antiquity of the scene and inspires that veneration which the ancients called *religio*. The oaks naturalise the house too, as if it originated, like everything else, from the landscape. The artificial cascade in the park descends by a 'natural fall', and all the careful hierarchical graduations of the scene owe 'less to art than to . . . nature'. Reiteration makes the sense emphatic. But the parkland serves more than this symbolic function. The trees – oak, beech, elm – are signs of fertility and prosperity, as any estate manager would know, and the sheep cropping the grass are not only natural and pastoral emblems, but feed the ground (by their very dung) as they crop. They too have economic utility. The picturesque river delights the eye, but is also a practical means of commercial communication, and the villages which 'adorn' the landscape have grown up because of the wealth of the estate, for which they provide the labour, and which feeds and protects them in return under the panoptic eye of Mr Allworthy. The scene finally closes by directing attention back from owner of the house to his Creator by means of the sublime mountains on the horizon whose tops are lost in heavenly clouds.

Apart from Allworthy the scene is empty of folk. No one tills the fields. Nothing stirs on the river. Not a servant is about the house. 'All that mighty heart is lying still.' Fielding has chosen dawn to reveal Paradise Hall. Absence, silence, stillness, are appropriate to the moment. It is an acknowledgement of the force of the ancient myth of the land bringing forth of its own volition. It is the viewpoint of Allworthy as possessor of the estate at a moment of leisure. But it is for a moment only. When the landscape fills with the characters of the novel – imprudent Tom, hypocritical Blifil, Thwackum and Square, false philosophers, Western, the petty tyrant – the image is no longer of paradise. On the contrary. *Tom Jones* is a satirical peregrination of eighteenth-century society. It is only in the 'fade out' into happy marriage at the end of the novel that one may again imagine paradise restored as Western's estate is joined to Allworthy's by the marriage of Tom to the wise Sophia, and the circle of goodness grows a little wider. But Fielding does not recreate his opening image. The isolation of this great passage in the novel, the isolation of Allworthy and the reader in the scene, are powerful indications that this is a visionary moment, the recreation of an idea of paradise with all the cultural and traditional power of myth imaginatively to order, explain, control human apprehension and activity. It is, as it were, an act of communion, that instant of purification which cleanses the ills of the world, though both before and after those ills have been and always will be.

There is no other moment so powerful and so formal in the reiteration of country house motifs in the prose fiction of Georgian society, though in poetry Thomson recreates similar images in the celebration of landscape, and the painters of the age will record house and owner and the land in comprehensive vision – idealised with the classic allusiveness of Richard Wilson's England, recreated in the image of Claude; or naturalised by Arthur Devis. Richardson, in *Sir Charles Grandison*, is Fielding's only serious rival in the novel in country house ideology as in so much else. The meticulous particularity of his description of his 'good man's house' in a long series of letters in his seventh volume provides a veritable checklist of desirable features given local habitation and a name. It runs the risk, however, of making the ideal ridiculous by too much detail. Richardson rarely knows when to stop.

Sir Charles is a man of taste and a Christian. As classic virtuoso he has collected pictures, statues, bronzes and busts from his travels, but as a lover of God he gathers his household about him in an elegant chapel, and as an example to all his people he worships in the village church. His familial piety is shown by his care for the dispositions of his father, and his reverence for his mother. Even an old gilt-framed cabinet 'will always be fashionable' because it was hers. The family portraits hang in the gallery. Though he has remodelled his house in the new classic style, the ancient 'Hall' is still a centre of care and hospitality. For Sir Charles's friends there are convenient 'lodging rooms' fit even for the 'best lord in the land'. For the tenants, or rather '*my* friends *my* workmen', there is a pharmacy and a salaried apothecary, and a surgeon who lives rent-free on this welfare estate, and even a library of improving literature kept for the loving domestic servants. Small wonder that the Hall is delightful in the prospects it commands of the prosperous and contented estate. In the park, which shows a just blend of art and nature, flourish the plantations of Sir Charles's ancestors. Flocks of fertilising sheep crop the grass, in the gardens grow apples and oranges, cherries, plums and peaches. Tenants and servants are 'sober' and 'diligent' and 'housewifely' and 'pious'. And so on, and so on.

What love he inspires in everyone, this Allworthy man, like God in His creation! So the 'prudent' housekeeper, Mrs Curzon, exclaims to Harriet Byron, who has wed this paragon:

Don't your ladyship see, how all his servants love him as they attend him at table? How they watch his eye in silent reverence – indeed, madam, we all adore him; and have prayed morning, noon, and night, for his coming hither, and settling among us. And now is the happy time; forgive me, madam; I am no flatterer; but we all say, He has brought another angel to bless us.   (VII, 8)

To which. what can Lady Grandison reply but 'The very servants live in paradise'. Their Lord, having been unfortunately absent, now dwells indeed! But one can see why Fielding detested Richardson. It is not just a question of artistic restraint, though Richardson runs on for dozens of pages, but rather that too much sweetness and piety cloys the palate – Sir Charles at the organ singing hymns while his wife weeps is one unforgettable moment. These unctuous servants are just too much. It suggests not an ideal made real – an estate can actually be like Grandison Hall in every particular – but rather hypocrisy: 'I am no flatterer; but we all say, He has brought another angel to bless us.' One celestial visitation is remarkable in this naughty world, but TWO angels in the house!

Fielding, who was a classicist, took his country house tradition direct from its sources. Richardson works at second hand. There is something about his writing of the assiduity of the examinee eager to put in everything he has been taught, and the 'bourgeois' writer here seems far more like a cultural lackey of the ruling classes than does Fielding, who belongs with the 'gentry'. Both writers, however, have purified their descriptions of that apparatus of learned allusions which had been so much the cultural code of the poets from Jonson, the imitator of Martial, to Pope, who follows Horace. It is choice in Fielding, ignorance in Richardson, but it extends the potential audience then as now. The eighteenth-century novelists for many readers provide the first point of entry to English literature freely available. They can be read directly for pleasure. Just as the architecture of the villa spread the country house ethos symbolically into suburbia, so the novel secures the territory of popular fiction.

It is a territory rapidly colonised after the example of Fielding and Richardson. Many of the devices of *Tom Jones* reappear in Smollett's *Humphrey Clinker*. Bramble Hall, like Paradise Hall, is the still centre round which the story wheels on its great peregrination of Britain, and the prickly, but good-hearted, Matt Bramble, in his way, has the same moral function as Mr Allworthy. It is he, especially, who restores the estate of Mr Baynard, formally 'a convent of Cistercian monks', but whose ancient virtue, symbolised by its great avenue of tall oaks, is threatened now by the luxurious innovations of a Timonesque wife, whose rage for fashion substitutes unproductive show for utility, and will lead to bankruptcy. Gradually Matt Bramble wins back the estate, and at last 'laughing Ceres re-assumes the land':

> With Baynard's good leave, I ordered the gardener to turn the rivulet into its old channel, to refresh the fainting naïads, who have so long languished among mouldering roots, withered leaves, and dry pebbles. The shrubbery is condemned to extirpation; and the pleasure-ground will be restored to its original use of corn-field and pasture.
>
> (Letter of 26 October)

The naturalistic form of the novel enables Smollett to enter at times even minutely into the practicalities of restoring an estate, both here, and in the account of Mr Dennison's 'experiments in agriculture, according to the directions of Lyle, Tull, Hart, Duhamel'. Only the learned reader will observe how much his satire on luxurious excess owes to Juvenal, and his praise of moderation to Horace and Pope.

Richardson, inevitably, appealed more to Jane Austen. Darcy's Pemberley has many of the characteristics of Grandison Hall, as Elizabeth Bennet comes to learn on her visit. Here too tenants and servants loyally recommend him as 'the best landlord and the best master'. The wisdom of antiquity is reverenced in the ancient library, and the old family celebrated in the picture gallery. Permitted to enter, from that privileged position, Elizabeth surveys the estate:

> Every disposition of the ground was good; and she looked on the whole scene, the river, the trees scattered on its banks, and the winding of the valley, as far as she could trace it, with delight. As they passed into other rooms, these objects were taking different positions; but from every window there were beauties to be seen. The rooms were lofty and handsome, and their furniture suitable to the fortune of their proprietor; but Elizabeth saw, with admiration of his taste, that it was neither gaudy nor uselessly fine; with less of splendour, and more real elegance, than the furniture of Rosings.
>
> 'And of this place,' thought she, 'I might have been mistress!'
>
> (*Pride and Prejudice*, III, 1)

House and estate, in the absence of their lord, still show his good qualities. There is no need to gloss the passage in detail. 'And of this place, I might have been mistress!' Compare the mistress of Penshurst, the great heiress of Wales, born and bred in 'the mysteries of manners, arms and arts'; or Maria Fairfax, whose marriage from greatness to greatness will reknit the unravelled state. Who is Liz Bennet compared with these? The empathetic reader, clutching the latest novel from the circulating library, imagines herself translated from pedestrian gentility to the elegances of Pemberley. The door of the country house opens to the aspirations of the (always rising) middle classes. Even further down the social scale a governess at Thornfield Hall will later exclaim, 'Reader, I married him', and a mere genteel companion will find herself mistress of the treasure house of Manderley.

That is for the future. For the Georgians the *topoi*, the commonplaces, of the country house tradition have securely transferred from poetry to prose, from neoclassical idealism to naturalistic forms. They are available for anyone to read, and become the material for common aspiration. But to continue to reiterate these motifs would be reductively repetitive, to follow Richardson, as it were, in ticking off a list: here is the doctrine of 'use' again in Austen, here Smollett has followed Pope out of Virgil and Horace. It also risks missing the wood for the trees. The conservative myth was always reactive. By the time Smollett and Austen were writing it has become deeply self-protective. The fundamental threats were first corruption from within; then destruction from without.

That was the Roman paradigm. It is no more than an enabling model. History does not repeat itself specifically. But it is a mode of ordering the nature of things which all classicists had inherited, and which passes on, inevitably, into popular fiction with the country house ethos itself. What destroyed the *ancien régime* in Rome had been *luxuria*, that passion for possession to which the acquisition of a great empire pandered. So the commonplace story ran. The gratifications of private wealth replaced public virtue. Hence the inner corruption of the *ancien régime* exposed it to destruction by barbarian invasion, Vandal hordes with freedom in their mouths, and swords in their hands (so Tacitus had written). The analogy with Georgian England was not difficult to make.

This concept of *luxuria* informs Pope's Mandevillean portrait of Timon. It underlies the redemption of Mr Baynard's estate in Smollett, or Fielding's castigation of Lady Bellaston in the new Rome of London in *Tom Jones* – where anything may be had for a price, even the souls of men. In fiction the old order reasserts itself. Baynard's lands are restored; Tom and Sophia return to paradise. But fiction is misleading, and Fielding is well aware that the providential order is the novelist's, not obvious in society. Look, by comparison, at the iconography of representative real houses outside the moral net woven by the composers of conservative myth – Holkham, Kedleston, Osterley, Syon, for example. These houses are declarations of 'taste', for subsequent generations the cynosure of aesthetic excellence. What has inspired their owners is not a vision of their homes as a moral norm, but an acquisitive passion for works of art which is directly analogous to the villa culture of ancient Rome, on which, in fact, much of the imagery of the houses is modelled (so the work of the Adam brothers). It is an aestheticism which transforms the concept of *luxuria* from a term of moral castigation to 'luxury', which is now a term of praise.

Contemplate the grand hall at Holkham, part basilica, part thermae, part temple (Pl. 25). One enters below a row of Ionic columns. We are not yet of their world. Between them, above, in hierarchic procession like the saints in a Byzantine mosaic stand the icons of classical statuary. The great exedra of the coffered ceiling mirrors the flight of steps which leads up to the level of the ancients and to the double doors of the entrance to the saloon and rooms of state, where ancient statuary comes alive in the person of the master of the house. This is the functional ceremony of power, but also an astonishing act of the aesthetic imagination. The wonderful hues of the warm Derbyshire alabaster and the vivid black marble of the decorated frieze to the podium convey an intense sensual, even sensualist, pleasure, and the enraptured imagination is translated from the present world to another order of existence of unlimited wealth perfected in classical beauty.

Examine the marquetry of the furniture in the library at Osterley, the care with which the grain of the veneers has been laid, the exquisite gradation of the colouring, the selection of decorative motifs: on the desk trophies of music and painting, lyre and flute, palette and brushes, garlanded and framed, and with them too the signs of architecture and music (Pl. 26). Even the very splats of the chairs display ormulu medallions inspired by classic gems, for Robert Child collected antique coins and medals, which repose in a medal cabinet, equally fine. At Kedleston the stoves which warm the house were designed by Robert Adam to resemble great classic urns in order that the totality of the design might not be impaired (Pl. 27). At Syon the patterned motifs of the floors conduct and control the apprehension of the visitor up to the ceiling which repeats Adam's design (Pl. 28). Or pick up any of Repton's red books and look out like Elizabeth Bennet through a window, and contemplate how the placing of a tree, a meander of water, the opening or closing of a vista, is as intrinsic to the wholeness of the aesthetic concept as a brush stroke to a painter, a key signature to a musician.

With this comes a discourse quite other than that of conservative morality:

The dressing room is papered and painted by Adam's decorative artist Pietro Mario Borgnis (1743–1801), to resemble an open loggia with 'Etruscan' terracotta and black arabesque trellis-work on a sky-blue ground. The Italian architect Giovanni Battista Piranesi (1720–78), in *Diverse Maniere D'adornare I Cammini*, 1769, had proposed the imitation of the Etruscan style by decorating walls with ornament inspired by ancient urns, bas reliefs, etc. However, this novel form of decoration, reflecting the influence of engravings of the Domus Aurea in Rome as well as being inspired by Italian Renaissance 'grotesque' decoration and the ornament and colouring of 'Etruscan' vases, was claimed by the Adam brothers in the preface to their *Works in Architecture*, Vol. II, 1778, to have first been introduced by them at the Countess of Derby's dressing room in Grosvenor Square. They also stated that Mr Child had been amongst the 'many persons of rank and fortune' who had been 'struck and pleased with the taste'.

That is from the Osterley Park guidebook (p. 87). It is a familiar language of scholarly connoisseurship working from Rome, through Italy to England by way of decorative motifs, source books, dates, artists; the *stemma* of influence. On one level it is pure aesthetic scholarship. It does not need to justify this kind of attention to these kinds of works. On another level it shows an aesthetic snobbery working upon the commercial market. 'Persons of rank and fortune' are obsessed with the acquisition of certain products as evidence of their taste. The brothers Adam, like any artists, are both creators of things of beauty – which are 'a joy for ever' – and in search of a market. It is no little recommendation that it was the Countess of Derby who first introduced Etruscan vases. There is a competition among those who claim status to be abreast of the latest development of fashion. Not to be so would be to lose face. It would betray a lack of taste; or a lack of the immense wealth necessary to display it.

There is a world far removed from Fielding's vision of Paradise Hall. If the novel merely held the mirror up to nature, then the pure aestheticism of Osterley Park and the economic basis of that passion for taste would be, of necessity, one of the central images reflected. But the moral imperative of the country house tradition in contemporary literature interprets the image differently. At best 'taste' is reconciled to virtue in a Grandison or a Darcy; at worst it destroys the good estate. One has to wait until the end of the nineteenth century before the sheer aesthetic beauty of the country house becomes centred as the subject of literature, pre-eminently in the novels of James, and in the movement to 'art for art's sake'. The sheer ugliness and brutality of industrialisation then privileges the country house as a sign of beauty purified by distance from the processes of mechanical production, like an island of the blest no longer of this world. It is, as always, a reactionary movement, but looking back in a different context from that of Jonson or Fielding or Smollett in the houses of their age. Paradise was always in danger of being lost, but for the late Victorian novelists and their successors the efflorescence of the country house as a sign of high culture occurs at a time when the old order is in terminal, even vertiginous decline, rented out, sold off, abandoned, overbuilt, destroyed by Darwinian economic law. Vandals had overrun the *ancien régime*.

Those vandals belong to the final part of the Roman paradigm of decline and fall. In July 1789 a barbarian horde 'with freedom on their lips and swords in their hands' had stormed the Bastille. The plunder of the country houses of the old order in France followed. The English ruling classes entered upon twenty-five years of war to suppress what was first called Jacobinism, then in the nineteenth century radicalism or socialism. It was said by Pitt at war with the French that the security of Europe was at stake. What was more the issue was the security of the English landed aristocracy. At Waterloo the old order appeared to have re-established itself. Stratfield Saye was the appropriate reward for the victor. But seventy years later English country house society was in terminal decline. The clock had been put back. It had not been stopped. The inner corruption of luxury, the outer threat of an ungovernable world, were to run their passage in England as in the old order of Rome.

In this context the *topoi* of the country house tradition acquire a different resonance. Familiar texts will not look the same. Whereas the initial part of this volume was the story of the growth of a convention, the second part is a history of preservation, of conservativism in increasingly difficult circumstances. Just as the classic culture of the country house survived the decline and fall of Rome, and intertwined itself with the Gothic world, so too, now, the country house ethos in England clings on in revolutionary times. This parallel between Roman and English experience is not a scientific analogy (history is not experimentally repeatable). The parallel is a structuring device. Just as the Roman story was used as an induction to the rise of the idea of the country house in English literature, so it will inform a narrative of decline and fall.

CHAPTER TWELVE

Jane Austen's houses

DREADFUL INTELLIGENCE has arrived from London. Murder and general mayhem are expected, and 'everything' of that kind. Picture the scene:

three thousand men assembling in St George's Fields; the Bank attacked, the Tower threatened; the streets of London flowing with blood, a detachment of the 12th Light Dragoons, (the hopes of the nation), called up from Northampton to quell the insurgents, and the gallant Capt. Frederick Tilney, in the moment of charging at the head of his troop, knocked off his horse by a brickbat from an upper window.

(*Northanger Abbey*, I, 14)

Every reader of Jane Austen knows the joke. Eleanor Tilney has translated into contemporary reality Catherine Morland's news 'that something very shocking indeed, will soon come out in London'. Catherine means a Gothic novel, Eleanor thinks she means a Jacobin plot. Eleanor's brother, Henry, apologises for her stupidity. 'The fears of the sister have added to the weakness of the woman; but she is by no means a simpleton in general.'

Henry Tilney's complacency is remarkable. Pitt had not shared it in the 1790s, the period of the composition of *Northanger Abbey*. He expected revolution. The year before the novel's publication, 1818, Habeas Corpus had been suspended. In 1819 the Manchester Yeomanry charged a 'mob' gathered in St Peter's Fields, Manchester. Drawing their sabres the Frederick Tilneys of that day cut down helpless men and women who had gathered to petition for parliamentary reform. It was said in justification of the killing fields that brickbats were afterwards found lying on the ground. The Six Acts (to control 'seditious' activity) followed, as did the Cato Street conspiracy (to assassinate the cabinet). Jane Austen's lifetime spans the years of Tory alarm at the international conspiracy of Jacobinism, and the most notorious era of repressive government in modern British history.

It is possible to read much of the Georgian novel and remain unaware of the French Revolution, and what that implied at home as well as abroad. Direct intrusion of politics into Jane Austen's novels is especially

101

rare. It is appropriate, however, that it occurs in her 'Gothic' novel, for Gothic fiction seems to act throughout her lifetime as a form of displacement for the 'Terror' of the Jacobin revolution and its threat to the stability of the country house order in England. Tyranny and superstition are the twin evils of the fiction of terror from *The Castle of Otranto* (1764) onwards. The castle is the sign of an oppressive landed aristocracy; Catholicism the religion of a benighted society. But such things are not here in England, but abroad. Or they are not now, but in some remote era of the past. In that way country house society suppresses uncomfortable home truths.

Remember that we are English, that we are Christians. Consult your own understanding, your own sense of the probable, your own observations of what is passing around you – Does our education prepare us for such atrocities? Do our laws connive at them? Could they be perpetrated without being known, in a country like this, where social and literary intercourse is on such a footing . . . where roads and newspapers lay every thing open? (II, 9)

So Henry Tilney weans Catherine from Gothic fantasy to a proper understanding of present 'security . . . in the laws of the land, and the manners of the age'. It is a lesson in Whig history. The Protestant religion, equality before the law, freedom of the press, the progress of education and literature: these are the guarantees of social security.

The other great conservative novelist of the time, Sir Walter Scott, would agree. In *The Heart of Midlothian*, Jeanie Deans, on her journey to London, sees a similar lesson in progressive history written in the architecture of the countryside as she proceeds from Scotland, disordered by the Porteous riots, to the secure Arcadia of the Thames, turreted in modern villas, embosomed in peaceful fertility. In *Waverley* it is the virtues of Whig law and commerce which restore the Gothic manor house of Tully Veolan destroyed by the romantic folly of the revolution of 1745 (for Jacobite read Jacobin). The marriage of the houses of English Waverley-Honour and Scottish Bradwardine enables the old manor house to be reconciled with the forces of progressive order, but in symbolic effigy only. The highland clans, the last semblance of the Gothic world in Britain, still march, but only in a 'large and spirited painting' on the wall. The old heraldic signs are set up once more, but only as signs; the fountain of hospitality flows with the intoxication of brandy punch, but just for one night's ceremonial feast. All is 'thoroughly repaired . . . with the strictest attention to maintain the original character', though now, writes Scott, given 'a lighter and more picturesque appearance'. In that way, when the subject of Gothic fiction comes home from the world of superstition and tyranny abroad, from Otranto or Udolpho, its architectural symbols in castle or old manor house are purged of their potential evil by the progress of British liberties, and enjoyed as romantic images of the picturesque. As Henry Tilney said, we remember of what race we are, and of what religion.

But Henry Tilney is not entirely right, even in terms of the deliberately narrowed world of Jane Austen's novel. His class and sexual complacency are undercut by the action of the story. In fact a form of domestic tyranny is exercised by General Tilney upon Catherine of an odious, even potentially dangerous kind. Every reader recognises that. If the great political issues of the day are suppressed, the actions of this man bring in question the ethics of his class. For General Tilney is a type of an aristocracy in which money is the sole measure of value, and the cult of taste has replaced ancient morality. He is Pope's Timon once more, but removed from the mythic structures of poetic satire to the everyday reality of England here and now, and at a time when the very existence of his order is radically at question.

The portrait of Northanger Abbey which is the frame for this moral action is more subtle than the set piece country house descriptions of the poetic tradition, for it is the stage for a naturalistic action. The narrative technique of the Georgian novel opens up the house as a series of significant *loci* (places) for a dramatic plot quite different from the more formally emblematic presentation and unified viewpoint of panegyric or satire. The House of Holiness and the House of Pride were traditionally opposed as different places. Pope's villa was the sign of true taste, Timon's of false. Penshurst was not the house of envious show, which is elsewhere, other. But the new naturalistic mode opens up dramatic multiplicity of viewpoint. That multiplicity is associated with an intimacy of psychological portrayal and a flexibility of narrative tone without precedent in the tradition as a means of representing complexity of social relationship. Northanger is seen from a variety of viewpoints – Catherine's, the General's, Henry's – and these views alter as the story develops. The Abbey is both the House of Holiness secularised – a seat of ancient simplicity, social utility and hospitality – and a House of Pride, the General's showpiece of luxury, taste and vanity. It is also a symbol of tyranny, not as fantasised in Gothic horrors, but here and now; but there is also an indication that such tyranny is merely wilful patriarchal arbitrariness, and in the marriage of Henry and Catherine (the upper and middle classes) the country house may be restored.[1]

What the reader first perceives at Northanger is seemingly an ideal house of the late Georgian period combining a delightful blend of picturesque Gothic with all the appurtenances of modern comfort and taste. Thus, iconographically, it represents the preservation of the best of old English traditions and progressive modernisation.

103

[Catherine] was struck . . . beyond her expectation by the grandeur of the Abbey, as she saw it for the first time from the lawn. The whole building enclosed a large court; and two sides of the quadrangle, rich in Gothic ornaments, stood forward for admiration. The remainder was shut off by knolls of old trees, or luxuriant plantations, and the steep woody hills rising behind to give it shelter, were beautiful even in the leafless month of March. (II, 7)

She is led thence not into a baronial hall, but, as modern custom would require, into 'the common drawing room', the present day focus of family life and the centre of hospitality for this visitor. Her eye searches for some traces of the Gothic order.

The windows, to which she looked with peculiar dependence, from having heard the General talk of his preserving them in their Gothic form with reverential care, were yet less what her fancy had portrayed. To be sure, the pointed arch was preserved – the form of them was Gothic – they might be even casements – but every pane was so large, so clear, so light! . . . The General, perceiving how her eye was employed, began to talk of the smallness of the room and simplicity of the furniture, where every thing being for daily use, pretended only to comfort &c. . . . (II, 5)

The reader, more sophisticated than Catherine, will recognise familiar signs of worth in place. There are the 'knolls of old trees', many of which we know are those of 'a grove of ancient oaks'. They naturalise the Abbey, provide shelter from storms (climatic or political) and combine utility with beauty.[2] There is (as with Scott) reverence for antiquity, tradition and continuity expressed by the preservation of Gothic 'ornaments', the signs of the past but purged from the superstition of Catholicism, and free too from Gothic discomfort, for this dwelling, like its plantations is 'luxuriant'. In that choice of word one sees the old idea of *luxuria* yielding to the new idea of 'luxury', the superabundant productivity of a successful commercial society.

Within Northanger the same blend of Gothic past and progressive present is shown in the windows, traditional in form, but now 'so clear, so light!' The enlightenment of the modern mind is shown even by the choice of glass, and the designation 'so large' testifies to the development of British manufactory science. The advance of luxury and taste is apparent likewise in the 'profusion and elegance' of the furniture, but lest it appear too luxurious, the General at once supplies the correct moralistic commentary. He 'began to talk of the smallness of the room and simplicity of the furniture, where every thing being for daily use, pretended only to comfort, &c. . . .' ''Tis Use alone that justifies Expense.' One recollects too from 'Appleton House' how important a word like 'small' may be. The General pretends only to simple comfort in his domestic life, though why should not everyday things be elegant?

The '&c.' gives the game away. The reader knows the kind of thing panegyric will say by way of moralising 'the use of riches'. The General is talking platitudes. They are not devalued as ideals – one will find in the parsonage houses of Austen's heroes a proper blend of elegant comfort and use – but in the General's mouth they are mere cant. He flattered himself, the description continues,

that there were some apartments in the Abbey not unworthy her notice – and was proceeding to mention the costly gilding of one in particular, when taking out his watch, he stopped short to pronounce it with surprise within twenty minutes of five! This seemed the word of separation, and Catherine found herself hurried away by Miss Tilney in such a manner as convinced her that the strictest punctuality to the family hours would be expected at Northanger.

The General's pride in his rooms is not only an act of self-flattery. He expects Catherine to encourage his vanity. Much in this is traditional matter of satire. The ostentation of gilded ceilings (and this is *costly* gilding) had enraged Seneca. The grotesque formal meal had always been the sign of false hospitality, and Catherine will be overwhelmed by the 'luxury and expense' of the dining parlour and the numerous servants. It is not as grotesque as Pope's Timonesque fantasy, but one need go back no further than Pope for the General's obsession with his watch: 'You drink by measure, and to minutes eat.' The deadening formality of the Tilney household is apparent to all readers. The General is living the ceremonial life of the *ancien régime* with his parade of servants and carriages, formal meals and regulated conduct. His children would enjoy, if they could, the more relaxed, democratic informality of the new age. But this is not truly a family. It is the fiefdom of a cold-hearted patriarch. The most significant sign of that lack of heart is the General's rejection of the portrait of his wife, which does not suit the canons of his taste. The rule of taste has replaced true *pietas*.

The General later takes Catherine on a tour of the gardens. The old ideal of the modest farm become country house appears again. *Beatus ille*, the classic poets had written: 'happy the man whose wish and care/ A few paternal acres bound.' The General, on the subject of greenhouses, asks

'How were Mr. Allen's succession-houses worked?' describing the nature of his own as they entered them.

'Mr. Allen had only one small hot-house, which Mrs. Allen had the use of for her plants in winter, and there was a fire in it now and then.'

'He is a happy man!' said the General, with a look of very happy contempt.   (II, 7)

One sign of the happy estate had been its sense of community, the reciprocal relation of landlord to tenant for the benefit of each. The General knows this too, in his mechanical and self-gratulatory way.

It is a rule with me, Miss Morland, never to give offence to any of my neighbours, if a small sacrifice of time and attention can prevent it. They are a set of very worthy men. They have half a buck from Northanger twice a year; and I dine with them whenever I can. (II, 11)

This is a ritual relationship which scarcely bothers to conceal the realities of power which lie behind it.

This is strong satire, and there is much in this text which, potentially, might be radicalised given the context of the age. Those rioting mobs, feared by Miss Tilney, would see in the General and the Captain their class enemy. The military profession of the family is a necessary form of defence of their land. This was first expropriated – the original monastery 'having fallen into the hands of an ancestor', as the owner euphemistically puts it – and is now being developed by a process of enclosure and demolition, so the text specifically tells us, the consequences of which are socially problematical. The General, meantime, is writing political pamphlets (so he tells Catherine). He claims that they are for the good of others. He means they are being written for the good of the Tilney estate.

Yet the strength of the country house myth had always been the great weight of adverse criticism of the House of Pride it could take on board, and yet survive. This remains true of *Northanger Abbey*. To follow Catherine on her tour is an education in Mandeville's economics: private vices, public benefits. After all, the entire community does benefit from the operation of the estate. Self-evidently, substantial employment is generated by the profusion of luxury. 'A village of hot-houses' is ridiculous, but must also provide far more surplus food than the Tilneys themselves can consume; the vast kitchen, on which the General (as always) prides himself, sounds as if it might feed a parish, as it formerly fed the monastic settlement. This kind of surplus originates in the policy of land enclosure, however insouciant. 'Modern invention' moves towards 'perfection' inspired by the 'genius' of the rich, providing by economic development something equivalent to the endowments of Christian piety in the past. Austen's language is ironically ambivalent. Good and evil grow up mixed in this world, and the novel is a more subtle form for revealing this truism than the idealisations of satire or panegyric. Jane Austen does not juxtapose the General's pride with an idyllic pastoral view of the charms of subsistence agriculture clinging to the verge of common pasture. Catherine admires. But she is alienated. If Northanger is not the fantasy house of terror and oppression of Gothic fiction (or radical polemic), it is not of her world either. Her preference is for the happy parsonage in the happy village of Woodston, the middle station in life, or 'home, sweet home' as it was to become.

The restoration of the Gothic house will come through the younger generation, Henry, Eleanor, and Henry's marriage to Catherine. It is Scott's solution also, or Charlotte Smith's in *The Old Manor House*. The younger Tilneys' good intentions are not in doubt. It is not their class which is at fault, but the General. Catherine's desire after all, is to marry up into country house society, and in this she is the typical heroine of female fiction. If the General, in a way, stands for the unacceptable face of the *ancien régime*, the personalisation of political issues into questions of individual morality makes reform also an individual matter. It leaves the country house, for good or ill, simply 'there', as a given reality, and an inherited system of values. In many respects those values keep even an imperfect man on the right track. The Tilney house and estate flourish with 'luxuriant' profusion, and if something of the tyranny of Gothic fiction has a real counterpart even in the southern counties of England, the virtues emanating from Woodston parsonage may redeem them through the practical piety of the better branch of the family tree.

This theme of conservation and renewal is one Jane Austen will return to repeatedly in her novels. General Tilney has, as his heirs, Lady Catherine de Burgh, horrified that the shades of Pemberley might be polluted by the fresh spirit of Elizabeth Bennet; and Sir Walter Elliott, posturing before the looking-glass of his own vanity at Kellynch Hall, to be replaced by the practical utility of Admiral Croft (whose only glass is his shaving mirror!). Catherine is the first of the series of heroines whose eyes are gradually opened to moral and social truth by a process of learning to understand the complex relation of fact to fiction and the nice discriminations which divide them. Only one of Austen's heroines, from the first, seems to have access to an integrated vision of moral truth which will sustain her on the long pilgrimage which leads, in fiction, to a happy marriage and a secure home. Fanny Price is the female Sir Charles Grandison, 'the good woman' who is an example to a troubled world. In the tradition of country house fiction she carries with her something of the redemptive symbolism of a Maria Fairfax or a Sophia Western. What sustains her are both the principles of Christianity and her power of imaginative sensibility. Her morality is the outcome of a conservative feel for the beauty of old things, and right action is as much the product of sensitive feeling as of correct tenets. In this way the threatened estate of Mansfield Park, after long suffering, is preserved by the love of a good woman.

Mansfield Park, Jane Austen's climactic country house novel, is a programmatic fiction. It is structured upon the fundamental binary opposition between the good and evil estates, though good and evil are potentially mixed in both, as at Northanger, for this novel permits no idealised territory, no vision of an Arcadian house or landscape somehow separated from society or time. Only the viewpoint is purified, for we see through Fanny's conservative and loving eyes.[3] But the conservative view, intrinsically, is conceived in temporal terms, in the way in which the present interprets the past, and moves forward to the future. That forward movement is necessary, though it carries with it reverence for the past. As at Northanger, the *ancien régime*, is decadent at heart. To adapt Paine's famous image, we admire the plumage, but perceive the dying bird.

The visit to Sotherton, Maria Bertram's future home, shows the decay of the old values. As the party from Mansfield are whisked through the purlieus of the estate, Maria Bertram chatters to impress Mary Crawford:

Here begins the village. Those cottages are really a disgrace. The church spire is reckoned remarkably handsome. I am glad the church is not so close to the Great House as often happens in old places. The annoyance of the bells must be terrible. There is the parsonage; a tidy looking house, and I understand the clergyman and his wife are very decent people. Those are alms-houses, built by some of the family. To the right is the steward's house; he is a very respectable man. Now we are coming to the lodge gates; but we have nearly a mile through the park still.   (I, 8)

Here still, potentially, is the proper country house society with church (and family tombs, we learn), alms-houses, diligent clergyman and steward gathered under the patronage of a great family: a nexus of economic utility, charity and morality. But Maria's attitudes are out of focus. The signification of the distance between church and house is moral, but she sees it merely as a matter of convenience. Churches are not built merely to be 'handsome'; clergymen and stewards are not to be judged merely in terms of respectability; cottages should not be a 'disgrace', and if they are they should be the first objects for the improvement of the estate. The very speed of this breathless transit through the village is wrong, and as a mile long drive is put between the visitors and the village, out of sight becomes out of mind.

Sotherton itself is now only a show house. Mrs Rushworth, extending her hospitality, discourses to her visitors like a National Trust guide.

The whole party . . . under Mrs Rushworth's guidance were shewn through a number of rooms, all lofty, and many large, and amply furnished in the taste of fifty years back, with shining floors, solid mahogany, rich damask, marble gilding and carving, each handsome in its way. Of pictures there were abundance, and some few good, but the larger part were family portraits, no longer any thing to any body but Mrs Rushworth, who had been at great pains to learn all that the housekeeper could teach, and was now almost equally well qualified to shew the house.   (I, 9)

One recognises a kind of William Kent formal house, and, indeed, the old forms of politeness had been kept up by its mistress. But it is empty formality. It means nothing to most of the visitors. Mrs Rushworth has had to learn her own family's history from the housekeeper, and merely to be able to show the rooms. Her son, who will inherit this, knows nothing of it; Maria's mind is set merely on the possession of Sotherton, if she can get it; Mary Crawford 'had seen scores of great houses, and cared for none of them'. That word 'cared' does not relate merely to taste, but to the moral responsibility of the owner of a house. But Mrs Rushworth has one delighted listener. Fanny is eager to 'warm her imagination' with a living sense of the past.

The moral implication of this becomes evident in the visit to the chapel.

They entered. Fanny's imagination had prepared her for someting grander than a mere, spacious, oblong room, fitted up for the purpose of devotion – with nothing more striking or more solemn than the profusion of mahogany, and the crimson velvet cushions appearing over the ledge of the family gallery above. 'I am disappointed,' said she, in a low voice, to Edmund. 'This is not my idea of a chapel. There is nothing awful here, nothing melancholy, nothing grand. Here are no aisles, no arches, no inscriptions, no banners. No banners, cousin, to be "blown by the night wind of Heaven." No signs that a "Scottish monarch sleeps below". . . .'

Mrs Rushworth began her relation. 'This chapel was fitted up as you see it, in James the Second's time. Before that period, as I understand, the pews were only wainscot; and there is some reason to think that the linings and cushions of the pulpit and family-seat were only purple cloth; but this is not quite certain. It is a handsome chapel, and was formerly in constant use both morning and evening. Prayers were always read in it by the domestic chaplain, within the memory of many. But the late Mr Rushworth left it off.'

'Every generation has its improvements,' said Miss Crawford, with a smile, to Edmund.

The languages of a National Trust guidebook, of Gothic sensibility and of moral cynicism are here brought into conflict. If romantic Fanny is, for a moment, a little like Catherine Morland, yet her imagination, fed by a love of literature, is infinitely preferable to the moribund antiquarianism of Mrs Rushworth's discourse of wainscot and purple cloth and the feelingless taste of 'It is a handsome chapel'. This is Tilney-like pride and complacency. As for Miss Crawford's 'Every generation has its improvements', this desire for 'improvement' involves the loss of all moral values. The Crawfords are rootless people, peregrinating from one house party to another. Henry does not reside on his estate. Mary knows nothing of the necessities of working one. Both see house and landscape merely as a vehicle for 'improvement', which is for them an expensive exercise in 'taste and money' to new dress an old house architecturally, to cut down old timber to refurbish a park, and specifically, here, to aid the Rushworths to transform Sotherton aesthetically into a shining new status symbol instead of 'a dismal old prison' as it is described. Theirs is the cult of immoral luxury. The ultimate condemnation is that, for Mary, the march of progress involves the discontinuation of family prayers.

The visit to Sotherton is so formally treated by Austen that the novel here is almost allegorical. Every sign is loaded with moral signification. That can be achieved with a specific episode. But Mansfield Park, as the place of the major action of the story, is of necessity a more complex *locus*. There is no tour of Mansfield. Perhaps that in itself carries meaning, for this house is to be dwelt in. It is not the object of a voyeur's visit. The only formal description we receive, appropriately, comes from Mary Crawford, and even from her we learn little more than that it is spacious, modern and set in a park of five mile circumference. Its modernity is shown by its sociability. The Bertrams frequently entertain the locality and set up smallish, familiar but select house parties. But too great a familiarity breeds contempt. The arrival of the vulgar Mr Yates will be a sign that things are going wrong. The large park does not suggest that Mansfield, any more than Sotherton, is hugger-mugger with farm or rural poor. The rectory, however, is a significant focus. The intercourse between Park and rectory will finally acquire cumulative moral significance when Edmund, in holy orders, and Fanny reside there.

There is nothing specifically to suggest that Mansfield, *per se*, is a better house than Sotherton. Its formality of manners, if anything, is severer. Sir Thomas has many of the attributes of General Tilney. His family tend to freeze in his presence. This is one cause of the defects in his children's education, for their father is not close to them (nor is their supine mother) and he reads the outsides of things for reality. The house reflects its owner. When Fanny first arrives 'the grandeur of the house astonished . . . her. The rooms were too large for her to move in with ease.' And even when later she is established in Mansfield as a home that she loves, even in a family affair like cards, one notices that when Sir Thomas is absent all is 'happy ease' but where he sits, 'steady sobriety and orderly silence prevail'. Ease dies in the presence of the *pater familias*. Order prevails.

But even that 'order' is askew. Sir Thomas's concern for rank, money, influence, render him blind both to the defects of the match between Maria Bertram and Mr Rushworth, and later to that between Fanny and Henry. Of Rushworth he thinks, 'It was a connection exactly of the right sort; in the same county, and the same interest', and he concurs most heartily even though he cannot refrain from saying to himself, 'If this man had not twelve thousand a year, he would be a very stupid fellow.' Yet it is not the quest for 'respectability and influence' which is so much a fault in Sir Thomas as his ignorance of the want of moral principle in his daughter.

Ambition, pride, coldness, formality. If owners make houses, then

Mansfield would seem the target of satire, not a house which Fanny Price can love, admire, reverence, by rational principle and moral imagination. Yet the praise of Mansfield is perhaps the most powerful conservative defence of the country house written in a time of revolution because it does not pretend that any human institution has ideal status, merely that this order of things, rightly directed, has immense worth. For without its 'master', for all his faults, Mansfield disintegrates, and with it all moral principle. Let the Crawfords in, with their taste for 'improvements', and the good customs of the house are broken up, and nothing put in their place. The resources of the estate are squandered, the proper function of the workers disturbed. When Sir Thomas's library makes way for theatricals, the very principles of culture, moral and imaginative, which books preserve, are broken up by a crass vulgarity ignorant of worth and morally degenerate. Mr Yates, who is discovered by Sir Thomas ranting (and backwards on!), is a kind of parody of a subversive demagogue.

It is the first function of Sir Thomas, returned from the care of his estates overseas, to restore necessary order and formality to his house, to have the innovations carted away, and to put things back to their proper old uses.

He had to reinstate himself in all the wanted concerns of his Mansfield life, to see his steward and his bailiff – to examine and compute and, in the intervals of business, to walk into his stables and his gardens, and nearest plantations; but active and methodical, he had not only done all this before he resumed his seat as master of the house at dinner, he had also set the carpenter to work in pulling down what had been so lately put up in the billiard room, and given the scene painter his dismissal.   (II, 2)

The centre of the house remains the communal meal. At the head of the table sits the master (and it is a warmer, more affectionate Sir Thomas who returns from absence), and the hierarchy of the household depends from there through his family circle, thence down to his servants (many of whose names we know, Baddely and Chapman, Ellis and Wilcox) and so even to his plantations abroad. As a proper master, business has come before pleasure, the management of house and estate through steward and bailiff, active and methodical examination and computation. One sees the entire economic hierarchy from master ultimately to the *servi* (for, of course, the plantations abroad are worked by slaves). The novel is so structured that the return of Sir Thomas, with all his faults, is like the arrival of the captain on the bridge of a storm-tossed ship. A firm hand on the wheel, and the ship has steerage way again. If the choice is Sir Thomas, or the ranting Yates, then the conclusion is clear.

It is this sense of order which Fanny comes to love. Fanny's 'place' within the house, literally and metaphorically, is her room. Even without fire at the beginning, it was her secure territory, and proper familial care soon adds comfort to security. It is the nature of a great house to possess many rooms, each with its proper role and inhabitant. Fanny's is far more than merely 'a room of one's own'. It is the museum of her sentimental feelings for the past, the repository where she gathers the treasures of memory which define the continuity of her being and her happiness at Mansfield. It was a school room, for the need of correct moral education is a leading theme of the novel; it is also a library, for the right choice of books is a necessary part of true education. This room of her own is also Fanny's protection, that secure space into which she can retreat should outside pressure become too great, and every entry into that space, whether by Edmund, or Mary Crawford, marks a significant moment in Fanny's life.

Thus, external order, even formality, is a safeguard of inner freedom. This is true of small things, like Fanny's life, as of great, the welfare of the house. One illustration will suffice. Fanny, harassed by Henry Crawford's attentions to her at one time, not knowing where to turn, is saved by the arrival of the butler and the train of servants who follow him to serve tea:

> The solemn procession, headed by Baddely, of tea-board, urn, and cake-bearers, made its appearance, and delivered her from a grievous imprisonment of body and mind. Mr Crawford was obliged to move. She was at liberty, she was busy, she was protected. (III, 3)

It could be satire. The phrase 'solemn procession' is mock-heroic. Pope might have written it. Here is, potentially, the cold formality, the over heavy solemnity of Sir Thomas's household at its worse. But it is personalised. The appearance of Baddely is a welcome sight. The very existence of the system grants Fanny her liberty. Without it she would be unprotected from Crawford, a predatory womaniser. Whereas Rushworth saw Sotherton as a 'prison', it is Mansfield's decorums that deliver Fanny from 'grievous imprisonment of body and mind'.

Sir Thomas is wise, therefore, in sending Fanny to Portsmouth to bring her to a just sense of the importance of Mansfield, for it is only a great house which can provide proper place and space for all its inhabitants. (The political implications of that are clear.) The experience of Portsmouth is a process by which Fanny learns to feel, as well as know, what it is that the master gives to Mansfield, a finding of her true father in Sir Thomas. All that formality, stiffness, hierarchical grandeur, which, in its negative manifestation, repels at Mansfield, now is longed for desperately among the tumult, impropriety and (it is bluntly put) circumscribed want of the proletarian household at Portsmouth. She longs for the 'times and seasons' of Mansfield – the phrase has Biblical resonances and speaks of the God-given processes of Nature – and for the care for 'everybody' there, the 'regulation of subject . . . propriety . . . attention' given to all:

112

she could think of nothing but Mansfield, its beloved inmates, its happy ways. Every thing where she now was was in full contrast to it. The elegance, propriety, regularity, harmony – and perhaps, above all, the peace and tranquillity of Mansfield, were brought to her remembrance every hour of the day, by the prevalance of every thing opposite to them *here*.   (III, 8)

The usual comparison reasserts itself between the good house and its opposite. But it is not, after all, Mansfield against Sotherton, for Sotherton could be another Mansfield with the right master (and mistress). It is the country house itself – Mansfield as the type – which stands in opposition to the vulgar, common, uncultured life of the Portsmouth house. Compare Sir Thomas, even in his stiffest vein, with Fanny's real father, and there is no doubt which way her feelings incline. She has learnt to belong to another part of her family. Even the charity she is eager to practise depends upon the beneficence of Sir Thomas. He had thought that she would miss 'the elegances and luxuries of Mansfield Park', and though Austen is chary of letting Fanny regret 'luxury', for the word is still hovering between good and evil, she undoubtedly longs for elegant propriety.

What purifies Fanny's longing is the generosity of her motives. She does not desire Mansfield's forms for their own sake, like a clockwork doll, but because they belong to the world of people she loves. The 'harmony' she requires, united with 'peace and tranquillity' is not the dull placidity of Lady Bertram's torpor. Fanny's role in the house will be closer to that of a ministering angel. Blessed are the peace makers. Harmony, as the consonance of strings melodiously struck together, is one of the usual conservative images (we have seen it in Sackville-West and at Stanway). Deprived of Mansfield, living now only on memories orchestrated by a sensitive imagination, she seeks to preserve what she can of her ideal country house even at Portsmouth. Thus, Fanny begins to educate Susan's moral sensibility and taste in the traditions of the Park.

That handing on of a tradition (from Fanny to Susan) is a more important act than 'our heroine' merely becoming mistress of Mansfield, which would be the conventional ending of female comic romance. This serious, sober, evangelical fiction has a different theme, for it is about the house itself more than the heroine. However much Fanny feels for the best values of Mansfield, she appreciates them most because she is an outsider. She loves the order, but she is not of it. Her role is to carry these values out into the wider world. It is a form of 'trust', her dedicated task. Hence the education of Susan, and hence the very existence of this novel itself. It is not directed at the Sir Thomases of the great world, but at the daughters of the middle classes who will learn from it.

The appropriate house for Fanny is Edmund's Thornton, that 'solid walled, roomy, mansion-like looking house, such as one might suppose a respectable old country-house family had lived in from generation to generation'. It is Henry Crawford's description, but he is not wrong in everything (merely in his desire, as usual, to 'improve' the property). Edmund's only significant change is to move the farmyard away from the house, otherwise his choice of home for himself and Fanny is the recreation of his father's house, only in more modest dimension. So the country house values move down the social scale, and gather moral earnestness with them, for this, besides being a gentlemanly dwelling, is also the home of a clergyman. Ultimately, Fanny and Edmund move to the rectory within the very 'view and patronage of Mansfield Park'. But they never possess the estate. They are, as it were, tutelary spirits watching over the house at the gate. Fanny, who loves with a sentimental moral passion a house to which she never fully belonged, is camped outside its walls and thus, only when part of Mansfield, but apart, can she keep alive the ideal she had most fully, most poignantly, when dispossessed at Portsmouth. Paradise is never here and present, but always at another time and place.

12 Wollaton Hall, from Joseph Nash, *The Mansions of England in the Olden Time* (1839–49)

13   Gillis van Tilborch, *The Tichborne Dole* (1670)

14   Hardwick Hall, the entrance hall, from Llewellyn Jewitt and S. C. Hall, *The Stately Homes of England* (1874)

15 The double cube room, Wilton House, with the Van Dyck portrait of the Fourth Earl of
Pembroke and his family, from the centrefold of the current guidebook

16 Alexander Pope's villa at Twickenham, after the painting by Peter Andreas
Rysbrack engraved by Nathaniel Parr

18 Sir Robert Walpole's villa at Houghton, from William Watts, *The Seats of the
Nobility and Gentry* (1779)

19   Holkham Hall, from William Watts, *The Seats of the Nobility and Gentry* (1779)

20   Chiswick villa, from William Watts, *The Seats of the Nobility and Gentry* (1779)

21   Blenheim Palace, the grounds of the old manor of Woodstock floated as a landscape lake

22   Stowe House, the garden front, from Benton Seeley, *Stowe, A Description* (1797)

23   Stowe, the Temple of Ancient Virtue, from Benton Seeley, *Stowe, A Description* (1797)

CHAPTER THIRTEEN

Norman Abbey

JANE AUSTEN'S political commitment to the country house order in an age of revolution is discreetly masked by her reputation as a writer of comic female fiction of parochial scope. Byron, on the other hand, is the most famous of English political poets. The later cantos of *Don Juan* poured in tens of thousands from radical presses in pirated editions. For every Susan weaned by a Fanny Price to a love of Mansfield Park, a Chartist petitioner shaped their vision of the decadent *ancien régime* from the verse of *Don Juan*, part Popeian satire, part Thackeray-like novel. Yet Byron is the writer of the last great poetic celebration of the English country house (Yeats's later meditations belong to Ireland), and that this celebration, even valediction, should occur at the very heart of a radical satire is remarkable testimony to the indestructability of the ideal. But, it might be said, English radicalism itself has always been intensely conservative, as deeply evangelical as Fanny Price, as respectful of the traditions of the constitution as any member of the House of Lords (where many radicals have ended their days).

Byron's description of Norman Abbey, the ancestral home of the Amundevilles, introduces the story of Don Juan at an English house party during the early days of the revolution in France. His 'hero' will quit the Abbey to join the revolutionaries, and be executed by them as an aristo. Such was Byron's plan. The Abbey is specifically modelled on the poet's own ancestral home, Newstead Abbey (Pl. 29).

> It stood embosom'd in a happy valley,
> Crown'd by high woodlands, where the Druid oak
> Stood like Caractacus in act to rally
> His host, with broad arms 'gainst the thunder-stroke;
> And from beneath his boughs were seen to sally
> The dappled foresters – as day awoke,
> The branching stag swept down with all his herd,
> To quaff a brook which murmured like a bird.

Before the mansion lay a lucid lake,
Broad as transparent, deep, and freshly fed
By a river, which its soften'd way did take
In currents through the calmer water spread
Around: the wild fowl nestled in the brake
And sedges, brooding in their liquid bed:
The woods sloped downwards to its brink, and stood
With their green faces fix'd upon the flood.

Its outlet dash'd into a steep cascade,
Sparkling with foam, until again subsiding
Its shriller echoes – like an infant made
Quiet – sank into softer ripples, gliding
Into a rivulet; and thus allay'd
Pursued its course, now gleaming, and now hiding
Its windings through the woods; now clear, now blue,
According as the skies their shadows threw.

A glorious remnant of the Gothic pile,
(While yet the church was Rome's) stood half apart
In a grand Arch, which once screened many an aisle,
These last had disappear'd – a loss to Art:
The first yet frowned superbly o'er the soil,
And kindled feelings in the roughest heart,
Which mourn'd the power of time's or tempest's march,
In gazing on the venerable Arch.   (XIII, 56–9)

The country house tradition in which Byron wrote is so rich that allusions crowd in. This is Fielding's Paradise Hall again where the social order seems as if confirmed by Nature and by Time. The very words 'happy valley' have paradisiacal associations, for Byron's phrase is directly derived from the description of the earthly paradise in which Samuel Johnson centred his allegorical novel *Rasselas* (1759). Beneath all is the old myth of the Golden Age when the soil gave freely of its fertility without labour. The metaphor 'embosom'd' establishes the land as fertile, the giver of the milk of life, the mother of the country house which is the natural product of the valley. The Druid oaks likewise protected Paradise Hall, and testify here to the duration of happiness from century to century. They are typical signs too of the free principles of the Gothic constitution which is the outgrowth of Nature. The house enparked is analogous to the Temple of Liberty at Stowe. The political allusion is clear from the reference to the patriot Caractacus, who resisted tyrannical invasion. It is popular resistance. The oak is a sign of a 'host' which is rallied – a political variant of Jonson's 'all come in' – and the 'dappled foresters' which now peacefully shelter in the woods might be read as signs of a protected and contented folk – after the manner of 'Appleton House'.

All signs of stress, whether past or present, are now suppressed within the natural order. The same process of visual elision as Fielding used to unite Paradise Hall with a monastic ruin here joins Norman Abbey and the Catholic remains in the landscape. But Byron's vocabulary pays special compliment to the Amundevilles. It was an 'old monastery' but an '*older* mansion', for the family were established before the monks. It is a sign, perhaps, of the Amundeville's Christian piety, as well as of their taste, that remnants of the monastery are preserved attached to the house (though apart from it). So the description tells, working its symbolic process upon Byron's recollection of the real remains of Newstead. But the 'new' in 'Newstead' would have the wrong connotations here. The chosen name of the country house takes the mind back to the Conquest – *Norman* Abbey. That is how old the family's claim to the land is. Then the allusion to ancient British freedom and Caractacus, by another act of elision, happily blends that Norman conquest with the even earlier free times. History, somehow, has reconciled many diverse matters in its processes – ancient British and Norman, Catholic and Protestant – just as the evolution of the house manifests 'a rich and rare/ Mixed Gothic'. Antiquity is the catalyst, and the justification. It suggests the ideology of Scott or Burke, for whom ancient trees, or ancient houses, were vital conservative symbols.

But the fundamental image is not political but maternal, developing from the original 'embosom'd'. The happy valley is a place of shelter – the deer are protected by the trees, the wild fowl nestle in their liquid bed upon the tranquil lake, and the picturesquely foaming cascade eventually has its turbulence 'allay'd', 'like an infant made/ Quiet'. It is appropriate, therefore, that over all, enshrined in the Abbey ruins, stands a maternal statue (so the poem goes on to tell). It is an image of 'The Virgin Mother of the God-born child,/ With her son in her blessed arms'.

> She made the earth below seem holy ground.
> This may be superstition, weak or wild,
> But even the faintest relics of a shrine
> Of any worship, wake some thoughts divine.   (XIII, 61)

Although the poet apologises for his superstition, none the less he establishes the religious sentiment. The park has been conceived as the natural paradise of the generative mother of mankind; now the house is under the tutelage of the mother of God. Nature and religion are reconciled. If paradise is regained, it is here in the fortunate British country seat of an ancient family, guardians of freedom, protectors of the fertility of the land, and defenders of the faith.

117

What follows, however, in the story of *Don Juan* is a massive satiric portrait of life within this idyllic house. For the household at Norman Abbey is a travesty of the ideals of the country house tradition which has been so formally invoked. The proud marionette, Lord Henry, the owner of the house, is Timon or Tilney once again. He is a feelingless connoisseur who buys taste in a commercialised market; and a politician who buys votes for his own interest. He is a false mirror of the mysteries of 'manners, arms and arts'. His wife, cold, unhappy, potentially adulterous Lady Adeline, is likewise a perversion of Jonson's wife: 'noble, fruitful, chaste withal'. Having begotten one heir, she has now abandoned all interest in her family. The grotesquely luxurious banquets over which husband and wife preside – and Byron describes two at length – are parodies of the communal feasts of the positive face of the country house tradition.

As for the rural community, Byron describes Lord Henry as a 'Sabine showman'. 'Sabine' was the classic term of praise for the simple farming life, but at Norman Abbey even agriculture is turned into display. My lord wants to carry off all the prizes, even at the local shows. He has more care for his prize pigs than his people. It is one of Lord Henry's tasks as the embodiment of Justice and of Peace to condemn two of his tenants to jail. They are the poachers who have been feeding on the spontaneous bounty of the land – that is their symbolic function. Radical readers would know also that the joint operation of the enclosure acts, from which Lord Henry's class had enormously profited, and the application of the Speenhamland system by the Justices of the Peace, had so impoverished the peasantry that a minor civil 'war' was even then in process between bands of armed poachers and the keepers of game.[1] This is why mantraps have been set up among the Druid oaks. The basis of wealth in force is viciously clear. Norman Abbey is a 'power house', and it is power ill-used.

It would be easy to continue at length in the same vein, and with contemporary parallels, for Cobbett's radical *Political Register* has close analogies with Byron. But that does not budge the ideal status of the passage on the happy valley. That celebration of what the great good place *might* be like also descends to those radical readers who bought Byron's poem. In this *Don Juan* is like *Tom Jones*, for the greater part of Fielding's novel is satirical. Yet it circles back to Paradise Hall, and its new Adam and Eve. So too the ideal status of Byron's passage on the happy valley stands, despite the alternative later shown – indeed, the very travesty of the ideal may reinforce it. Nor is the religious sentiment of the pious image of the Virgin undercut.

None the less, even within the depiction of the ideal there are certain absences. As in Fielding, the landscape in Byron's formal description is empty of folk – symbolised, perhaps, in the 'dappled foresters' who sally forth, but only symbolised, and remotely. And compared even with Fielding's unpeopled estate, there is no Squire Allworthy risen with the sun. Then, as the reader moves among the abbey ruins, the sense of absence grows stronger. An elegaic, even sinister note develops in the verse. Though the tutelary statue of the Virgin is a powerful presence, she presides over a ruin, and at the centre of the description of the ruin is a void: the great stained glass window which has vanished, a

> mighty window, hollow in the centre,
> Shorn of its glass of thousand colourings,
> Through which the deepen'd glories once could enter.   (XIII, 62)

Something was once there which we now no longer perceive. What it was one may only vaguely imagine, and as the imagination comes into play, the classic mode of the description of the park gives way to the Gothic.

> But in the noontide of the Moon, and when
> The wind is winged from one point of heaven,
> There moans a strange unearthly sound, which then
> Is musical – a dying accent driven
> Through the huge Arch, which soars and sinks again.   (XIII, 63)

But if the description of the house is symbolic, is not this also? The 'noontide of the Moon' is the polar opposite of the sun rising upon Allworthy, though the moon is still 'one point of heaven' – a divine sign within Nature, like the lamenting wind. 'Nature' (the elements) and 'art' (the window) combine, and the 'dying accent' is the lament for what is no longer depicted in the glories of the shattered glass. The Virgin Mary is the *genius loci* of this ruin. What is being lamented (put in the simplest terms) is the destruction of the former monastery by tyranny, and the demise of Christian morality (even if that were superstition) which the ruins represent. Compare the rectory which stands whole and entire at the gates of Mansfield Park.

The sense of the lost ideal of the monastery is always present in the description of the house party in the cantos which follow. Byron returns repeatedly to the figure of the guardian spirit of the Virgin Mary, part of the Amundevilles' house, but apart, and to the story of the dissolution of the religious house. Thus a travesty of the Virgin appears in a major symbolic episode in the sixteenth canto. There he tells the tale of 'a country girl in a close cap/ And scarlet cloak' who is 'left in the great hall' waiting to be summoned before Lord Henry in his capacity as Justice of the Peace. She is with child. Her 'crime' is illegitimate fertility, for she has been a 'poacher upon Nature's manor', Byron writes – thus linking her with the tenants caught in the mantraps.

> The present culprit was extremely pale,
> Pale as if painted so; her cheek being red
> By nature, as in higher dames less hale
> 'Tis white, at least when they just rise from bed.
> Perhaps she was ashamed of seeming frail.
> Poor soul! for she was country born and bred,
> And knew no better in her immorality
> Than to wax white – for blushes are for quality.   (XVI, 64)

Byron gives seven stanzas to the scene. It is the only incident set in the great hall – in Jonson the heartland of the united community; now it is the place where a solitary girl waits for punishment. That reference to 'nature's manor' links her clearly with the traditional theme of the productivity of the soil which gave birth spontaneously in the Golden Age. This spontaneity is now a 'crime'. But the strongest symbolic link in the poem is with the image of mother and child which presides over the ruins of the Abbey, and the resonances are multiple. Although the scarlet cloak links the country girl with the whore of Babylon, that, surely, is the outlook of a hypocritically censorious ruling class. One might propose instead Mary Magdalen, for this is a repentant harlot. But dare one suggest that she is most closely related to the Virgin Mother of God herself, depicted like the girl in this poem with a child, but without a visible father? The whiteness of the girl's cheek is a sign of her real purity set against the corrupt world of the 'quality', whose blushes are artificial.

The other major link with the Virgin is the purest of all Byronic heroines, Aurora Raby. She is the mysterious beauty whom Don Juan meets and admires at the house party, but finds impervious to seductive charm. In this she stands like Fanny Price to Henry Crawford, and her function, like Fanny's, is that of a saviour figure. But, unlike Fanny, she is not a character who acts in a narrative. Her role is merely to be, and to remind of what has been. Like the statue of the Virgin, she is part of the house, yet apart, and like the statue, she is a religious symbol. Part of her significance is that she is a Roman Catholic; thus she is like the dwellers in the monastery of old. She is 'sincere', 'austere/ As far as her gentle heart allow'd', and the follower of a 'fallen Faith':

> she had something of sublime
> In eyes which sadly shone, as seraph's shine
> All youth – but with an aspect beyond time;
> Radiant and grave – as pitying man's decline;
> Mournful – but mournful of another's crime,
> She look'd as if she sat by Eden's door,
> And grieved for those who could return no more.   (XV, 45)

This representation of Aurora is as close as the poem comes to re-constituting the spirituality of the lost window of the Abbey. It seeks to restore what was absent. In the original description of what was lost Byron had written that the colours of the window once streamed 'off the sun like seraph's wings'. So Aurora's eyes like 'seraph's shine'. Here is an association of an ideal figure with sunlight after the manner of Fielding's Allworthy. Her very name, Aurora Raby, is allegorical. Through the void of the abbey window the Aeolian wind had blown 'sad but serene', and Aurora, recalling paradise lost, has an aspect 'grave . . . but mournful, but mournful of another's crime' as she grieves for those never to return to Eden. The ruin and the Catholic maiden both lament a disaster. The specific word Byron chooses is 'crime' – and that criminality is the dissolution of the monastery – the loss of paradise. Aurora's quiet sadness, her solitude and her potential redemptive role as the ray of a new dawn are an essential part of her relation to the old Catholic order which the 'novel power' of Lord Henry's class destroyed. The new capitalism expropriated the property of Aurora's ancestors to build Norman Abbey. What Fielding elided by a picturesque device at Paradise Hall is here, in the symbolic person of Aurora, on the verge of re-emerging as a religious and social issue.

The expropriators of the monastery seek to pass off their arbitrary crime in the usual way. One remembers the tales of duck's blood at Stanway, or the falling in of the lands at Appleton by 'escheat'. So, at Norman Abbey, this history of expropriation is rendered by way of an evasive frippery. Lady Adeline, Don Juan's hostess, has composed a Gothic pastiche, 'The Song of the Black Monk', which she sings to Juan. But lurking within her Gothic fantasy is substantial revolutionary potential. 'Tyranny', one finds, is here and now in England – and in this use of the Gothic *Don Juan* resembles *Northanger Abbey*:

> When the Lord of the Hill, Amundeville,
> Made Norman Church his prey,
> And expelled the friars, one friar still
> Would not be driven away. . .
> But beware! beware! of the Black Friar,
> He still retains his sway,
> For he is yet the church's heir
> Whoever may be the lay.
> Amundeville is lord by day,
> But the monk is lord by night,
> Nor wine nor wassail can raise a vassal
> To question the friar's right.   (XVI, 40)

If Byron had completed the poem, the ominous nature of the song would be more apparent, for the friar's appearance is always proleptic of the death of an Amundeville. But the symbolic status of the image is already established. The monk repossesses his own at night, and it was at night too that the Aeolian window of the Abbey moaned with 'a strange unearthly sound' and in 'a dying accent'. It is as if some mysterious force laments the wrong done in the happy valley, and Juan is vouchsafed a vision of the dispossessed Black Friar stalking Norman Abbey, which may be beyond rational explanation. If that suggests something of the mystic religiosity of *Macbeth*, the text reminds the reader that Juan, like Shakespeare's protagonist bound for hell, is more in need of the divine than the physician (XVI, 33). Rulers may hold power by force for awhile, but divine retribution awaits them after all.

A series of religious allusions, thus, focuses upon the ruins of the Abbey. The former monastery is attached to the Amundeville's house, but not of it, standing in a rural paradise the very antithesis of the corrupt house party of Lord Henry and his guests. The solitary, pregnant girl in the great hall is a sign of a trust, a responsibility, a duty betrayed, just as the Virgin and Child of the ruins are a sign of a lost faith. An act of expropriation underlies the Amundeville's possession of the estate, and, as the story of the poachers shows, a further act of expropriation is continuing to deprive the people of such vestiges of communal property as yet remain. The ideal imagery is that of mother and child, of maternal and religious care. The reality, as represented, is of two nations, the rich and the poor. And it is an ominous state, full of potential violence should the expropriated strike back. Revolution had already broken out in France.

But this is to make explicit what is only tentatively explored in the poem. There is a pull in *Don Juan* between an inherited ideal of the happy, rural estate, and a cynical, destructive view of the way in which the hypocritical ideology of the possessors of the land masks the selfish brutalities of power. Between the two a different kind of idea is beginning to form in symbolic shapes and connections. But the very ruined form of the Abbey is representative of the imperfect nature of Byron's conception. What is it that might be put in the place of that acquisitive capitalism which had destroyed the happy valley? There is a window, whose imagery we cannot see; a seraphic heroine, Aurora Raby, who (unlike Fanny Price) will not redeem the great house; an avenging force in the Black Monk, but burlesqued in comic song.

But, as the nineteenth century developed, the argument passed into other hands. The idealisation of a Christian and medieval state, the reconstitution of a lost ideal of community, welfare and responsibility, but within the existing orders of society: these were to become the shaping ideas of the Young England movement[2]. The 'two nations', the rich and the poor, were to be reunited by the recreation of the ancient organic society of the country house restored. Such is the theme of the social novels of Byron's admirer and imitator, and future conservative Prime Minister, Benjamin Disraeli. Radicalism has grown conservative. In Aurora Raby one may perceive Disraeli's redemptive figure, Sybil, coming into being, for the eponymous heroine of Disraeli's most famous novel is a descendant of the last abbot of Marney whose lands had been plundered by Henry VIII's followers to build their new country houses.

CHAPTER FOURTEEN

Young England and old houses

MOWBRAY CASTLE was a Victorian mansion built on the great estate of the late Lord Fitz-Warene. It dominated what had been an obscure village now grown into a large and flourishing manufacturing town, a circumstance which trebled 'the vast rental of its lord'. The Norman name of the Fitz-Warenes was spurious, like the castle, for the founder of the family fortune had been plain Mr Warren. The new title, and the castellated form of new house, linked the rich man deliberately with the conquering arms of William I.

At the end of *Sybil* (1845) this 'House of Pride' is plundered by an enraged mob. Lord Fitz-Warene, now Earl of Mowbray, is stoned to death and the artistic treasures gathered in the castle are scattered promiscuously by the rioters, who are searching only for money and liquor. The drunken vandals, who call themselves 'Hell-cats', under the leadership of a demagogue called the 'Bishop', then themselves expire, burnt to death in the very fire they had started. As Disraeli phrases it, 'the splendid mimickry of Norman rule' is destroyed along with 'the ruthless savage' who styled himself 'the Liberator of the People'. It is a fit image of the self-destructiveness of social division and disorder. The Victorian novelist translates to English soil the threat of Jacobinism. There were native portents enough: the Gordon riots; the burning of Nottingham Castle; physical force Chartism.

It need not be like that. At an earlier stage of the disorder another mob invaded the park of another neighbouring squire. Instead of being met by Lord Mowbray with bayonets at his back, they were greeted by the squire's wife and her children. Perceiving the people were hungry she sent for food and fed the multitude:

When all was over, [a] deputation waited again on the lady to express to her their gratitude; and the gardens of this house being of celebrity in the neighbourhood, they requested permission that the people might be allowed to walk through them, pledging themselves that no flower should be plucked and no fruit touched. The permission was granted: the multitude, in order, each file under a chief and each

124

commander of the files obedient to a superior officer, then made a progress through the beautiful gardens of their beautiful hostess. They even passed through the forcing houses and vineries. Not a border was trampled on, not a grape plucked; and, when they quitted the domain, they gave three cheers for the fair castellan.   (VI, 7)

Disraeli adds, 'the writer speaks from circumstances within his own experience.'[1] There seems no reason to disbelieve him. The idealisation of the country house is essentially English. This place is of 'celebrated' beauty. The folk delight to explore the grounds, as if this were Blenheim or Chatsworth today on any Sunday afternoon. The people are content because the owner of the house has fed them from her bounty. It is the theme of the Tichborne dole. The hierarchy of the social order is strongly emphasised, for even the people have their officers, and at the end of the day they cheer the Christian charity of their hostess.

Thus the House of Holiness replaces the House of Pride. But the great social question for the conservative imagination was how might the little community of the good country estate still serve as a model for an industrial nation and its great cities? Of old, the virtuous man had quit the smoke, the noise, the riches of Rome or London and retired to his villa; hence satire of the city or panegyric of the country. But now the city is everywhere, and, like Wodgate in *Sybil*, is hell upon earth, a no-man's land without government, religion or education, the home only of hunger, disease, violence. Hence the revolutionary underclass, led by their 'Liberator' vent their anger upon the rich. The degeneracy produced by the industrial revolution poses as great a threat as Jacobinism. Disraeli's heroine, Sybil, cries out:

When I remember what this English people once was; the truest, the freest, and the bravest, the best-natured and the best-looking, the happiest and most religious race upon the surface of this globe; and think of them now, with all their crimes and all their slavish sufferings, their soured spirits and their stunted forms; their lives without enjoyment, and their deaths without hope; I may well feel for them, even if I were not the daughter of their blood.   (II, 14)

By 'daughter of their blood' she means 'Saxon'. She embodies the same concept of pristine freedom architecturally represented by the Temple of Liberty at Stowe. The enemy are the 'Normans', those who treat the soil of England as if it were the conquered fiefdom of the rich, to be controlled by force, not united by communal love.

However naïve Sybil's view of history, there is no doubting the sincerity of her emotion. Responsibility for the corruption of the estate of England is not a buck to be passed to socio-economic causes. The usual argument of the insouciant rich in Disraeli's novels is that the land is overpopulated. If only the poor would cease to breed so rapidly... So Malthus was recruited to justify the doctrine of passing by on the other side.[2] After all, if the poor were any better off they would merely breed more children and be poor again. Or there was the not unfamiliar argument of 'the market', the hand of Providence operating by economic laws to make the rich, inescapably, richer, and keep the poor in their place. But for Sybil the responsibility for social ills is individual. It lies at the door of the wealthy and the selfish. The clear intention of the novelist is to dissolve the aura of 'mystification' (Disraeli's word) with which the propertied class invest themselves, and to show self-regarding dishonesty for what it is.

The root of this conservative critique springs directly from the apostle of Jacobinism himself. Disraeli accepts the argument of Paine's *The Rights of Man* that the landed aristocracy of England originate in military conquest, reinforced by political corruption. The argument of *Sybil* is that 'we are divided between the conquerors and the conquered', and that this 'spirit of Conquest has adapted itself to the changing circumstances of ages, and however its results vary in form, in degree they are much the same.' As an example of that adaptability of 'conquest', the Tudor expropriation of the monastic lands showed the rich blatantly becoming richer by taking what should have belonged by Christian duty to the poor. Such is the foundation of the fortune of the hero of *Sybil*, Charles Egremont, whose ancestor, Baldwin Greymount, a confidential domestic of one of the favourites of Henry VIII, made a financial killing from the privatisation of the Church, and changed his name with his social status to 'Norman' Egremont. Thus to the conquest of the Saxon people is joined the plunder of the Christian commonwealth. Actions which were praised by Marvell in the Fairfax family, discreetly passed by at Paradise Hall, or burlesqued in Gothic parody at Norman Abbey are now rawly presented as an historical scandal. An ancient name is a sign not of fame but of infamy.

Disraeli's use of architectural setting to convey this strong message is formal and programmatic in his paired novels on the condition of England, *Coningsby* (1844) and *Sybil*. The great political centre Monmouth House is one sign of the corruption of the *ancien régime*. Lord Monmouth is found among the colossal busts of the Caesars, imperious tyrants and monsters of sexual depravity whose images are emblems of corruption masquerading as the taste for the antique. The walls display in fresco the loves of gods and heroes, types of the licentiousness of the aristocracy; every quarter breathes an air of 'luxurious repose' – and Disraeli uses *luxuria* in the old moral sense. Even the Venetian girandoles, which in Pope might have recalled the life of the Palladian villa, here are signs of that rigid and decayed 'oligarchy' of Venice which had presided over the long years of decline of the famous, now infamous, commercial republic – a *memento mori* to England.

Coningsby Castle may be easily 'read':

[The] air of habitual habitation . . . was entirely wanting at Coningsby. Everything, indeed, was vast and splendid; but it seemed rather a gala-house than a dwelling; as if the grand furniture and the grand servants, had all come down express from town with the grand company, and were to disappear and to be dispersed at the same time. And truly there were manifold traces of hasty and temporary arrangement; new carpets and old hangings; old paint, new gilding; battalions of odd French chairs, squadrons of queer English tables; and large tasteless lamps and tawdry chandeliers, evidently true cockneys, and only taking the air by way of change. There was, too, throughout the drawing-rooms an absence of all those minor articles of ornamental furniture that are the offering of taste to the home we love. . . . The modes and manners of the house were not rural; there was nothing of the sweet order of a country life.

(*Coningsby*, IV, 9)

This castle is a mere hotel, lacking those signs of love and true taste which mark a home whose lord, as Jonson wrote, 'dwells'. In traditional form the virtue of the country is contrasted with the town, though that virtue is now expressed by the phrase 'sweet order', which is suggestive more of what Yeats was to call 'the ceremony of innocence' than of those heroes of old who smelled of sweat from the plough (as Seneca imagined). This is a genteel country life compared with the vulgarity of the 'cockney' furniture, imported like the guests. It suggests something of the snobbery of an Evelyn Waugh, even the aestheticism of James. But it is so formally traditional in the comparisons it evokes that we recognise the devices at once. It is a little mechanical, even *déja vu*.

It is Marney Abbey which is the most significant of the proud houses of the old order. It is like Byron's Norman Abbey, for Disraeli sets up the same tension between the signifiers of the ideal country house and the deplorable state of the real world. The house is presented in a long, formal description at the beginning of Book Two of *Sybil*, and is given the old, right symbols, for it is set within a parkland of ancient trees, itself an ancient (Jacobean) dwelling, but tastefully and conveniently bought up to date.

The portal opened to a hall, such as is now rarely found; with the dais, the screen, the gallery, and the buttery-hatch all perfect, and all of carved oak. Modern luxury, and the refined taste of the lady of the late lord, had made Marney Abbey as remarkable for its comfort and pleasantness of accommodation as for its ancient state and splendour. The apartments were in general furnished with all the cheerful ease and brilliancy of the modern mansion of a noble, but the grand gallery of the seventeenth century was still preserved, and was used on great occasions as the chief reception room. . . . It occupied the whole length of one of the wings; was one hundred feet long, and forty-five feet broad, its walls hung with a collection of choice pictures rich in history; while the Axminster carpets, the cabinets, carved tables, and variety of easy chairs, ingeniously grouped, imparted even to this palatial chamber a lively and habitable air.

127

This is a splendid, but pleasant house, especially an hospitable dwelling. The preservation of the old hall, in all its detail, carries particular resonance. For the old is not merely for show. On great occasions the rooms revive their ancient function. Even the long gallery is filled. This cheerful and brilliant home is not only aesthetically charming, set 'in the midst of a beautiful park' remote from the ills of the city, as Lord Mowbray enviously comments, but the same nobleman tells us that it is 'surrounded by a contented peasantry'. It might be thought that Marney, raised from the stones of the old abbey like Paradise Hall, carries forward the best of monastic piety into a consciously progressive modern world, rich in history, like the paintings, and benefiting from all that is best in that history.

Disraeli calls Marney Abbey 'beautiful'. He qualifies his epithet. It is a 'beautiful illusion'. For this is like one of the palaces of *The Faerie Queene*, seeming fair without, but foul within. After the picturesque tour of Marney Abbey, the narration takes the reader to the country town of Marney, dependent on the 'Abbey'. It is the kind of description more familiar in Irish literature than English. The thatch of the rotting tenements resembles more the dunghill than the cottage. Within, water streams down the walls, and the family of the house huddle together in the promiscuous squalor of home, sweet home. There is no sunlight, no sanitation, and everywhere disease. Typhus strikes father and newborn child alike. With disease stalks famine.

This town of Marney was a metropolis of agricultural labour, for the properties of the neighbourhood having for the last half-century acted on the system of destroying the cottages on their estates, in order to become exempted from the maintenance of the population, the expelled people had flocked to Marney, where, during the war, a manufactory had afforded them some relief, though its wheels had long ceased to disturb the waters of the Mar.   (II, 3)

The responsibility for this is placed squarely on the landed estates. In contrasting Marney Abbey and Marney it is as if we have been shown, for example, an ideal villa of classic description, and then, unexpectedly, been taken to the pits where the slaves were chained. The very discourse changes. Disraeli writes in the language of a government inspector.

These wretched tenements seldom consisted of more than two rooms, in one of which the whole family, however numerous, were obliged to sleep, without distinction of age, or sex, or suffering. . . . These hovels were in many instances not provided with the commonest conveniences of the rudest police; contiguous to every door might be observed the dung-heap on which every kind of filth was accumulated, for the purpose of being disposed of for manure.

The intention is to shock, and part of that shock arises from the deliberate breach of the conventions of the country house idyll. Why this should come so late in the day is problematical, for the rural poor had always been there. But, in part, the formulaic nature of literature itself had controlled the nature of discourse. The convention of satire was to contrast the *ills of the city* with the *virtues of the country*. As late as 1738 Johnson could think of no better way to castigate London than by writing an imitation of Roman Juvenal in which the satirist pauses at the city limits to speak his mind before leaving for a rural retreat. This was not unreasonable. Rome and London were both aberrations in pre-dominantly rural societies. Within the country itself the bad estate often seems aberrant also because it has imported the evils of the city into Nature – hence the criticism of *luxuria*. The good estate thus remains the model of right social organisation. If the poor appear in the picture, then the productivity of the estate and the charity of the rich will bring personal relief. One thinks of the heroines of female fiction donning their pattens to walk through the mud with a basket of provisions over their arm for some old widow woman dying alone in her cottage. These formulaic descrip-tions, self-evidently, belong to the literature of the possessors, not the poor. That is easily perceived in retrospect. But, considering the present condition of the global village, as the world is now called, one might reflect on the parable of the mote and the beam before waxing self-righteous about this ancient image of charity.

At Marney Abbey the signs of the good estate of old are taken as if they were real, but are false. It is the villain, Lord Mowbray, who praises the 'contented peasantry'. The ritual image and the ritual language are invoked, but only to be demystified. The talismans are devices to conceal the gross economic oppression on which the façade of picturesque per-fection is based. In this Disraeli is closer to Marx or Engels than he is even to the previous generation of poets of the rural poor, Clare or Crabbe, Goldsmith or Wordsworth. The social problems of industrialisa-tion had grown greater, were growing day by day. If rural Marney is foul, it is a small centre of disease in the countryside. Wodgate is worse. It is a whole landscape of urban dereliction. Industrialisation is the exacerba-tion and multiplication of the ills of a town like Marney to monstrous, uncontrollable, size. There is no longer one nation but two, the rich and the poor. And the rich are to blame. One thinks of the way Dickens links the aristocratic Dedlocks in *Bleak House* to the dereliction of Tom-all-Alone's. The symbolic punishment of evil there is death by disease. Disraeli is more political. At the end of the chapter in which the lot of the rural poor is described, the first incendiary fire is lit, 'a beacon to the agitated parish'. The English Revolution has begun.

But Disraeli's criticism is written from within the ethos and the tradition of the country house. The English political novels are crowded with significant houses, Monmouth, Coningsby, Marney, moralised, contrasted one with another, and by implication in relation to the whole ancient pattern which goes back to the Caesars. Marney Abbey is the nadir of the tradition because it is a whited sepulchre. But the purpose of the future Lord Beaconsfield of Hughenden House was to touch bottom only to strike out again to revitalise what seemed on the verge of revolutionary extinction. Only by recognising the degree of mystification upon which the beautiful illusion depended might mystery and beauty be made positive forces for good again. It is one of the major claims of this imaginative fiction that human beings are not the products merely of the means of production and exchange, or mere creatures of the market, but souls stirred by sentiment and emotion, by faith and reverence, and that very power of the imagination upon which all literature works.

Beyond Marney Abbey – which we are told is far removed from its original site – there lies the ruined monastic settlement where Disraeli first writes of the creation of the 'two nations'. It is the equivalent of the ancient Choir at Norman Abbey in *Don Juan*, and here Disraeli's heroine, Sybil, takes on the role Byron had given to the symbolic stone of the Virgin Mother with her Child. Disraeli first sets the scene with the usual picturesque detail of mead and wood and water, of farm and mill and moss-grown stone. He tells of the old 'rights of hospitality', and of the charity of the monks 'at whose gate, called the Portal of the Poor, the peasants of the Abbey lands, if in want, might appeal each morn and night for raiment and for food'. This picturesque scene and quaintly moralised history then yield to a more intense symbolism.

From the west window, looking over the transept chapel of the Virgin . . . the eye wandered down the nave to the great orient light . . . through a gorgeous avenue of unshaken walls and columns that clustered to the skies. On each side of the Lady's chapel rose a tower. One, which was of great antiquity, being of that style which is . . . called Norman, short, and thick and square, did not mount much above the height of the western front; but the other tower was of a character very different. It was tall and light, and of a Gothic style most pure and graceful; the stone of which it was built, of a bright and even sparkling colour, and looking as if it were hewn but yesterday. At first, its turreted crest seemed injured; but the truth is, it was unfinished. . . . The abbots loved to memorise their reigns by some public work, which should add to the beauty of their buildings or the convenience of their subjects; and the last of the ecclesiastical lords of Marney, a man of fine taste, and a skilful architect, was raising this new belfry for his brethren, when the stern decree arrived that the bells should no more sound. And the hymn was no more to be chaunted in the Lady's chapel; and the candles were no more to be lit on the high altar; and the gate of the poor was to be closed for ever; and the wanderer was no more to find a home. (II, 4)

Each side of the Lady's chapel rises a tower. The allegory demands interpretation. The one, Norman and inferior, is a sign of conquest and the Norman aristocracy. But it is united by the Lady's chapel, and thus by symbolic marriage and by love, to the other tower which sparkles as if hewn yesterday, though it is unfinished Gothic work, a belfry to call the faithful to the house, a memorial to beauty and to utility. It is this unfinished work that the new generation is imaginatively called to complete as an act of faith in God and by practical charity, expressed by hospitality to all and care for the welfare of the poor. Egremont, our hero, is told that these monasteries were the old country houses of England.

There were on an average in every shire at least twenty structures such as this was; in this great county double that number: establishments that were as vast and as magnificent and as beautiful as your Belvoirs and your Chatsworths, your Wentworths and your Stowes. Try to imagine the effect of thirty or forty Chatsworths in this county, the proprietors of which were never absent.... They expended their revenue among those whose labour had produced it. These holy men, too, built and planted, as they did everything else, for posterity: their churches were cathedrals; their schools colleges; their halls and libraries the muniment rooms of kingdoms; their woods and waters, their farms and gardens, were laid out and disposed on a scale and in a spirit that are now extinct; they made the country beautiful, and the people proud of their country. (II, 5)

Compare with these houses of refuge the Union workhouse now and the gaol. Then there was true community, now there are the two nations, but 'it is community of purpose that constitutes society.' That is the idealistic message Egremont is taught.

This is a rhapsody among ruins. It was said by the apologists for the country house that it had taken over the better functions of the monastic order. Now we are told that the Golden Age was to be found in the monasteries themselves. Disraeli distances himself from this idealism by giving it to another. The symbolic mode of writing at this juncture is obviously 'poetical', and the language of the Chartists who instruct Egremont is Arcadian rather than documentary history. Sybil, the Virgin come alive from the Lady's chapel, is no more real than Marvell's new Eve, Maria Fairfax, or Byron's Aurora Raby. The very intrusion of this mode of writing into a novel which elsewhere uses the language of a documentary Blue Book obviously draws attention to its mythic status. But myths are not necessarily false in the way Marney Abbey is. They are potent driving forces. They exist, and because they exist, they constitute part of reality.

The 'ideal' house of these novels therefore has something about it of the quality of a dream, though it is modelled on Victorian archetypes. It is given a religious name, St Geneviève. Coningsby 'progresses' to this mansion from the political liberalism of Beaumanoir house, and that journey, thus, is akin to a pilgrim's progress.

131

In a valley, not far from the margin of a beautiful river, raised on a lofty and artificial terrace at the base of a range of wooded heights, was a pile of modern building in the finest style of Christian architecture. It was of great extent and richly decorated. Built of a white and glittering stone, it sparkled with its pinnacles in the sunshine as it rose in strong relief against its verdant background. . . . The valley opened for about half-a-mile opposite the mansion, which gave to the dwellers in it a view over an extensive and richly-cultivated country. . . . The first glance at the building, its striking situation, its beautiful form, its brilliant colour, its great extent, a gathering as it seemed of galleries, halls, and chapels, mullioned windows, portals of clustered columns, and groups of airy pinnacles and fretwork spires, called forth a general cry of wonder and of praise.
(III, 4)

This is a typically new, Gothic, Christian Victorian country house. Pugin's ideal design for Garendon Hall is traditionally associated with St Geneviève (Pl. 30). From the real world, Alton Towers (Pl. 31), Eaton Hall or Tortworth Court might serve equally well, or Scarisbrick where the tower soars like that of some medieval cathedral to heaven. At Alton Castle the Gothic complex combined hospital, chapel, school, warden's lodgings, hall, kitchen, library, lodging for 'poor brethren' and a community hall. This was the 'true thing', claimed Pugin, the real recreation of the medieval community. At Scarisbrick the owner chose to be painted in Tudor costume, and the house was thickly decorated with pious texts.

But the story of the Gothic Revival and its relation to the Young England movement is well known[3]. Though the fictional Eustace Lyle, owner of St Geneviève, is modelled on the real-life Ambrose Lisle Phillips, it is not a base in social realism that is sought in this description. St Geneviève is a house transfigured, as if the former religious settlement of Marney Abbey were rebuilt but changed into a country house. The site suggests something of those choice locations of retreat selected by the monks of old by a river (among a wood in which the wild deer stray as at Norman Abbey), but that opening view into the richly cultivated countryside is the sign of commitment to the welfare of the estate. In this location the house sparkles with light, its pinnacles are airy, its colour brilliant, it calls forth a general cry of wonder and of praise. There is something of magic about this, of transfiguration, something which, like the terrace on which the house is raised, is 'lofty and artificial'. This new Christian architecture which recreates the old in halls and chapels and galleries, portals and pinnacles and spires is something like Matthew Arnold's vision of Oxford through the imagination of the scholar ggypsy. It is not quite real.

It is appropriate, even inevitable, that 'merry Christmas' should be spent in this house. The master and his guests celebrate in full the rituals of that great Victorian invention with Boar's Head dinner, Lord of Misrule and Christmas Carol, and the text (like the Kelmscott Chaucer) breaks into Gothic type. The yule log burns 'on every hearth in that wide domain, from the hall of the squire to the peasant's roof'; for a week 'all comers might take their fill, and each carry away as much bold beef, white bread, and jolly ale as a strong man could bear in a basket with one hand'; there is a red cloak for every woman and a coat of broad cloth for every man. This is not mere Utilitarian charity, it is said, but the way to win the affection of the people. Nor is it mere fantasy. Sound cottages, village halls and schools, restored almshouses and churches testify throughout the countryside to the commitment of Victorian landlords to the community they controlled.[4] The great country house celebrations of the times for Christmas and coming of age, for marriages and the funerals of the great are well documented, and a vast sea of folk gathered about the house gaze out at us now in the documentary realism of estate photographs. Behind the festivities one recognises that sense of community which is ritually expressed by the formal giving and receiving of presents.

For at St Geneviève Christmas is, as it were, the culmination of the everyday. Almsgiving occurs twice each week throughout the year, and the first thing the visitors see on approaching the house is a long queue for what the Romans called 'the dole'.

They came along the valley, a procession of Nature, whose groups an artist might have studied. The old man, who loved the pilgrimage too much to avail himself of the privilege of a substitute accorded to his grey hairs, came in person with his grandchild and his staff. There also came the widow with her child at the breast, and others clinging to her form; some sorrowful faces, and some pale; many a serious one, and now and then a frolic glance; many a dame in her red cloak, and many a maiden with her light basket; curly-headed urchins with demure looks, and sometimes a stalwart form baffled for a time of the labour which he desired. But not a heart there that did not bless the bell that sounded from the tower of St Geneviève!   (III, 4)

At first sight the most striking thing in this portrayal of the 'deserving' poor is its picturesque quality. The text invites the reader to see with an artist's eye. The documentary mode of the social reformer, used among the tenements of Marney, yields here to something akin, for instance, to the work of George Morland, who would likewise have picked out that widow with a child at her breast and others clinging round. One couple in this composition we have met before. That mother bringing with her a daughter carrying a light basket is as old as Martial, and has a key role as an icon at Penshurst. But in Jonson this was part of the celebration of the fertility of the land, for the daughter was carrying a basket of provisions as a spontaneous offering, and her mother was in search of a husband for her. As the lady of Penshurst brought forth heirs to the estate, so too did the people multiply. But in Victorian England mother and daughter now come as beggars. The light basket is empty, and cannot carry much away.

Fertility itself is now the social problem, discussed by the rich in Malthusian terms. The people multiply too fast, and the surplus population is driven off the land and out of work. In keeping with the medieval ceremony of alms-giving this procession of the poor is called a 'pilgrimage', but compare the vigorous prosperity of Chaucer's fair field of folk on the way to Canterbury with this long dole queue. And this is merely the people of a good estate. Beyond lies the town of Marney, then Wodgate, Manchester, Dickens's London. Are even forty monastic Chatsworths in every county – if one could even imagine such a thing – a real solution to the problems of overpopulation and industrialisation in the great hunger of nineteenth-century Britain?

Disraeli's portrayal of St Geneviève is both a celebration of the medieval, even mystic fervour of Young England idealism, and his farewell to a movement already overrun. The whole artifice of the description of the house, the celebration of Christmas ritual, the picturesque image of the poor, distances the great good place as a work of art and of the imagination. To lose contact with the sources of this pious care would be an impoverishment of the spirit, but to depend upon perpetual Christmas in the country as a cure for massive social ills would be a dereliction of common sense. When the text breaks into Gothic the very typeface indicates the break between the everyday and reconstituted medievalism.

These are the novels of a practical politician, and a future Prime Minister. He cannot remain at St Geneviève. But what is remarkable is the degree to which the ideal of the country house carries over when he addresses himself to the depiction of the reforms necessary to solve fundamentally the problems St Geneviève placates only locally. For there are other, and new, country estates in England, more practical and more productive. They are the industrial complexes established by the new men Mr Trafford, 'on the banks of his native Mowe', and Oswald Millbank, 'in a green valley of Lancaster'. In both these places 'their lord dwells', in close relation to their factories, and, in Trafford's case, tied to the land by sentiments of childhood affinity. His factory is almost a cathedral, for the style is Christian Gothic, and his two thousand workers are a family community, 'the child under the eye of the parent, the parent under that of the superior workman; the inspector or employer at a glance can behold all.' It is the panoptic eye of Mr Allworthy again, or God in His creation, served now in an industrial temple: 'The roof of groined arches, lighted by ventilating domes at the height of eighteen feet, was supported by hollow cast-iron columns through which the drainage of the roof was effected' (*Sybil*, III, 8). Here is nave and clerestory, but also the most advanced sanitary convenience, the new Gothic order completing, as it were, the tower unfinished at old Marney Abbey.

Both Trafford's and Millbank's industrial estates are model communities, villages gathered around factory and country house. Millbank's is

remarkable for the neatness and even picturesque character of its architecture, and the gay gardens that surrounded it. On a sunny knoll in the background rose a church, in the best style of Christian architecture, and near it was a clerical residence and a school-house of similar design. The village, too, could boast of another public building; an Institute where there were a library and a lecture-room; and a reading-hall, which any one might frequent at certain hours, and under reasonable regulations. (*Coningsby*, IV, 3)

Trafford's estate is the same, a cluster of 'homes' and gardens, with public baths and schools, a church, and hence a prosperous and moral people. His own house, which is in the Tudor style, the Gothic church, the gardens round each house, and the sparkling (unpolluted) river against a sylvan background together form an ideal image of what Disraeli calls the 'baronial principle' recreated in 'community'. This is Penshurst, or Paradise Hall, or Grandison Hall restored. The factory now gives forth, like the land of old, more than the estate requires, and the land itself has now become a natural park and picturesque background to great house, church and village related in one society. The tending of each garden has become a ritual reminder of the organic relation of home to soil (and a useful source of fresh food). Nor, as at Grandison Hall, is the welfare of the mind and soul forgotten in library and reading room and church. But it is a sign of the new age that Millbank has no great ancestors. He fills his picture gallery, therefore, not with pictures of his aristocratic forebears, but with the fine, free landscapes of Lee, the animals of Landseer, the homely pathos of Wilkie and 'specimens of Etty worthy of Venice when it was alive' and was a famous commercial republic. Finally there is a reminder of the great republican ideal which underlies all, for Millbank's hall is both capacious, as fits the greatness of its owner, and 'classic' too.

A final touch is added to this symphonic harmonisation of traditions when Coningsby enters the hallway:

the sweetest and the clearest voice exclaimed from above, 'Papa! papa!' and instantly a young girl came bounding down the stairs. . . . Mr Millbank waved his hand to her and begged her to descend. She came down slowly; as she approached them her father said, 'A friend you have often heard of Edith: this is Mr. Coningsby.' (IV, 4)

Of course our hero will marry our heroine in the best traditions of romantic fiction. But another tradition is operative too. Here is the pledge of the fertility of her father's house: as Maria Fairfax to her father, so Edith to Millbank. In practical terms it means that the family business will continue in this house. It will also be a symbolic union, for Coningsby is a branch of the old, decadent aristocracy, and Edith the offspring of the new capitalism. Their marriage will be 'earned' by Coningsby learning to work for her (a quasi-Biblical parable). When they are united, it is a sign that the old order and the new are reconciled in the conjunction of Coningsby Castle with Hellingsley.

There is a firm social reality underpinning this image of the better world to be. Richard Arkwright had built a model village for his mill workers as early as 1776. Akroyd, at Copley, followed his example (1849) in the Gothic style, because 'This taste of our forefathers pleases the fancy, strengthens the house and home attachment, and entwines the present with the memories of the past', and he chose as his architect the leading exponent of the style, Gilbert Scott. At Saltaire (by 1872) there were 820 model houses, a park, church, chapel, school, hospital, public baths and laundries, an evening institute and 45 almshouses. Bromborough Pool, Port Sunlight, Bournville, New Earswick, followed, and thence the whole Garden City concept. William Lever, George Cadbury, Joseph Rowntree, might serve as real-life counterparts for the exemplary Millbank or Trafford. Nor is the merging of commercial money with aristocratic title an uncommon phenomenon. How far the fictional idealisation of the country house creates the moral imperatives of such industrialists, how far it reflects their practice is a nice (and unsolvable) issue.[5]

But the work of the imagination does not end in reform. There is an obsession with the country house in Disraeli which runs beyond the remodelling of industrial England as a new village community. The ultimate dream of Millbank, as of many real-life contemporaries, is to retire to a place in the country. The aim is not to run a rural estate – he has spent a life running an industrial one – but to find the perfect old English house, sanctified by the generations of the passing ages:

One of those true old English halls, now unhappily so rare, built in the time of the Tudors, and in its elaborate timber-framing and decorative woodwork indicating, perhaps, the scarcity of brick and stone at the period of its structure, as much as the grotesque genius of its fabricator, rose on a terrace surrounded by ancient and very formal gardens. The hall itself, during many generations, had been vigilantly and tastefully preserved by its proprietors. There was not a point which was not as fresh as if it had been renovated but yesterday. It stood a huge and strange blend of Grecian, Gothic and Italian architecture, with a wild dash of the fantastic in addition. The lantern watch-towers of a baronial castle were placed in juxtaposition with Doric columns employed for chimneys, while under oriel windows might be observed Italian doorways with Grecian pediments. Beyond the extensive gardens an avenue of Spanish chesnuts at each point of the compass approached the mansion, or led into a small park which was table-land, its limits opening on all sides to beautiful and extensive valleys, sparkling with cultivation, except at one point, where the river Darl formed the boundary of the domain, and then spread in many a winding through the rich country beyond. (VII, 3)

Perhaps after so many formal descriptions the longed-for English country house comes with too much familiarity – old trees in a fertile landscape, river and garden and venerable history from the classic to the Gothic. Yet, in a context in which Disraeli has constantly and programmatically moralised his houses, what is remarkable about Hellingsley is the absence of moral gloss. Just as Millbank has bought out from his industrial estate, so too this house is separated from society. The word 'hall' signifies antiquity, not use. Though the land is fertile, you look upon it as something 'beautiful', like the great Spanish chestnuts which blossom so remarkably in spring. These are not the raw material of imperial and commercial navies. What is valued here is that the house is 'rare', and the rarity of something so old has been preserved by different 'proprietors' who have preserved a valued work of 'architecture'. Families come and go, the architecture is valued for its unique quality. Millbank does not want to own the mass-produced or commonplace. The strange blending of classic and Gothic detail, which has been so much the substance of symbolic reading in the country house tradition, is here detached as architectural description for its own sake, inspired by aesthetic pleasure in picturesque form, – Doric columns as chimneys, Italian doors with Grecian pediments. Millbank has come here to enjoy all this in well-earned repose. One thinks of Monypenny and Buckles' account of Disraeli himself at Hughenden. *O! quid solutis est beatius curis?/ Cum mens onus reponit, ac peregrino?/ Labore fessi venimus larem ad nostrum? / Hoc est, quod unum est pro laboribus tantis.* It is a sign of the world we have lost that as late as 1929 it was not thought necessary to translate this commonplace.[6]

The potency of a myth like this does not reside in the accuracy with which it reflects socio-economic structures. As a mode of apprehension and a creator of desire it transfigures the process of getting and spending. Something is moving in these novels of Disraeli more powerful even than the wish to heal the divide between the two nations, the rich and the poor, and to make whole the community. They are works of longing for a country home: *O rus, quando ego te aspiciam?*[7] Millbank buys Hellingsley not because he is a social climber, nor to play out a fantasy of old style squirearchy, but because he wants the house itself. He who has spent for utility until utility is supplied will now begin to spend for the things of the spirit. There is something about the house which is talismanic. It is 'true' because it is old, writes Disraeli. It recalls 'happier images' and 'better recollections' seen in the 'beautiful' light of an English summer's day. There is a joy and a form of truth in beauty and in antiquity itself. Elsewhere house and estate have been given moral justification, but this is a mysticism beyond morality. When morality is satisfied there remains another aim, to preserve, to enjoy the object of desire.

137

CHAPTER FIFTEEN

Kelmscott House
News from nowhere

THE WELL-ORDERED revolutionary multitude in *Sybil* had protected the beauty of a country house they loved. Disraeli claimed that the episode was true. English radicalism was at heart conservative. The Utopian vision of a later revolutionary socialist supports the claim:

Yes, friend, this is what I came out for to see; this many-gabled old house built by the simple country-folk of the long-past times, regardless of all the turmoil that was going on in cities and courts, is lovely still . . . and I do not wonder at our friends tending it carefully and making much of it. It seems to me as if it had waited for these happy days, and held in it the gathered crumbs of happiness of the confused and turbulent past.   (*News from Nowhere*, 31)

William Guest had rowed up the sylvan Thames from Hammersmith, past Hampton Court and Mapledurham (where Pope had known the Blounts), beyond the medieval halls of Oxford and come with the woman he loves at last to Kelmscott. It is a house, like Penshurst, built with 'No man's ruin, no man's groan', but raised by the simple country-folk as a type of happiness and loveliness free from the turmoil of London. Here is no pride of ostentation, but, as Guest will declare, this many-gabled house, raised to meet the needs and express the love of the folk of old, is 'a piece of natural beauty'. Nature confirms the true happiness of the house. It is a symbol of the Golden Age.

But the Golden Age is not in some long-lost past paradise, but in the future. For William Guest's dream, and his journey from Victorian Hammersmith to Kelmscott, is an imaginative pilgrimage which shows in Utopian vision the coming of communism. The wage-slavery of the capitalist market has ended (not without great suffering and conflict). The apparatus of State bureaucracy has withered away – the Houses of Parliament are now a dung market (at last performing a useful function) – and Promethean human nature is unbound. It is a particularly English version of communism, owing as much to Pugin and to Ruskin as to Marx, and to the Victorian idealisation of medieval Gothic as natural, national and pious.[1] It is deeply imbued with the tradition of the literature of the country house. The very name 'Guest' repeats one of the dominant themes of 'To Penshurst', and the English version of the brave new world culminates in a communal feast in the countryside at Kelmscott. The last vision bestowed on William is of happy husbandmen and women, labourers and artists, gathered in the parish church within the demesne of the great house which is now their trust. William Morris's *News from Nowhere* (1890) is one of the most remarkable instances of how fundamentally the love of the country house has entered into the English spirit.

One of the major idealisations of the country house tradition has been the way in which it suppresses the element of labour, its golden fiction being that the land brings forth *sponte sua*. When the happy workers appear they too give spontaneously to their lord from the superabundant fertility of Nature. Radical writers have seen this as deplorable 'mystification'. But it is not an issue for Morris, for the extraordinary vision of *News from Nowhere* accepts both the traditions of *sponte sua* and of the happy worker, and redefines them. An unspecified scientific 'force' has done away now with the slavery of capitalist (and communist) production lines. 'All work which would be irksome to be done by hand is done by immensely improved machinery.' Thus it comes about that 'in all work which it is a pleasure to do by hand, machinery is done without' (15). It is easy to see what Morris's arts and crafts socialism itself suppresses and mystifies (would that atomic energy and the microchip might operate so benignly), but the intensely idealistic and moving proclamation of his gospel is that in the future men and women freely working for themselves and their community will rejoice in what their hands make, and, by the natural instinct of humanity, bring forth things of beauty – fine clothes, so that even Boffin the dustman is golden, fine handicrafts, and above all fine houses, of which Kelmscott is the measure.

Rural England has become the *locus amoenus* (the pleasant place) of which poets wrote. The scenes William perceives on his journey resemble the sentimental scenes of picturesque art, and he sleeps 'in small cottage chambers, fragrant and clean as the ideal of the old pastoral poets'. Everywhere 'dear Guest' is met with spontaneous and free hospitality (for money is unknown). In every house of sufficient size the great hall has become once more the focus of community; witness Hammersmith Guest House, under whose 'open timber roof' the pilgrimage begins:

It was a longish building with its gable ends turned away from the road, and long traceried windows coming rather low down set in the wall that faced us. It was very handsomely built of red brick with a lead roof; and high up above the windows there ran a frieze of figure subjects in baked clay, very well executed, and designed with a force and directness which I have never noticed in modern work before. (3)

Guest thinks of a meal on high table in an Oxford college hall as he eats, and later he is told that the great houses scattered in the country 'are more like the old colleges than the ordinary houses as they used to be'. At Hampton Court, and at Mapledurham, his journey again takes him to the communal hall. He begins to feel at each place as if it were his own. Martial, or Jonson, would understand what he meant.

> The people whom we met there had an indefinable kind of look of being at home and at ease, which communicated itself to me, so that I felt that the beautiful old place was mine in the best sense of the word; and my pleasure of past days seemed to add itself to that of to-day, and filled my whole soul with content. (22)

This communist future is founded on an intense nostalgia for an ideal past, as though all England were collegiate Oxford or one great monastery: a commonwealth of social harmony and culture. That nostalgia is as much aesthetic as political: 'I felt that the beautiful old place was mine in the best sense of the word.' For Guest, the house would not be so beautiful were it not old, and if it were not beautiful it would not appeal. The sense of possession is idealised, for this place belongs to the whole community because it belongs to no one master. One can perceive not only communism but the idea of a National Trust coming into being here.[2] The past is the legacy of the future to be lovingly transmitted for the benefit of all. (So at Goodrich today any villager may see Morris's ideal in the community hall of Tudor brick and tile, gable and exposed beam, and wide hearths for roaring fires. But what real history has not left to the village – for the oldest building there is the grimly picturesque ruin of the castle – imagination has recreated for future generations in the symbolism of ancient architectural form. Goodrich's Tudor hall is, in fact, contemporaneous with *News from Nowhere* and a tribute to Morris's influence.)

As Guest eats in hall there enter to him comely womenfolk, again as tradition required. It was the especial praise of the mistress of Penshurst that she was a good housewife, and that she was fertile also.

> Come, now, my friend, ... don't you know that it is a great pleasure to a clever woman to manage a house skilfully, and to do it so that all the house-mates about her look pleased, and are grateful to her? (9)

This is what women do best, despite the views of some who foolishly despise the keeping of a house or the rearing of children. In the communist world of the country house,

> How could it possibly be but that maternity should be highly honoured amongst us? Surely it is a matter of course that the natural and necessary pains which the mother must go through form a bond of union between man and woman, an extra stimulus to love and affection between them, and that this is universally recognised.

140

The discrimination of the sexes is part of the same natural order as the house in its fertile garden and estate. This is not a discrimination culturally determined, but part of the universal order, as in classical antiquity, so at Penshurst, so in the millennium. Women will keep the hearth and rear the children. It is 'natural' and it is 'necessary'.

At Penshurst the comely daughters of the land, bearing fruit, came seeking husbands. So when Guest falls in love with Ellen he sees her in a similar emblematic image, walking from the hay field to the garden:

> I saw a light figure come out of the hay-field higher up the slope, and make for the house; and that was Ellen, holding a basket in her hand. . . . I looked, and over the low hedge saw [her] shading her eyes against the sun as she looked toward the hay-field, a light wind stirring in her tawny hair, her eyes like light jewels amidst her sunburnt face, which looked as if the warmth of the sun were yet in it.   (23)

A woman standing in a garden is the traditional image of Eve, mother of mankind; the emblems of the harvest, and the very warmth of the sun which burns in Ellen, make her too the natural image of Venus, goddess of love and fertility.

Thus Ellen, accompanying Guest, comes home again to the country house as the couple reach their journey's end at visionary Kelmscott, peopled by 'bright figures', set among 'ancient elm-trees'. The trees, as always, are signs of conservative continuity, but unlike the landscape of Paradise Hall, this is celebrated now as a fair field full of folk (as that other 'William', the poet Langland, had expressed it).

> Over the meadow I could see the mingled gables of a building where I knew the lock must be, and which now seemed to combine a mill with it. A low wooded ridge bounded the river-plain to the south and south-east . . . and a few low houses lay about its feet and up its slope. I turned a little to my right and through the hawthorn sprays and long shoots of the wild roses could see the flat country spreading out far away under the sun of the calm evening, till something that might be called hills with a look of sheep-pastures about them bounded it with a soft blue line. Before me, the elm-boughs still hid most of what houses there might be in this river-side dwelling of men; but to the right of the cart-road a few grey buildings of the simplest kind showed here and there . . . my heart swelled with joy as I thought of all the beautiful grey villages, from the river to the plain to the uplands, which I could picture to myself so well, all peopled now with this happy and lovely folk, who had cast away riches and attained to wealth.   (30)

Kelmscott itself is still no more than a glimpse of mingled gables, but is the centre of the landscape. Nothing closes the vista except the distant hills as the *locus amoenus*, 'this pleasant country place', extends as far as the eye can see, and as far as the imagination desires. Of course those hills are the pastures of sheep – that has not changed since Arcady – and the mill is the only sign of mechanised industry in sight, the one thing necessary to process the bounty of the land and produce the staple of bread. It is driven not by the mysterious 'force' whose factories are always nowhere to be seen in this Utopia, but by the waters of sweet, salmon-crowded Thames.

There is something strange about this landscape of communist industry. Though Guest celebrates a land of happy and lovely 'folk' (the good old Saxon word), yet the conventions of aristocratic landscape art have conditioned his imaginative eye. For though we see the simple houses of the folk, they themselves have now disappeared. Guest deliberately 'disentangles' himself from the 'merry throng', he tells us. He looks out on the 'picture' as if seen through a Claude glass,[3] for the whole is suffused with an evening glow, like Claude's 'The Enchanted Castle', which so moved Keats, or Francis Danby's 'The Enchanted Island'. Hawthorn sprays and long shoots of wild roses frame the scene, not unlike the borders of a Morris print. It is the aesthetic eye of a cultivated, leisured mind which composes this elegaic image (elegaic for it will soon be lost as the book terminates and Morris awakes from his dream). It is appropriate, therefore, that the journey's end is not one of the simple cottages, but Kelmscott, Morris's own country house. All men have equal rights, as Burke himself admitted, but not, even in Nowhere, to equal things. Ellen, like Guest, 'detaches' herself from the people and enjoys the house alone. They explore the place and find 'no soul in any room'.

Kelmscott itself provides the frontispiece to the book, framed, like the landscape, with a continuous wreath of foliage, designed by Morris himself and symbolic of natural beauty: 'This is the picture of the old house by the Thames to which the people of this story went' (Pl 32). The chosen façade is the east front (because the oldest) of the 'U'-plan house of *c.* 1570. The stone path of which the text speaks leads past the English roses Guest admires to an unpretentious porch. Kelmscott was not built for envious show. The door led to the screens passage; to the left the kitchens, to the right, of equal dimensions, the hall. Beyond that, in the wing (1670), would have been the private quarters of the family. The garrets above, so Guest says, would once have been the dwelling of the tillers and herdsmen of the estate, but are now, in his dream, the sleeping-place of children (though they too are strangely invisible). The furniture was sparse 'and that only the most necessary, and of the simplest forms' (no *luxuria* here) for the house itself 'and its associations was the ornament of country life'. That word 'associations' is the key. For Kelmscott, despite the mill and barns, is no longer a working place, nor a centre of communal life, despite the hall. Mill and barn are there, like the roses and the lichens, for the associations of country life they call to mind:

How I love the earth, and the seasons, and weather, and all things that deal with it, and all that grows out of it, – as this has done. (31)

So Ellen cries, touching the lichen that has grown from the stone of the wall of the house as if to embrace it. This is not communism, nor community, but an expression of sheer romantic love. 'And the house itself was a fit guardian for all the beauty of this heart of summer.'

It is a dream, as Morris himself insists. Kelmscott is like Pope's Twickenham, or Stowe, the embodiment of an idea in symbols. Reality was never like that. In fact Morris did not live permanently at Kelmscott. He could not, any more than Guest. It is one of the grandest of English holiday cottages, leased for twenty years at a cost of £6,000. The cash came from the successful commercial exploitation for the capitalist market of Morris's handicrafts. There is an additional irony in the presence in the attics of the 'rustic simplicity' of Ford Madox Brown's dressing tables, washstands and towel horses, for, as the guidebook comments, they 'are the only ones of their kind to survive. Perhaps elsewhere such rustic simplicity has not insured preservation.' Precisely so. Crude socialist artefacts command little value in the market. But the house now contains the Cabbage and Vine tapestry which is the only piece Morris ever wove entirely by himself, investing 516 hours of labour in the process. It is interesting to speculate on the sale room value of this. Morris made a fortune from selling art. Pope, a capitalist poet, would have celebrated the fact. He delights to tell how he got the money for Twickenham. The dream of *News from Nowhere* suppresses the market element of labour.

Of course, Morris's ideas both on medieval architecture and on practical socialism are more hard-headed than this simple summary suggests, and *News from Nowhere*, self-evidently is a Utopian fantasy perceived by the mind of a fictional character, William Guest. Yet the emotional drive of this fiction is towards turning a real, old country house into a symbol of the imagination, and Kelmscott had a special role for Morris which protected the actual place from the harsher light of history. He himself took a 'pilgrimage' similar to Guest's from Hammersmith to Kelmscott in a boat which he christened 'the Ark', and his own account of the voyage tells, at length, of a spiritual journey from the oppressive world of the city into a picturesque countryside praised as an honest 'work-a-day world' – through which he comes to Kelmscott with a lover's rapture: 'presently the ancient house held me in its arms again.'[4] Likewise, his long account of Kelmscott in *The Quest* (November 1894) reiterates his pleasure in the 'loveliness' and the 'charm' of a place which is not a power house but at one with the soil and the community: 'so much has the old house grown up out of the soil and the lives of those who lived on it'. The idealisation of the house is obvious, too, in the way the socialist turns social signs of class or work into aesthetic attributes, so that 'the coat-armour' on the mantel is 'by no means inelegant', and the farm buildings form a delightful group among which stands 'a very handsome barn of quite beautiful proportions'. He ends appropriately with a testament to his 'love', though he adds, 'a reasonable love I think'. But in the same decade both Aymer Vallance and J. W. Mackail in their biographies of Morris conflate romantically his factual and fictional accounts of the house, further eroding the boundary between imaginative love and the world of reason.

The driving force of this extreme idealism is such that it has translated itself from the beautiful and moving fiction of *News from Nowhere* even into the would-be merely descriptive prose of the Society of Antiquaries guide (1977):

Kelmscott 'Manor' is a beautiful and unspoiled example of the local architecture of the stone-building region extending from Oxfordshire westward into Gloucestershire and north-westward into the Cotswolds. . . . The intrinsic merits of the house are alone sufficient for admiration, but the special interest of Kelmscott in the literary, social and artistic fields is that it was the home of William Morris, the writer, socialist, artist, craftsman and manufacturer, from 1871 to his death in 1896, and contains most of his possessions and many of the products of his genius.

The leading word remains that of *News from Nowhere*: 'beauty'. It is a quality that compels 'admiration', and a quality too that here, in the heart of rural England, may be found in an 'unspoiled example'. This is the language of Keatsian aesthetic romanticism. 'A thing of beauty is a joy for ever.' One preserves such things for their 'intrinsic merits', and only remote from the city, in country life, are they likely to remain unspoilt. It is the 'genius' of the real artist which reveals this intrinsic beauty in his work, and thus, to Keats, one may join Plato, for there exists, it seems, an inherent and permanent concept of beauty which the artist reveals and the connoisseur appreciates. This connoisseur is, moreover, an 'antiquary', and, as the guide makes clear, unspoilt beauty is found in the things of the past, old tapestries and paintings, rich cassone and illuminated manuscripts, and the possession of such taste separates even the communist from the untutored proletariat. The guide tells, therefore, that the new decorative style at Kelmscott 'drove graining and marbling to the public house', and it is clear that the vulgarity of the *public* house has no place in the privacy of Kelmscott's hall. It is appropriate, therefore, that today Kelmscott is opened to the public only 'on six advertised days of the year'. One would not want 'an ancient and beautiful house' trampled to death by mere day trippers. Until all the world are arts and crafts socialists, Kelmscott is best preserved by antiquaries.

None the less the guide pays honour (and properly so) to the common people Morris would have admired: the local craftsmen who, 'entirely devoted to their charge' have restored Kelmscott as a memento of Morris. These good workmen, however, may not fully understand what is meant when the guide writes: *Maxima res effecta, viri; timor omnis abestol Quod superest.*[5] Which Latin tag may indicate, again, from what roots the country house still sucks its nourishment. This is the language of the leisured and learned class who love and understand the nature of art. The dignity of labour is celebrated, but in Morris's dream William Guest toils not, neither does he spin, but is fed and clothed by the loving generosity of his friends in his search for Paradise Hall. What is most appreciated in this new medieval world are the artefacts made by the hands of artists, beautiful clothes, fine carvings, beautiful buildings. It is appropriate that the dream house of the pilgrimage is now a museum whose function is to refine taste and to inspire the (few) visitors with a love of beauty. The function of the house is not political – that communistic community ideal is indeed nowhere – but aesthetic. The house is (to use a word of Henry James's) a repository of 'spoils' – the artefacts of the past gathered for the delighted passion of refined sensibility. Kelmscott is no longer a social sign, but an artistic one, not grounded in an estate, but a creation of the imagination.

News from Nowhere is a potent work. It is part of the spirit of the age. The National Trust has its origins in the same decade, though it was some years before the first country estate with its encumbent house was taken on board.[6] The original aim was to preserve vernacular tradition unspoilt, that ancient and beautiful England which Morris celebrated. From the same period dates Edward Hudson's *Country Life*, the journal of record of the English country house. It is more than a record of things as they were. A large part of the journal is devoted to offering old artefacts and old houses for sale. At a price, anyone can buy the visible signs of age and beauty. There is a mere commerce to that (there always is), but the commerce could not take place were there not a driving hunger of the imagination to possess things of beauty, of which the pre-eminent example is the country house.

What the past cannot supply, for the stock is limited, the present recreates. The perfected expression of the aesthetic and elegaic mode in imaginative architectural form is found in the work of Morris's contemporary and successor, the last of the great English country house architects, Edwin Lutyens. 'In architecture, close as it is to men's lives and their history, the visible result of time is a large factor in the realised aesthetic value, and what a true architect will in due measure always trust to.' The words are those of Walter Pater, but the principles are Lutyens's, so Lawrence Weaver wrote in his famous celebration.[7] Lutyens's work

145

bridges the divide between the vernacular tradition of the early National Trust and the greater houses of *Country Life*. There is a passionate concern for 'legitimate' material (Weaver's word): oak aged by sand-blasting and steeping in lime, old furniture bleached and scrubbed, old building techniques renewed in cruck and newell. At the same time the whole repertory of the past is invoked, whether in neo-Tudor mansion nestling in Gertrude Jekyll garden, neo-Baroque palace or neo-Palladian villa, or Gothic castle springing in picturesque sublime on remote hilltop.

Lutyens's houses are not mere formal pastiches but are intended to call into imaginative play the apprehension of the passage of time. So at Marshcourt 'classical' Corinthian pilasters in the hall stand on 'vernacular' brick pedestals, as if different strata of history challenged each other to declare which had superior authenticity of age. At Overstrand the masonry pavilions of the house are constructed to suggest that they are the fossilised towers of an earlier fortified dwelling. Conversely, Castle Drogo, a brand-new fortress, appears, from a distance, to be lapsing into decay for part of the *enceinte* is incomplete. But perhaps most remarkable of all, at Homewood the mass of an elm weather-boarded cottage is cut back to show the white-rendered Ionic façade of a classical villa within. Nature's growth and civilisation's decay are paradoxically joined in a metaphysical conceit. Then, as the oldest of signs, above the entrance porch of Crooksbury house (built in vernacular wood and brick as Morris himself would love) there stands the primitive hut of Laugier's imagination, mankind's first home, paradise recalled.[8]

Lutyens's clients were (in the main) the *nouveaux riches*, and the houses were the rural retreats, the weekend hotels of families divorced from the old aristocracy of the land, each one, in its different way, another Kelmscott. The need was to create in symbolic form that continuity, tradition, community, history, which was their England. This is both 'aestheticism' and associationism, for it reads architecture through the spectacles of books and through our own moral needs. Weaver, in his essay, regrets the 'impurity' of this, but admits its inevitability.

Nowhere is this historical ideal more beautifully and symbolically revealed than in Deanery Garden, Sonning, built for Edward Hudson, proprietor of *Country Life*. It is minutes only by train from Paddington, but secluded from suburbia by its redbrick wall beside the Thames. Within the domain Lutyens preserved the old fertility of an apple orchard, Eve's garden without the forbidden fruit, and the very name Deanery Garden makes this a holy settlement: for the pleasure of a man of business, whose business is the celebration (and the sale) of old houses.

The principal room, as tradition now demanded, is the great hall, massive with ancient beams. the interstices filled with chalk. and rising the height of the house. A huge open fire heats the room, a superb bay window of forty-eight lights invites the eye out into the garden. There, in symbolic design, a moat protects the inner wall of the Deanery, an ornamental drawbridge, never to be raised, leading to a lower terrace. The semi-circular steps beyond, linking formal garden with orchard, themselves constitute an inner gatehouse, and emphasise how the house stands raised above the site, lovely to look upon in its rich, red vernacular brick – recalling Philip Webb's work for William Morris at Bexley Heath[9] – and lovely to look out from into this symbolically fortified refuge.

It is a 'playful' design (Weaver's word), even 'paradoxical' (in the conception of a more recent writer).[10] To unite church and great house, castle and Garden of Eden in one conceit for the proprietor of *Country Life* is an historically appropriate act. The sign of the country house is divorced from the continuity of family and estate – this is the suburban retreat of a man of commerce – yet Deanery Garden shows the potency of the aesthetic yearning for a place of beauty which preserves the past within the countryside. It is Kelmscott new built for the needs of a new age (capitalist not communist), and the work of Lutyens, self-evidently, is the pattern book for a thousand suburban imitations since.

But there is another resonance in Deanery Garden which neither a term of rhetoric like 'paradox' nor a term of art like 'aesthetic' fittingly expresses. As an historical process works itself through and the ancient orders of English society change and decay, in this poetic architecture one finds again the same patterns of symbolic apprehension which marked the ultimate decline of that earlier classical civilisation to which the English country house is so much indebted. The interchange of the symbolism of church and castle at Deanery Garden has direct analogy with Sidonius's praise of the castle of Pontius Leontius at the end of the Roman era. This was first defined by the language of religion and then of war. There the divinities had chosen a fortress for themselves, an enclosed home sanctified by Nature in its garden, and where an old way of life might still continue amongst the works of art a family had gathered as signs of their wealth and of their culture. It is a tradition now belonging only to the rich who understand it through the medium of art, but celebrated even by the poor, so the poet claims, who hold up their hands to rejoice at such things outside the castle walls. It is remarkable that a millennium and a half later, even at Deanery Garden, in suburban Sonning-on-Thames, this language of conquest is not yet eradicated.

It requires a valediction.

CHAPTER SIXTEEN

Cardiff Castle

THE WAR WITH revolutionary Jacobinism gave a new significance to the English castle. To restore, or build, a castle after the fall of the Bastille cannot be seen as an act of mere aestheticism. What had once been a picturesque motif for a jaded architectural taste now acquired a clear, patriotic resonance. The most notable, and influential, example was the refurbishment of Windsor at great expense by George III, and the elaborate rituals of the Garter acted out in the renovated fortress. The spirit of chivalry went forth to defeat France as it had at Crecy and Poitiers. George III was a new Edward III. Great banquets were served in St George's Hall, and after the crowning victory of Waterloo, the Waterloo Chamber was established in climactic place in the sequence of armoured rooms of state. George IV continued what his father had begun at an ultimate cost of more than a million pounds.

The annual pilgrimage of sightseers to Windsor testifies to the success of the programmatic and triumphalist icon. It is only one among many. At Belvoir Wyatt's 'picturesque' rebuilding revived the *donjon* almost upon the original site, but recruited images of religion to support the aristocracy militant. Thornton's guard room and adjoining galleries reproduce Gothic motifs from Lincoln Cathedral as the setting for the arms of the Leicestershire militia. The Duke and Duchess, recalling ancient patriotism, chose to have their portraits painted in Tudor costume after the style of Joseph Nash,[1] and after the Congress of Vienna Belvoir became the centre of a more social congress as a Wellington or Esterhazy, Mutescewitz or Rokeby was entertained with extraordinary splendour to the strains of martial music.

The movement continues from the revolutionary epoch to the onset of the First World War. John Nash's castle-building dates from the 1790s, Smirke's and Lugar's from the first decade of the nineteenth century. At Bayons Charles Tennyson (who preferred to be known as d'Eyncourt) built a complete *enceinte* to his property with bridge, drawbridge and fortified gatehouse. Peckforton Castle dates from the 1840s where in more than medieval discomfort Lord Tollemache lived out the pageant of his feudal generosities. Alnwick and Horsley Towers date from the 1850s; Cardiff Castle from the 1860s, Arundel was gigantically restored in the 1880s and 1890s; Lutyens's Castle Drogo belongs to the twentieth century.

If these are the signs of a revived chivalric idealism,[2] they are also manifest images of social control. The rigid class and sexual hierarchy of the Victorian country house (formalised in the long corridors of power) is most obviously expressed by the revival of the imagery of the castle. Medieval rituals, whether mock tournaments or competitions of archery, medieval celebrations of the estate in communal feastings, testify to an idealisation of a world free from the taint of revolution, whether radical or industrial. As late as 1859 the Percy dependants, at their annual dinner, sang in praise of the family and 'Those relics of the feudal yoke . . . That binds the Peasant to his Lord.'[3] That loyalty was subsequently to be put to real test. Throughout the countryside simple village memorials testify to the death of what were the last feudal armies to volunteer to fight and die under the command of the gentry in the war of 1914–18. The ritual slaughter of the shooting parties of the estates was made real. It is fitting that the greater public cenotaphs should be designed by the architect of the last great country houses, Edwin Lutyens.

> Fall if ye must, ye Towers and Pinnacles,
> With what ye symbolise; authentic Story
> Will say, Ye disappeared with England's Glory.[4]

The heraldic symbolism of Scott's manor house, Abbotsford, with its armoury and baronial fantasies of chivalry, is the strongest architectural link of the times with literature. The popularity of Scott's novels in the nineteenth century is in reciprocal relation with the idealisation of the middle ages. But the most literary of actual castles is that restored for the Marquess of Bute at Cardiff, with its hunting lodge at Castell Coch. Bute's coming of age, with its enormous medieval pageantry, and his conversion to the Roman Catholic Church are the subject of Disraeli's sensationally popular novel, *Lothair* (1870). Bute himself was a deeply literary man, conversant with many languages ancient and modern, and in commissioning William Burges to restore his castles for him he set about creating one of the most detailed and complex literary and iconographic programmes of the age.

Cardiff Castle (Pl. 33) and Castell Coch deliberately eschew connection with the people. The smooth dressed stone of the walls excludes the mob. It is a provocative sign, for in Wales the English castle always reminds of original conquest. To protect the new Bastille (at Castell Coch) there are drawbridge and portcullis, even an apparatus for pouring boiling oil upon intruders. The numerous towers of both fortresses picturesquely break the skyline, rising higher even than their Norman originals. The principal windows look inward to the keep, not outward to the landscaped park. But, on higher levels, smaller outlets scan the entire countryside; to the south are the docks loading Bute coal in what was then the busiest seaport in Britain; to the north, up the valleys, the Bute mines. The castle and its lodge, seen at a distance, geographical or historical, are highly romantic in their play of pinnacle and cone and crenellation among parkland trees. Closer to they are exclusive, introspective, grim.

In Cardiff on the Taff, as in France between the Dordogne and the Garonne fifteen hundred years before, an aristocrat of an imperial power had chosen to build a fortified home – Bute, moreover, built on the site of a legionary camp. The historical connection with Rome is unbroken. 'No siege engine, nor ramp, nor catapult-shot, nor scaling ladder' could shake the walls of the home of Pontius Leontius, whose towers, like Cardiff's, expressed pomp and power. Practical necessity dictated to Leontius. That was less urgent for Bute, whose defensive symbolism, accordingly, is an act of choice. But Nottingham Castle had been burnt in Reform riots, and the Chartists in Wales had marched from the valleys to occupy Newport. Matthew Arnold saw a new barbarianism loose in Victorian society; Marx and Engels wrote of a new slave economy. It is not an entirely remote parallel to liken those underground pits where Roman country gentlemen kept their *servi* of old with those other pits a few miles from Castell Coch which helped make the Marquess the richest man in Britain. Burgus Pontii Leontii and Bute's two castles are all places of authority ringed by alien forces.

There is the same ostentation of opulence within. Cardiff Castle, like Leontius's, has its summer and winter rooms. The taste of the owner for luxury is in both cases expressed in gilded roofs. Cardiff is encrusted with gold. At Leontius's fortress the women were represented (ritually) at their spinning and embroidery, for these were the signs of the good Roman housewife. At Cardiff, in equally ritual sign, the Chaucer room incorporates the poet's *Legend of Good Women*. Above the fortresses reside the appropriate deities: for the Roman, Dionysius and Phoebus; for Bute, the Virgin Mary herself, a fountain ornament in the roof garden, generative Venus made Christian. Throughout the castle angels and prophets mingle with warriors: King David (poet as well as hero) and his medieval equivalent, the chivalric knight Robert the Consul, shown in the banqueting hall riding forth from his fortress. Beyond his walls Leontius had planted vines, sign of both the Dionysiac fertility of the land and the happiness of the owner's slaves. In the Victorian home the joyful servants were carefully kept out of sight, if not out of mind, but on the hillsides above Cardiff Bute felt it right to plant his own vineyards, a symbolic act productive of a peculiar communal wine.

These parallels between Bute and Leontius are not those of deliberate allusion (like Pope's to Horace), but it is not fortuitous that Bute built on a Roman site. Common elements link the ancient and the modern world, and similar circumstances create similar patterns of imagery from the inherited store. The Roman villa had changed, of necessity, to the proto-feudal castle. In Cardiff the classic tradition of the English country house, as it approaches its end, draws its imagery and inspiration from that very feudalism into which the ancient world had merged. Bute's fantasies, like Sidonius's poetic images, belong to the end of an epoch.

The two fortresses at Cardiff are extreme examples of the country house separated from an estate, whether that estate were agricultural manor or the more complex administrative unit of the Honour in which a market town would form an essential part (so the relation of Arundel Castle to its town). The rural estate at Cardiff exists only as an icon. It is symbolised by the decorative park; around Castell Coch there is a forest, the appropriate setting for a hunting lodge. Bute's industrial investments now take the place of the old administrative Honour. Both fortresses seemingly control strategic points (as they had of old). Castell Coch dominates the direct line of communication to the coal-bearing valleys, and their potentially rebellious workers; the castle in Cardiff dominates what was the old Roman road west and the new seaport.

Although the fertility of the land has no real relation to the houses, embedded in an urban and industrial setting, yet greenery without and painted images within indicate how important the signs of the old order remained. The superabundance of Nature is expressed in a riot of colour in Burges's designs. At Castell Coch the blue heavens of the drawing room swarm with birds flocking among the stars; they nest in painted trees on the walls and small game sport beneath. The images are utterly charming. In Cardiff fertility is expressed in more solemn images. In the domestic dining room, above the fire, Sarah, in lifelike effigy, beholds the visitation of the three angels, a Biblical image both of the promise of children in marriage and of the spiritual 'children of the promise'.[5] It is of especial significance in the light of Bute's conversion to Roman Catholicism, and relates to the image of the Mother of God herself which presides over the castle. Secular literature supplements the divine. 'The Parliament of Fowls' is celebrated in the Chaucer room, a poem on the festival of St Valentine's Day where the marriage of the birds is presided over by Dame Nature herself, harmonising and controlling under God the hierarchy of society. In lighter vein, elsewhere, the castle portrays the winter and summer pursuits of lovers.

Just as the fertility of the land is continued from park and forest outside to painting and statuary within, so too the dominance of the land by the feudal family is repeatedly expressed in visual signs. The Bute coat of arms occupies a central position in the library, its supporters a horse and stag, signs of the mimic war of the chase, the motto *Avito viret honore*: he flourishes with ancient honour. The banqueting hall is devoted to Robert the Consul, conqueror of Glamorgan, whose figure in coat of chain mail is shown leaving his castle gate while his servants blow trumpets in celebration in every tower (an image Sidonius would understand), the women of his family wave their handkerchiefs and the Church blesses (Pl. 34). Above, from the roof, angels look down. This seems the idealisation of 'a very perfect, gentle knight' (Chaucer's phrase) set out to right wrongs, succour the distressed and serve God. The Victorian country gentleman embraced the highest traditions of service and piety, called by Providence to fulfil his high duties to Church and State.[6]

This romance is touchingly ideal. The eye is translated to the world of poetry by the shimmering colours, the life-like effigies of glittering saints and knights, the superabundance of the natural world which crowds the walls. It is as if we were the Lady of Shalott working upon a glowing tapestry, and never daring to look out of the windows of the imagination to the world outside. For outside the loads of coal, hacked by blackened men from dangerous and twisted seams, daily clanked down iron rails beyond the castle walls. The intensity of the idealistic introversion seems a direct inversion of the images outside. This shutting out of barbarity is also a shutting in. Compare the open portico of any Whig Palladian villa inviting ingress and egress, or the easy passage through the windows of a Repton House from drawing room to lawn. At Cardiff there is a retreat into the realm of the imagination which suggests that the mind itself, however richly decorated with images from art or literature, has become its own Bastille.

There is something deeply disturbing in the way that the decorative symbolism will never let you alone, as if Bute feared that a blank space on the wall, a window opening onto a railway line, might provide a freedom of thought, the possibility of imagining another world which would shatter the loom of art. This is typical of Victorian decorative art, which crowds every space with the products of manufacturing capacity and wealth, but it seems particularly expressive here of a lack of confidence even within extraordinary wealth and power.

The images of fertility, for instance, spin off into quirks and fantasies. Though love is celebrated, the images of matrimony show two dogs pulling in different directions, and another pursuing a cat into a tree. Though barren Sarah is promised children, the offspring of the house are not shown. There is no place for them on the walls. She looks out not only on angels, but on a monkey's face with a nut for a bell push in its mouth.

On the staircase a slithering crocodile is about to eat a child. In the Arab room are eight of Burges's favourite birds. They are parrots, which he admired, he said, for their 'grotesque motions . . . fine colouring and . . . great intelligence'.[7] It might be read as a symbol both for the aristocracy and for the designer. Compare this quirkiness with the iconography of Georgian Clandon Park, where, in traditional imagery, one sees above the hall fireplace a willing bull brought to sacrifice in the classic world (Pl. 35), from medieval time in tapestry the happy harvest of rejoicing workers in the fields, and then, in family portraits, celebration of the fertility of the women of the house. Cardiff, by comparison, is uncertain what its imagery is about.

Bute and Burges, perhaps, thought of those grotesque images which intrude even into the architecture of medieval cathedrals. Quirkiness is part of the reconstitution of their ideal. Or if the castle at Cardiff were a 'metaphysical' poem, the visual oddities would be the equivalent of the 'wit' for which such works are noted. If Marvell were the architect, not Burges, he might have similar devices in the form of the tortoises, bees and quails of 'Upon Appleton House'. But there is a danger in yoking together heterogeneous ideas, blessed angels and comic crocodiles, knights and parrots. Multiplicity may lead to confusion, and confusion to contradiction unaware of the way it subverts itself.

It is the great hall which is most problematic in this respect, for the symbolic centre of communal life was also the real centre of old of the armed force which controlled the community. The image of Robert the Consul (the sign of chivalry) is of an armed man, because the Normans took what they wanted by conquest. When the eye eventually travels down from the knight to the foot of the crenellated towers of the iconographic fireplace, it perceives the grated window of a dungeon through which a prisoner gazes up at the knight. It is Robert of Normandy who died a captive in 1134. (So, at Castell Coch, a real dungeon is supplied as part of the 'appropriate' apparatus of a gentleman's residence.) If one settles down to read the mural paintings of the great hall the imagery grows darker yet. The tale of Robert concerns two matters: the knight's dishonesty in shifting allegiances between Stephen and Matilda, and civil war in England. There is depicted also the violation of the sanctuary of the Church, and Robert's eventual death with nothing resolved. Upon this scene the angels in the roof look down. It is surprising that they do not weep.

There are many ways of reading this history. One is as record of fact. These things happened in the story of the castle. Now they are past. But if allegory and symbol are insistently present elsewhere, as in the tale of Sarah and the Promise of the Seed, how might one read this in a nineteenth-century context? Property is held by force; the word of the powerful is worthless; religion is a sham; the nation is divided against itself. That is the story of Robert. Let those who dine here celebrate the new medievalism. Burges was even witty on the violence of chivalry. The castle motif of the fireplace in the great hall is repeated in my lady's room at Castell Coch in a majestic twin-towered washbasin. The hot water runs out between the towers, just as, in the age of Robert the Consul, boiling oil would have poured down on outsiders. Take warning.

This grotesque irony seems out of kilter with the pious Catholic mysticism of Bute. Yet the trains of imagery of the castles are so introverted, remote and alien that they are detached from any relation to the outer world, and if brought back into relation to that world they seem disturbed, even a little mad, as conquerors and crocodiles, angels and parrots compete for attention. The houses are pure symbols, and that symbolism has become disordered fantasy. But this example, *in extremis*, is typical of the period. The Victorian country house has no style, but is formed from any permutation of baronial castellan, Tudorbethan manorial, Gothic ecclesiastical, Italianate republican, or fetch and carry from the Loire, scene individable and style unlimited. Everything is on offer because no man is sure of what he should do, except, like Burges's parrots, to imitate other voices and display glorious plumage at enormous expense.

Bute's castles are now show houses, superbly kept by the citizens of Cardiff, no mean city, and eloquently displayed by well-instructed and kindly guides. Like some Diplodocean creatures, the houses were not fitted to survive as living entities. Visitors admire the plumage, and forget the dying bird.

CHAPTER SEVENTEEN

Decline and fall

THE CAUSES OF the decline of the country house are commonplaces. The radicalisation of politics and progressive acts of parliamentary reform undermined the power base of the old aristocracy. So too did the new industrialisation. The agricultural crisis beginning in the 1870s damaged the economic foundations of property based upon land. Death duties and heavy taxation accelerated the decline; the Great War of 1914–18 shattered the last vestiges of feudal community and service. After the war many of the gentry sold up. Ruined houses and the site of lost houses are now the archaeological markers of a departed order.

The process is not one of absolute decline and fall, but a Darwinian culling of those least fitted to survive, whether the excesses of Victorian architectural fantasy which required a small factory of servants to run, or isolated manor houses deprived of their land and inundated by industrialisation. Houses have always been lost, some in a very short space of time, as the vanished palaces of Tudor and Jacobean pride testify, and the process in the twentieth century has been mild indeed compared with the absolute brutality of the dissolution of the monasteries. The institutions of feudal Church and State are still in place in Britain in monarchy, House of Lords, and ancient universities and public schools, and the riches of the landed aristocracy still command enormous influence and power.[1] The current list of historic houses open to the public extends to more than 1,300. This is only a fraction of the whole. Nor has the process of building ended.[2] It might be said that the cry that the country house is in danger has been but another act of mystification to conceal the facts of economic power. England has changed merely to stay as it was.

The decline and fall of the country house, none the less, has been one of the obsessional subjects of modern literature from the late nineteenth century onwards. It is powerfully foreshadowed by liberal criticism, witness George Eliot's *Felix Holt, The Radical* (1866), and the visionary radicalism of Dickens, whose ruined Satis House, and sterile bride, Miss Havisham, devoted to death, is one of the most powerfully subversive images of the old *topoi* of the fertile estate. But country house literature

155

had always been critical and shaped by outsiders' voices which are as much satirical as hortatory or idealistic. Dialectical argument, and the flexible ambiguities of language, allowed the tradition to absorb adverse criticism. Moreover, a bit of complaint from writers with a chip on their shoulder has little effect on the wealthy. The new Victorian rich continued to put their money into new country houses for all Dickens or Eliot might say.

Yet something is gnawing away even from the *inside* of conservatism. The idealism of Disraeli's Young England fiction is excessive, and that excess is a reaction to a sense of extreme threat to an unregenerate old order. Cardiff Castle has merely pulled up the drawbridge on an outside world it does not wish even to acknowledge. The social cause is self-evident. But there is a literary cause as well. The usual mode of the nineteenth-century novel is that of a quasi-scientific naturalism, and the very employment of that mode tends to strip the country house of allegorical or symbolic signification. The mere existence of a convention that what is depicted is real blocks the construction of the ideal. For much of the naturalistic fiction of the age the house is simply 'there' as a setting for an action when the action moves into the countryside. Thrushcross, Ullathorne, Queen's Crawley, Lowick, De Stancy Castle, Riversley, Woodview, have social, even psychological, significance, but not the ideal status of a St Geneviève or Kelmscott. The same is equally true for the *mise en scène* of a Jones or a Pinero as dramatists of high society.

The concomitant to a loss of idealism is cynicism. It is an obvious quality within Trollope, the most prolific, and still the most popular, of the conservative country house writers of the age. The great series of the Palliser novels constitute a far more subversive portrait of the rot destroying the old order in England than any of the more fervidly excited satires of Dickens, for this is a portrait from within, without praise or malice. Trollope merely seems to hold the mirror up to nature, mirror after mirror in seemingly inexhaustible sequence, and chronicles the passage of the age. In so doing he shows too the passing of all that traditionally had recommended the old order. If he were not so verbose, if he had more than one plot (one grows so tired of the tale of who will marry whom), the major theme might be more apparent.

The old chivalric aristocracy has already quit the scene in the Palliser saga —so much for the dream of a return to Camelot. Ancient Grex Castle is little more than a picturesque ruin and Mabel Grex, who might be the fertile source of renewal of the old, is condemned to frustrated spinsterhood. That tale is almost an aside in the history of the time. But Plantagenet Palliser and Lady Glencora, the great centres of the political wheel of these novels, are destined for extinction too. Theirs is the old Whig/radical aristocratic tradition which, while acknowledging the justice of Paine's critique of the origins of aristocracy in conquest and corruption (so Lady Glencora herself says), sought at least to mitigate the divisiveness of inequality. The 'young England' which replaces them is not Disraeli's conservatism, but the new Toryism of Plantagenet's son, Silverbridge, the heir to Gatherum Castle and future Duke of Omnium. His aim, he tells his saddened father, is to protect wealth against the radicals and communists. It is a simple class war of two nations between rampant Toryism and left-wing extremists. There is no middle ground. You protect your own class. 'The people will look after themselves, and we must look after ourselves. We are so few and they are so many, that we shall have enough to do.' (It seems as if the Tory has taken warning from Shelley's 'The Masque of Anarchy'.) It is a sign of the new cynicism that whereas his father serves his country honourably (though with little effect) as Prime Minister, the son loses a fortune on a horse given the same title. He knows how to spend riches, and how to pick them up, for he acquires a fortune by marriage to the daughter of an American capitalist.

A writer in the old country house tradition, like Pope, would moralise the tale. A rotten apple like Silverbridge would fall from the tree, but the stock would remain good. Or, in darker vein, Pope would show how the whole barrel might grow corrupt. But Trollope merely describes in neutral prose the people, and the *locus* of their actions. It is appropriate to this new conservatism that the novels are full of new properties. They suit the new age. Though Matching Priory is built upon the site of an old monastic settlement, that conjunction has no moral significance; it matches 'the way we live now'. Picturesque Loughlinter spreads its romantic domain as far as the eye can see. But it has no relation to the land or its people. The tenants merely sing of their lord: 'Here in summer, gone in winter.' Crummie-Toddie has no tenants at all. It is just an estate where animals are bred for gentlemen to shoot. Most important of all the houses is the Duke of Omnium's new castle, Gatherum, a place so monumentally uncomfortable 'no one would ever think of living there', Lady Glencora says. Silverbridge puts up at the local inn, and the most regular visitants are the tourists who come to see 'one of the British sights', a new monument to the old order.

Lady Glencora seeks to bring Gatherum back into use. (Trollope, as usual, is socially accurate.) Her aim is that hospitality should flow 'like a fountain' from the castle to the new retainers of her husband, not feudal knights, nor the folk of the estate, but those who will be useful to the Prime Minister in his political career. On the lawns outside the ancient sport of archery is revived; inside there are never less than forty to dine. In a remarkable scene her husband, coming 'home', finds himself bewildered in the house. The front doors, 'so huge and so grand' that they were seldom used, are open and the Duke goes out onto the terrace from the hall built altogether for show and in no degree for use or comfort . . . turning to the left towards the end of the house he came upon a new conservatory. The exotics with which it was to be filled were at this moment being brought in on great barrows. He stood for a moment and looked, but said not a word to the men. They gazed at him but evidently did not know him. How should they know him, – him, who was so seldom there, and when there never showed himself about the place? (*The Prime Minister*, 19, 'Vulgarity')

This is Timon's villa once again, and if the writer were Pope it is obvious what moral comment the poet might make upon a front door rarely open, upon the exotica of the conservatory, and on a lord who thinks even of himself as a thing of show, and whose very workmen do not know him. The very word 'use' cries out its associations. But the text makes no allusions, offers no moral gloss. The point of view is Plantagenet's. It happens to differ from that of his wife. Their disagreement is resolved in the husband's favour, but not on moral grounds. The Duke eschews 'vulgarity'. He does not want the place turned into a kind of Grand Hotel where anybody may sit down and dine with him because they have money. That is the kind of man he is. That is the way we live now.

It is typical of Trollope's fiction. One 'merely' hears and sees. On the evidence of what we hear and see, the major preoccupations of the English ruling classes might be said to be fox-hunting (even above politics), the efficiency of the central heating (if any) and the improvement of the profitability of estates, especially by keeping down the wages of labour. As for culture, as Jeffrey Palliser expresses it, 'Nobody ever goes into a library to read, any more than you would go into a larder to eat.' Occasionally the writing seems to offer what might be interpreted as a moral symbol. At Matching there is 'a grand old ruin of an oak tree . . . within a skeleton of supporting sticks', but then that is the kind of thing that old parks do contain. It might, or it might not, be satiric comment on country house society. It certainly could not apply to the rampant conservatism of Silverbridge. More overt are Lady Glencora's Painite accounts of the English aristocracy as based on corruption, favouritism and robbery. But her 'fast and furious' prattle is just Lady Glen's talk. She is no democrat, but a great society hostess. One day, meeting a party of tourists head on, she does not stop to speak to them, but beats a fast retreat to the privacy of her tasteful boudoir. That is the way she is. The reader can turn the Janus-faced text either way, as laughing at her, or at Paine. The novels are either a naked celebration of the way the ruling class stays on top come whatever, or they are a naked revelation of the selfishness of the rich. It depends where you stand. Trollope remains apart paring his finger-nails.

There is something refreshing about this lucid cynicism. No one could accuse Trollope of writing cant. But once establish this kind of transparency and it is difficult to draw the veil of mystery over things again. Trollope's political novels left the country house stripped naked. The next generation take up the subject where he left off, but moralise the theme. As the old order enters into the crisis of the 1880s the nature of country house society, its struggle for survival, its decay or corruption, become a central subject for English fiction.

The world we have lost is not depicted, on the whole, as one to lament. Wilde described the polish of the high society his plays depict as 'a horrible painted mask', an elegant veneer which covers idleness, extravagance and a predatory immorality. The beautiful house, Branshaw Manor, in Madox Ford's *The Good Soldier* (1915) is merely the carapace of a decadent order, sustained only by squeezing the tenantry of the estate and decreasing the charities of the rich. So 'life peters out'. Huxley's *Crome Yellow* (1921) mocks the pretensions of the literary house (a Garsington Manor or Beckley Park), and prophesies the passing of country house society: 'Fifty years and the country-side will know the old landmarks no more. They will have vanished as the monasteries vanished before them.'[3] In Isherwood's *The Memorial* (1932) Vernon Hall is sold as a building plot, its demise symbolic of the moral as well as material bankruptcy of a class now driven into southern European hotels. In Waugh's *A Handful of Dust* (1934) the last of the Lasts camp among the abandoned rooms of Hetton Abbey, breeding silver foxes for the luxury market, while above the Abbey a crazy clock no longer keeps time, but by its clanging keeps the inmates awake. The symbolic rooms at Hetton – Launcelot and Guinevere – mock the Victorian longing to return to Camelot and remind of the common pastime of the rich, adultery. Promiscuous sexuality is the common pursuit of Waugh's vile bodies, as it was of the masked comedians of Wilde. In Lawrence the paralysed sterile husband of an unfaithful wife in *Lady Chatterley's Lover* (1928) is the extreme, but representative, symbol of a decadent class unable to renew itself. There is no longer even honourable death in battle for such people, as Guy Crouchback finds in Waugh's *Sword of Honour* (1952-65).

What survives is a mummified culture. The Tory credo expressed in Galsworthy's *The Country House* (1907) satirises a conservatism which conserves only privilege:

I believe in my father, and his father, and his father's father, the makers and keepers of my estate; and I believe that we have made the country, and shall keep the country what it is. And I believe in the Public Schools, and especially the Public School that I was at. And I believe in my social equals, and the country house, and in things as they are, for ever and ever. Amen.[4]

If the satire of that is a little too blatant, the insider's picture in Victoria Sackville-West's *The Edwardians* (1930) is a sadder variant on the same theme. The protagonist of the novel, Sebastian, is trapped by the old order once commendable, now exhausted. We are sympathetically shown the old-fashioned loyalty of servants to the house, the rituals of gift giving at Christmas, the personal relation between master and servants, his (guilty) care for his 'people' ('guilty' because the new Toryism despises such old-fashioned paternalism) and the historical continuity on the estate (represented by the laying down of timber from generation to generation by an old carpenter). But all this is now an elaborate anachronism. Nobody but Sebastian cares any more. The underservants no longer recognise even their mistress and the young men leave to work in the greater freedom of industry outside. The vast substructure merely props up a life of vacuous pleasure and ritualised promiscuity. 'All their days were the same; had been the same for an eternity of years. . . . With what glamour this scheme is invested! and upon what does it base its pretensions?' (1) The question is rhetorical. There is no longer a worthwhile foundation. The novel ends with the coronation of George v, an act symbolic of the entrapment of British society in the rituals of its dead antiquity.

Time and again the last post seems to have sounded. At the end of Shaw's *Heartbreak House* (1919), his Chekovian portrayal of the gentry as a useless chattering class, bombs rain down from heaven upon such people. House after house had long since gone up in flames: Thornfield, Riversley Grange in Meredith's *Harry Richmond* (1871); Stancy Castle in Hardy's *A Laodicean* (1881); and Poynton in James's *The Spoils of Poynton* (1897); Daphne du Maurier's Manderley was to follow. Some are torn down, as Kings Thursday in Waugh's *Decline and Fall* (1928), others pass into alien hands, like Bladesover in *Tono-Bungay* (1909) or Robin Hill 'to let' at the end of *The Forsyte Saga* (1922), or lose their ancient function, like Hetton Abbey, or Llannabba Castle in *Decline and Fall*, which becomes a type of the bad public school. In symbolic fall, down too come the old trees, the signs of historical continuity. At Groby, in Madox Ford's *Parade's End* (1924-28), when the great tree in the garden comes down, the house itself is shaken. And everywhere the spread of the urban landscape blots out the old England. So the famous apostrophe in *Lady Chatterley's Lover*:

England my England! But which is *my* England? The stately homes of England make good photographs, and create the illusion of connection with the Elizabethans. The handsome old halls are here, from the days of Good Queen Anne and Tom Jones. But smuts fall and blacken on the drab stucco, that has long ceased to be golden. . . . Now they are pulling down the stately homes, the Georgian halls are going. . . . One England blots out another. The England of the Squire Winters and the Wragby Halls was gone, dead. The blotting out was only not yet complete.

What would come after?[5]

Yet Lawrence's obsequy was premature. For the apparent demise of the country house in the real world as a subject of modern fiction becomes its salvation in the world of the imagination. The house, separated from the social order which once sustained it, will become itself a pure symbol. It escapes from Nature, and from naturalism. This is a process which was already apparent in the writing of Disraeli and Morris where the great house became first spiritualised as a sign of community, and then an aesthetic home loved for its own sake. It was in vain that traditional conservative/liberal writers like Mallock (*The Old Order Changes*, 1886) or Mrs Humphrey Ward (*Marcella*, 1894) concerned themselves with the reform of the actual. Modernise the estate; bring in new money. True enough, but the great fictional subject was the fall of the country house and Ward – a fine novelist – and Mallock have been passed over. But the very focus of fiction upon the decline and fall of the country house allows the idea of the great good place to become imaginatively disassociated from actuality. Gissing, in *The Private Papers of Henry Ryecroft* (1903), expressed the new idealism plainly:

Can we, whilst losing the class, retain the idea it embodied? Can we English, ever so subject to the material, liberate ourselves from that old association, yet guard its meaning in the sphere of spiritual life?[6]

For Gissing the spiritual idea was that of community centred upon the country house: 'the instinct which made an Englishman – tying together village and great house'. Such idealism will run strongly in the writings of Sackville-West and Woolf in time of war, and is expressed by the motto of Forster's *Howard's End*: 'only connect'. But the 'spiritual life' acquires a resonance which is aesthetic too, as the house becomes a unifying sign of culture, a test of the ability of the intelligent mind to comprehend and love things of beauty for their own sake. Thus it is Platonised into a world of pure idea. The English country house, wrote Gissing, is 'perfect of its kind',

it has the dignity of age, its walls are beautiful, the garden, the park about it are such as can be found in England 'lovely beyond compare'.

Thus the beauty of the house is the sign of the loveliness of England, and aestheticism and patriotism are at one. While the country house was the social focus of society, for good or ill, such an idea would always be in collision with the real nature of things. But as pure idea, with the country house written off as a vanishing social phenomenon, there is nothing to check its growth and elaboration in the mind itself. It is appropriate that the torchbearer for the new mysticism should be a writer from outside English society, a purely detached and imaginative observer. As the country house order declines and falls in fiction, it is recreated again in the novels of Henry James.

CHAPTER EIGHTEEN

Dream houses

IN A SHORT STORY, 'The Author of Beltraffio', Henry James tells of a young American author's discovery of the English country house. The American records how he saw England as if the reproduction 'of something that existed primarily in art or literature. It was not the picture, the poem, the fictive page, that seemed to me a copy; these things were the originals, and the life of a happy and distinguished people was fashioned in their image.' By choosing an outsider as his centre of consciousness, James draws attention to the way the country house tradition is preserved by onlookers; and by selecting a writer, he indicates how much the house is seen through the spectacles of books, not as it is (whatever that may be) but as the imagination wishes to perceive it.

The naïve outsider of this tale is only one step removed from James himself. His *Notebooks* tell of a typical country house visit:

I went down into Somerset and spent a week at Midelney Place, the Lady Trevilian's. . . . Very exquisite it was (not the visit, but the impression of the country); it kept me a-dreaming all the while I was there. . . . It was the old houses that fetched me – Montacute, the admirable; Barrington, that superb Ford Abbey, and several smaller ones. Trevilian showed me them all; he has a great care for such things. These delicious old houses, in the long August days, in the south of England air, on the soil over which so much has passed and out of which so much has come, rose before me like a series of visions.[1]

This passage shows a strange mixture of snobbery and romantic gush. Like Pope before him, James likes to drop a noble name. But the nobility are here no longer seen as public figures. Trevilian's role is that of a showman and custodian of ancient houses, and before James's enraptured gaze these 'delicious' places dissolve first into dream, then into 'a series of visions'. But it is more than a portrait of the aesthete as a young man that James offers. He is an artist looking for future material. He goes on: 'I thought of stories, of dramas, of all the life of the past – . . . . It is art that speaks of these things.' He means both the writers of the past and his own writings. The *Notebooks* are contemporaneous with *The Portrait of a Lady* (1881).

The fictional 'author' of Beltraffio had soon discovered that the ideal

162

vision of the English country house had no correspondence with the life of the people within. The tragic story tells of a struggle between an aesthetic father and a philistine and puritanical mother. Her sick son is allowed to die rather than grow to maturity under the influence of his father. Thus the fertility of the house is extinguished in a sterile conflict between art and morality. The tale is typical of the country house theme in James. His subject is the idealisation of the high civilisation, culture and aesthetic beauty of the English house as both perceived and created by a sensitive, literate consciousness; and the contrast between that ideal and the men and women of a decadent and dying order. There is Mertle in *The Awkward Age* (1899), the crystal cage of Newmarch in *The Sacred Fount* (1901), Matcham in *The Wings of the Dove* (1902) and *The Golden Bowl* (1904), and, best known and most sinister, Bly in *The Turn of the Screw* (1898), where the ghosts of Gothic fiction have found a home in England with a vengeance and corrupt even the age of innocence. 'Your lady's chaste' wrote Jonson of religious Penshurst, but in James's country house adultery is the fashionable pursuit, and the new religion is that of Mammon. The weekend parties of 'The Real Thing', 'The Death of the Lion', 'Broken Wings', 'The Two Faces', are parodies of the old idea of the happy community.[2]

The old order is in dissolution. The country property of England is up for sale, and the contents of the stately homes of old are on the march to the auctioneer's room and the museum. Old Mr Longdon in *The Awkward Age* is shocked by the promiscuous renting out of Mertle. It is a sign of the times, 'this sudden invasion of somebody's – heaven knows whose – house' and the 'violation' of the 'home' 'just for money'. Medley, in *The Princess Casamassima* (1886), is rented by the promiscuous Italian of the allegorical title for three months only, who gets a musty old place cheap. Even Gardencourt, that second Eden demi-paradise of *The Portrait of a Lady*, has passed from English to American hands. The very furniture in *The Spoils of Poynton* (1897) – the 'spoils' of the title – is twice packed into removal vans before being ultimately destroyed at the burning of the house, now owned by 'philistines'. Perhaps only Mr Longdon of Beccles is the exception that proves the rule, for here 'the long confirmation of time' represented by the house corresponds to the morality of the owner 'The "taste" of the place . . . was nothing more than the beauty of his life':

Beyond the lawn the house was before him, old, square, red-roofed, well assured of its right to the place it took up in the world. This was a considerable space – in the little world, at least, of Beccles – and the look of possession had everywhere mixed with it, in the form of old windows and doors, the tone of old red surfaces, in the style of old white facings, the age of old high creepers, the long confirmation of time.   (24)

This has something of the effect Edwin Lutyens strove for at Deanery Garden, or Lutyens and Jekyll together at Great Dixter.

But it would be sentimental to see such a Jamesian passage as normative, however much it expresses a longing in the artist and in the age. It is the very lack of the 'right to place' of the possessors of the great houses that creates the imperative to aestheticise the house itself, its 'works of art and furniture', and to separate the intrinsic value of the artistic ideal from the manifest decadence of the possessing classes. It is the problem of the relation (if any) between taste and morality to which James obsessively returns, for taste itself is not a guarantee of morality. Mrs Gareth in *The Spoils of Poynton* has made her home the most 'complete work of art' in England, but to preserve that art all normal humanity and mundane morality are sacrificed to the pietistic contemplation of arranged perfection. Poynton is 'an impossible place for producing; no active art could flourish there but a Buddhistic contemplation'. Mrs Gareth chooses a woman as the inheritor of the house, for her son is unworthy, but Fleda Vetch is not chosen because a woman is fertile, but for her taste. She is offered only 'the long lease to a museum'. It would make her, like Miss Havisham, a bride of death, and like Satis House, Poynton too burns. The beautiful objects, pursued around the countryside like some antiques roadshow, are consumed as well. 'Poynton's *gone*?' asks Fleda, to which the ironic reply from a common workman is, 'What can you call it, miss, if it ain't really saved?' The word 'miss' draws attention to Fleda's maiden situation, and the phrase 'really saved' is laden with implications. Does the mere existence of a house, even in all its beauty, truly save it? Houses are not museums. As soon as one speaks of saving them, they are, in a sense, already 'gone'.

The question, who shall inherit Poynton, is one aspect of the larger issue Lawrence was to raise. Who shall inherit England? If 'England' was the country house, to whom shall that tradition be handed on, and in what way? It is put acutely by James in *The Princess Casamassima*, a programmatic, even allegorical, novel which raises the social issue directly. It is the story of a young revolutionary socialist, Hyacinth Robinson, the bastard offspring of the nobility, raised in shabby gentility on the very verge of the London underworld, whose violent purposes are blunted by his visit to the great house of Medley. Lost between two worlds, one dead, the other powerless to be born, he kills himself.

The corruption of the old order is not in doubt. It is the Princess, at the great house, who says of English high society:

It's the old régime again, the rottenness and extravagance, bristling with every iniquity and every abuse . . .; or perhaps even more a reproduction of the Roman world in its decadence, gouty, apoplectic, depraved, gorged and clogged with wealth and spoils, selfishness and scepticism, and waiting for the onset of the barbarians. (22)

This brings the Gothic and classical traditions together, explicitly linking the Jacobin revolution in France with the fall of Rome before the barbarians. The country house is part of the 'spoil' of the fall of the empire, and she is speaking to Hyacinth, a 'Jacobin', who is even now committed to the overthrow of the aristocracy. The adulterous Princess is herself the very embodiment of the corruption she describes, a collector of lovers as well as of bibelots, and for her there is an added 'Gothic' frisson in bedding revolutionaries.

The Princess is, perhaps, a little *outré* in her attitudes. It is the 'continental' aristocracy that she represents. England had prided itself in avoiding the excesses of the *ancien régime*. James, accordingly, offers by way of comparison Inglefield, the home of the ironically named Lady Aurora (a socialist gentlewoman). But it is Dickens's Chesney Wold again where 'the rain drips, drips, drips from the trees in the big dull park':

When one's one of eight daughters [Lady Aurora exclaims] and there's very little money (for any of *us* at least) and nothing to do but to go out with three or four others in mackintoshes, one can easily go off one's head. Of course there's the village, and it's not at all a nice one, and there are people to look after, and goodness knows they're in want of it; but one must work with the vicarage, and at the vicarage are four more daughters, all old maids, and its dreary and dreadful and one has too much of it, for they don't understand what one thinks or feels or a single word one says to them. Besides, they *are* stupid, I admit, the country poor; they're very very dense.   (15)

This is the nadir of the old idea of community, whether feudal, or Morris's socialism, before the cold, wet light of novelistic realism. It is dreary plodding around with old maids in the rain doing good to the poor, and 'goodness knows they're in want of it'. These unmarriageable virgins (themselves complaining of want of money) are intellectually as well as biologically sterile. Lady Aurora does not represent a new dawn, even though she is heralded by one of the recipients of her charitable attention as 'one of the saints of old come to life again out of a legend'. She is ashamed of being rich, and of the life of 'parties and races and dances and picnics and cards and life in great houses', but depressed by her mundane charities. Thus she flirts with the idea of socialism and wonders why 'the lower classes didn't break into Inglefield and take possession of all the treasures in the Italian room'. Those treasures mean nothing to her.

The paradox of the novel is that the inheritor of the treasures of the rich, in an imaginative sense, is a member of those very lower classes. Hyacinth Robinson is shut out from what he imagines is the exquisite fineness of a loftier world by poverty and bastardy. But he aspires in his imagination, and expresses his longing by his work, for he is the kind of craftsman who of old turned the idea of the beautiful house into reality. His is the 'exquisite art' of the bookbinder, and he imagines connoisseurs in future ages handling his work with admiration. He is, like Morris, an arts and crafts socialist. But it is one of the many tragic ironies of this story that in the great library at Medley he finds the books on the shelves thick with the 'dust of centuries'. The owners of great houses have no use for culture. He sits down at a magnificent desk there to practice his penmanship, and finds that he has nothing of value to write. His penmanship is beautiful. But it is form empty of content.

It is through Hyacinth's ravished consciousness that we see the 'treasure house of Medley' in an episode James uses as the fulcrum of the novel. It is one of the most elaborate, longest and most formally developed of country house descriptions. As the living body of the house dies, the literary tradition becomes intensely self-reflexive as the spirit of things enters the imagination. It is as if James gave full rein to that naïve tendency to gush he indulges sometimes *in propria persona*, but this is now firmly contained within the creative matrix of fiction as Hyacinth is substituted for himself. The young artist wakes to the dawn and to Medley – his first visit to the country and to a great house – and his first hours are spent in a rapturous exploration of this brave new, and old, world.

At one end of the garden was a parapet of mossy brick which looked down on the other side into a canal, a moat, a quaint old pond (he hardly knew what to call it) and from the same standpoint showed a considerable part of the main body of the house – Hyacinth's room belonging to a wing that commanded the extensive irregular back – which was richly grey wherever clear of the ivy and the other dense creepers, and everywhere infinitely a picture: with a high-piled ancient russet roof broken by huge chimneys and queer peep-holes and all manner of odd gables and windows on different lines, with all manner of antique patches and protrusions and with a fascinating architectural excrescence where a wonderful clock-face was lodged, a clock-face covered with gilding and blazonry but showing many traces of the years and the weather. (22)

This is the English country house as natural, organic form, an accretion of love and time, the historical process mellowed and harmonised, beautiful like a picture. The weathered clock-face makes this scene an emblem of time, or rather timelessness, for the last thing Hyacinth asks is 'what o'clock?' He sees blazonry and gilding weathered by years, and in the love for the patina the climate has created one forgets the social significance of the golden coat of arms which spoke once of power, pride of rank and forceful possession. So too the moat is now indistinguishable from a canal (or is it a pond?) for successive stages of landscape gardening (jumbled in Hyacinth's enthusiastic ignorance) have turned a defensive boundary into a formal ornament, and then into a naturalised element. So too the house has undergone many developments of sprouting chimney and gable and window, like England itself, and this long-mellowed organic process will blunt the thrust of Hyacinth's revolutionary purpose.[3] Now dense ivy climbs over all, naturalising the house by uniting it with the English green of the garden (it might be Tintern Abbey as Wordsworth saw it), but suggestive too in James of that picturesque decay which characterises the condition of a declining nation. Thus Hyacinth's room looks out from the back of the house. In class terms, the proletarian guest has been given an inferior lodging, and in symbolic mode, this lover of old houses has an outlook which is retrospective.

As the young socialist forgets to look forward at Medley, he is moved to tears of love by the recollections of the old. 'His whole walk was peopled with recognitions; he had been dreaming all his life of just such a place and such objects, such a morning and such a chance.' The word 'dream' is an obvious warning that this is something of a romantic rapture, like Catherine Morland at Northanger, but it is a far more intense romanticism than hers. It is more like Adam's dream, as Keats described it. He awakes that spring morning, and finds the dream true. Here are old books and great tapestries speaking of deep learning and high culture. Sheltered in the garden is a Chinese pavilion, whose very wallpaper depicts, in symbolic image, the unity of civilisation among a leisured class, for it shows the ancient ritual act of the communal tea ceremony. Such a retreat, too, a Pliny might have enjoyed in his classic villa. Hyacinth recalls an earlier 'vision':

the vision of societies where, in splendid rooms, with smiles and soft voices, distinguished men, with women who were both proud and gentle, talked of art, literature and history. (9)

Here, now in the flesh, is the Princess herself, whose beauty recalls something he has seen 'in a statue, in a picture, in a museum', and whom he perceives in a transcendental moment seated at a piano, playing for him alone.

Two or three times she turned her eyes on him, and then they shone with the wonderful expression which was the essence of her beauty; that profuse mingled light which seemed to belong to some everlasting summer and yet to suggest seasons that were past and gone, some experience that was only an exquisite memory. . . . That was the beginning of the communion – so strange considering their respective positions – which he had come to Medley to enjoy. (22)

This gives, and yet denies. There is a plangent yearning for the perfection of civilisation, that 'serenity of success' and 'accumulation of dignity and honour' which are the prerogative of the highest achievement of rank and culture (this could be Burke on Marie Antoinette), and yet the recognition that this is only a dream, or rather, as the text suggests, a memory of something that was once present and has all but been lost.

167

It is an almost mystic experience. The word 'community' has now become 'communion'. Jonson at Penshurst, and Morris at Kelmscott, had seen the great house harmonising the divisions of society. For writers like Pope that society had been smaller. His feast of reason and flow of soul had embraced only like-minded men of rank. Now it is a community of two, and as the number shrinks the numinous word 'communion' inflates the significance, as if the laying on of the rhetoric, like supreme cosmetics, may conceal the cracks in the skin beneath. It is for Hyacinth an almost religious moment, a revelation of what civilisation might be, yet it trembles on the verge of mere sordidness. The Princess is an adulterous flirt, playing with the young man's sensibility out of idle curiosity. She belongs not to a world of high culture, but to a class which is 'idle, trifling, luxurious'.

There is a constant interplay at Medley (as at Northanger) between 'dream' and 'reality', but here it is the imaginative world which has the higher value. The house itself is dead, kept alive only by sympathetic vision. The 'vast high hall' is the setting only of Hyacinth's solitary supper, served by an 'automatic' butler; the chapel is a 'queer transmogrified corner'; the tapestries for 'show'; the library deep in dust; the whole place going cheap because 'musty', as the Princess says. The old order is passing away in bad smells and tales of ghosts, and transitory promiscuity of possession. Yet the cultural inheritance is passed on in the realm of the imagination. It is as if, separated from what Hyacinth knows is the 'want and toil' which had been necessary to create the 'happy few', the ideal of Medley can make the world spiritually a richer and a better place. The transfer of that ideal is no longer from one member of the ruling class to another; the rulers know too well the reality of their houses. It belongs now to those outside. Hyacinth carries his vision of Medley with him even into his tragic suicide, and when he thinks of the place he imagines it in terms of a richly bound work of literature, or as a beautiful painting. Art has transformed it, but since it is a work of art, it can never be the substance of life.

His last week at Medley in especial had already become a far-off fable, the echo of a song; he could read it over as a romance bound in vellum and gold, gaze at it as he would have gazed at some exquisite picture. (29)

Hyacinth's suicide comes a little too pat to end the tale. It is a predictable formal resolution, but it speaks of fiction. The closure of life is not so neat as the closure of a novel. In this *The Princess Casamassima* weakens the conclusion of *The Portrait of a Lady* written some five years before. James's greatest novel in praise of the English country house had ended with the choice of life, not death, with the world still all before us. Isabel Archer, the lady of the portrait, will never possess Gardencourt, but she carries the memory of her days there as preciously as Hyacinth remembered Medley, and it is the strength of those memories which helps her to live and to endure. It is an inheritance passed on to generations of readers. *The Portrait of a Lady* has had a central place in the rise and institutionalisation of English studies this century, and thus in the communication of the country house ethos. It is appropriate, therefore, that the popular Penguin Modern Classics edition should cite on its paper cover the words of a member of the feudal university of Cambridge claiming that this is one 'of the two most brilliant novels in the language'. The same edition joins ancient religion to ancient university in likening the work to a great cathedral. It is appropriate that the old order should give classic status to a work in praise of ancient culture.

The tale begins in paradise, and Isabel's story is too well known to bear detailed reiteration. The Garden of Eden was lost, so too will Gardencourt be. The emblematic significance of the gathering on the lawn is lovingly and formally created. To this moment Isabel will return again at the end of her pilgrimage of knowledge gained through suffering. One knows the house almost without description. It is 'a picture made real', an expression of that 'beautiful old England' which has through literature become a living tradition. The very name of the place, compounded of the 'garden' and 'court', unites the 'high civilization' of well-mannered, cultured people with the benediction of the original natural order. 'Sacred Gardencourt', Isabel will call it. The moment of perfect communion with which the story begins takes place betwixt the worlds of art and of nature, upon the lawns outside the house on the banks of a river.

It stood upon a low hill, above the river – the river being the Thames at some forty miles from London. A long gabled front of red brick, with the complexion of which time and the weather had played all sorts of pictorial tricks, only, however, to improve and refine it, presented to the lawn its patches of ivy, its clustered chimneys, its windows smothered in creepers. The house had a name and a history; the old gentleman taking his tea would have been delighted to tell you these things. . . . The front of the house overlooking that portion of lawn with which we are concerned was not the entrance front; this was in quite another quarter. Privacy here reigned supreme, and the wide carpet of turf that covered the level hill-top seemed but the extension of a luxurious interior. The great still oaks and beeches flung down a shade as dense as that of velvet curtains; and the place was furnished, like a room, with cushioned seats, with rich-coloured rugs, with the books and papers that lay upon the grass.

It is an English summer afternoon, perfect, upon a perfect English lawn. The day has waned a little, but 'real dusk would not arrive for many hours'. The shadows are long, but the light is of the finest and rarest quality. It is a moment of stasis, of 'leisure' and 'innocent pastime'. We see before the house an old man holding an exquisite cup in his hand. He is serving tea to a young maiden. It is a typically English thing to do. But the formality of the description makes afternoon tea in the garden into a ceremony of innocence. It is the sign too of the transmission of a tradition from the old to the young.

Almost every word in these opening pages reverberates with resonances back to the very origins of the country house tradition. The appeal to Nature is fundamental. This is a country villa, the retreat of a man of business retired from affairs. (Mr Touchett, the host, is a wealthy banker now devoted to the care of Gardencourt.) If this were a Latin text the word 'luxurious', used without prejudice, would tell us we were late in the tradition. The luxury is a sign of the exquisite taste of the owner of the villa. So books and papers lie scattered on the lawn, emblems of culture and learning (and within the house is an extensive collection of rare and beautiful pictures). The host, like a latter day Pliny, enjoys the 'privacy' of his well-ordered property, sharing that privacy with a few choice souls. Only one element among these ancient motifs might tell that this is Gothic civilisation, not classic. It is the presence of the young and beautiful maiden through whom, traditionally, the fertility of the feudal line would be handed on.

Gardencourt is an old house, as ancient in its origins as the reign of Edward VI. Red brick and gables and chimneys have been mellowed by time; and creeper and ivy, as at Medley, blend house with landscape. In its growth the pattern of English history may be traced, and, as so often, the house is taken as a sign of the constitution of the state. Elizabeth slept here on a royal progress (of course); Cromwell's revolutionaries bruised it, but failed to level the house; the Restoration enlarged the house; and the eighteenth century modernised it. The French Revolution and the industrial revolution have passed Gardencourt by. The present owner is an American, a man from the New World, therefore. Though he had at first grumbled at 'its ugliness, its antiquity, its incommodity', now:

at the end of twenty years, [he] had become conscious of a real aesthetic passion for it, so that he knew all its points and would tell you just where to stand to see them in combination and just the hour when the shadows of its various protruberances – which fell so softly upon the warm, weary brickwork – were of the right measure.

Thus even an heir of the American Revolution has fallen in love with all that an old English house represents. It is home for him, secure in the 'home' counties, and where his son Ralph, in the tragic ending of the tale, returns to die, for he also, like his father, wishes to end his days 'at home'.

Upon this scene the light of the long summer day is beginning to wane. Those lengthening shadows on the lawn, though adding to the exquisite nature of the beauty, tell that Gardencourt's time is passing. It is no longer sustained by a great family, but has been bought by a new man as 'a great bargain' – who but the *nouveaux riches* can keep up an establishment like this nowadays? The emphasis upon the house in its garden says something about the relation of this emblem of ancient beauty to the land. The estate, and the men and women who worked it, have gone. There are a dozen house servants and 'an old woman curtsying at the gate', that is 'all'. Gardencourt, like Lutyens's Deanery Garden, has shrunk even from the possession of a park. Community has declined to a communion of two, and that Jamesian religious word is only metaphoric. The feast in hall has become tea on the lawn; even the philosophical symposium is now no more than the chat of an old banker to a young woman, and if she is given something of the significance of a latter day Eve, eager to 'know' in every sense of the word, yet, at this moment, she is little more than charmingly naïve. Mankind will not fall with her, though this paradise will be lost. The old man will soon die, his son Ralph, who loves Isabel, will die soon also without an heir, and Isabel, the spiritual heir of Gardencourt, will contract a loveless marriage to a cold and corrupt aesthete. The house, in a spiritual sense, is left to its ghost, which Isabel is privileged to see, as a sign that she has come to maturity through suffering. This scene on the lawn at Gardencourt is like a painting of antiquity by Claude, or of the *ancien régime* by Watteau. It is beautiful, but with the loveliness of an elegaic dream.

A practical 'real' English house is set in contrast to Gardencourt: Lord Warburton's Lockleigh. Gardencourt is a place constructed by the imagination of outsiders; Lockleigh is the actual ancestral home of an aristocracy which has lost its old function and is unable to discover a new. Warburton is 'a nobleman of the newest pattern, a reformer, a radical, a contemner of ancient ways' – in theory. The paradox of his position in practice is that he can 'neither abolish himself as a nuisance nor maintain himself as an institution'. He is a character something in the same mould as the extravagant aristocratic revolutionaries of *The Princess Casamassima*. His radicalism is an amusement pursued only so long as it will not damage his position. If socialism should come, Warburton would be left with his half dozen houses, his seat in the Lords, his elegant amusements and his tenantry. Politically it is a true prophecy. British radicalism has preserved the old order, loyal to the conservative constitution. Isabel, in rejecting his proposal of marriage, rejects too 'the peace, the kindness, the honour, the possessions, a deep security and a great exclusion' which Lockleigh represents. Were she his wife, she would be, she concludes, no more than 'a picturesque loyalist'. In terms of the opposition between two houses, Gardencourt and Lockleigh, it is the choice between the preservation of a paradisiacal dream as a country of the mind, or absorption into a great, but meaningless, aristocratic establishment.

When Lord Warburton showed her the house, after luncheon, it seemed to her a matter of course that it should be a noble picture. Within, it had been a good deal modernized – some of its best points had lost their purity; but as they saw it from the gardens, a stout grey pile, of the softest, deepest, most weather-fretted hue, rising from a broad, still moat, it affected the young visitor as a castle in a legend. The day was cool and rather lustreless; the first note of autumn had been struck, and the watery sunshine rested on the walls in blurred and desultory gleams, washing them, as it were, in places tenderly chosen, where the ache of antiquity was keenest. (9)

The elegaic note is as strong here as at Gardencourt, though the centre of consciousness is now not that of the mature novelist but the innocent enthusiasm of young Isabel. The phrase 'as a castle in a legend' is, perhaps, too fairy-tale (too Catherine Morland), but the soft, deep weather-fretted hue, the tender gleams of the sunshine, the 'ache of antiquity' of the house, have all the same quality as the longer description of Gardencourt. But it is a house expressive of a different kind of society. Lockleigh is feudal. Though 'modernized' (like Warburton), it still stands in its ancient defensive moat. It is expressive too of the Norman union of Church and State, we shall learn, for Lockleigh church is in the family gift, and given to a muscular, unspiritual younger son of the family. As Henrietta Stackpole, Isabel's friend, comments later, Warburton, who owns half a dozen seats, also 'owns' his 'thousands' of tenants, and the ownership of the enclosed park of Lockleigh is marked by 'a gigantic iron fence, some thirty miles round'. Miss Stackpole is not the most accurate narrator of the European scene – elsewhere that fence becomes a wall of stone! – but there is a difference between the lawns of Gardencourt sweeping down to the Thames, and the moated ancestral seat of Lockleigh. On the castle 'the first note of autumn' has been struck – one reads the emblem in the same way as the lengthening shadows of the summer's day of the earlier description, but this later season is now 'cool and rather lustreless'. Such distinctions continue later. Warburton's sister complains that there is no picture gallery at Lockleigh, unlike Gardencourt. The Touchett's much-loved house, though only a recent acquisition, contains a rich sediment of paintings from the past. The modernized feudal castle, though a family seat, lacks an ancestral portrait gallery. In this, as by radical politics, the Warburtons are culturally deracinated. Isabel will not remember her time here as she will at Gardencourt. She returns to Gardencourt impelled by loving memory; but she will not marry feudal Warburton, and that nobleman eventually retreats into the exclusivity of his caste by marrying one of his own kind.

Warburton is an honourable man. The villains of this tale are Osmond (Isabel's mistaken choice as a husband), one of the coldest most trivial, and most cruel of James's aesthetes, and the predatory, parasitic Madame Merle, a sponger on the hospitality of great houses, envious of the 'spoils' of other people's property, and 'never idle' at her work. 'I was born before the French Revolution. Ah, my dear, *je viens de loin.*' So she describes herself. She is also Osmond's former mistress. Promiscuity remains one of the great signs of decadence in country house fiction. The moral growth of the heroine in relation to such people, and her acquisition of experience through suffering, is the humane centre of this story. At the end there comes the return to Gardencourt where the climactic episodes occur: the death of the friend of Isabel's youth, Touchett's sick son Ralph; a final, vain proposal from honest Caspar Goodwood; the last meeting with Warburton; Isabel's resolve to return to her husband.

There seemed to Isabel in these days something sacred in Gardencourt; no chapter of the past was more perfectly irrecoverable. When she thought of the months she had spent there the tears rose to her eyes.   (47)

The word 'chapter' is self-reflexive. It recalls the reader to the first chapter of the novel now ending, and recalls too the idealisation of the 'perfect' house itself as a fictive creation of the imagination. What is 'perfect' about it is that is is 'irrecoverable'. Hence the tears. To enter into this imagined world again would be, as it were, to live, but the very process of living would of itself render perfection imperfection. Ralph, instead, must die there, 'in one of those deep, dim chambers of Gardencourt where the dark ivy would cluster round the edges of the glimmering window'. Yet there had been in Isabel's life a moment of stasis, free from the past, un-committed to the future, which she perceives now only in retrospect, where in the ceremonies of an old and loved place something perfect had been felt, communicated by place to person, from age to youth, from the history of past generations to the present. It is deeply interwoven with the experience of death. The ivy which overgrew the house will shortly grow over the body of Ralph, and the light, always symbolic in these descrip-tions, now no more than glimmers in deep, dim chambers. Yet it shines through the window. This is still Ralph's 'own dear house'. It is where he belongs. Just as much as at Penshurst, here too 'thy lord dwells', even in death, and the loving imagination testifies to this in life, and by the living words of literature.

This is close to mysticism, and it is vulnerable to the charge of being mere obscurantism. To get the true feel one needs the whole experience undergone by sharing Isabel's life throughout the story. Gardencourt's especial status now is that it is for her a 'sacred' place. It is the House of Holiness re-established, and where that House originally existed in *The Faerie Queene*, not in the literal world, but in the consciousness of a wayfaring soul. Gardencourt belongs to her memory and her imagina-tion. It is irrelevant who shall inherit the actual building. The people who mattered to her are gone. But they, and their house, which for a little time she shared, live on as long as her remembrance survives. They live too as long as this fiction, which creates the semblance of her mind, speaks to readers of English, to those who sympathise with the fate of Isabel and feel and see as she does.

There is a clear line of inheritance from James to Forster, Woolf, T. S. Eliot, Waugh of *Brideshead Revisited* (1945), and Cary in *To Be A Pilgrim* (1942), whose very title links Tolbrook house to a 'house of holiness' in history, that medieval priory from which Cary's country house originated. All have a sense of 'the great good place', that phrase of James's describing in a short tale some unnamed dwelling, part country house, part convent, part grand hotel, part hospital, which meets an undefined 'great want' with a 'dream' of 'sweetness', a world of 'reason and order', very 'paradise' itself, were it not dependent on the wealth of this world. The names Forster, Woolf and Eliot link this mysticism inextricably with the heartlands of 'English literature', that great national subject in large measure invented this century, and which Eliot, by his criticism, helped to create. If it is difficult to envisage the idea of 'English' without these writers, then the houses they celebrate are part of the national inheritance: Howards End, Poyntz Hall, Knole, 'Burnt Norton', though perhaps best known of all at this moment (1992), thanks to the images of television, is Waugh's Brideshead, popularly associated with Castle Howard (Pl. 36).

The Jamesian theme is that of inheritance, the transfer of a mystic legacy from one soul to another. It is dependent, as it is described, upon the possession of a certain kind of conservative imagination, and the existence between the fiction and the reader of a shared culture. It is the ultimate development of a process which was initiated when eighteenth-century idealist novels separated a Paradise Hall or a Grandison Hall from actual houses, conceiving the idea of a place rather than the place itself. In its twentieth-century context the theme especially takes up the question, 'who shall inherit England?' It is not just a question of the once green and pleasant land. As the skies darkened in the 1940s, the very survival of England itself became a matter of life and death in time of war.

'Only connect', wrote Forster to the people of England, and to all humane readers. He needed to make such an appeal, for *Howards End* (1910) is full of loose connections, and misconnections. The cement of community has gone in the class divisions of the modern world. But there is one firm link in the tale. It is that between Mrs Wilcox and Margaret Schlegel, the older and younger generations. It is Mrs Wilcox who is the keeper of the spirit of the country house of the novel's title, though it is typical of the dislocation of the time that this becomes a rented place. Her family belong to what Forster calls 'the civilization of luggage', and it is an appropriate symbol of the nature of modern 'improvements' to an estate that the erection of a garage at Howards End (to house the transitory apparatus of a transitory people) damages the roots of the wych elm in the garden (the sign of age and continuity in one place). By cutting off the garden round the house from the meadow outside they sever too the link (only symbolic now) between house and productive Nature.

But Mrs Wilcox is in tune with the true spirit of the place. She is depicted as a kind of latter day *genius loci* or fertility spirit with her arms filled with hay from the meadows, her heart replete with love for the garden and house. In Margaret she perceives a fellow sympathiser to whom she may offer a home in the rootless modern world. ('Can what they call civilization be right, if people mayn't die in the room where they were born?' she asks, longing to establish continuity of connection.) It is as if by sympathetic magic that the doors of the house open to Margaret alone when the key is lost; it is she who sees the magic pigs' teeth in the bowl of the wych elm; and when at last she rightfully 'inherits' the place, the tree flourishes once more and the opening into the meadow is restored. Thus Mrs Wilcox, now dead, lives on in the house. 'She is the house and the tree that leans over it. . . . I cannot believe that knowledge such as hers will perish with knowledge such as mine. She knew about realities.' So Margaret says, and it is clear that by 'realities' she means things of the spirit. At the end that spirituality is close to pantheism as the great red poppies in the garden reach out towards the lesser poppies in the meadow. The garden fills with the laughter of children, blessed by the fertile benediction of Nature itself. The novel ends with a celebration of harvest and the excited cry, 'it'll be such a crop of hay as never'.

That word 'never' suggests that this is another tale of 'news from nowhere'. Such things never were – except in fiction. In this mystic world the cutting of the hay is not essential to the welfare of the estate (as it is even in Marvell's equally symbolic 'Upon Appleton House'). Nor has the connection of Mrs Wilcox with the spirit of the place any significant relation to those processes of inheritance intrinsic to the historical role of a Barbara Gamage or Maria Fairfax as great heiresses (even though Wilcox and Schlegel are now intermarried). The old signs are still there, but divorced from social structures. The spiritual is made real only by the connection of mind to mind, Mrs Wilcox to Margaret. The apprehension of the spirit of the place, house and land, is the role of those who lovingly preserve and understand, and that function falls especially to women.

Understand what? There is an obvious mushiness about this. Have a hole in a hedge, poppies and pigs' teeth ever before carried so much spiritual significance? There is a strong element of suburban fantasy about this vision of the house in the country, even a fey whimsicality. Compare the elaborate and deeply rooted iconographic system of Pope's Twickenham. But the more trivial the signs, the more striking the feeling.

It is like the preservation of a lock of hair from the head of a loved one when the beloved has gone. Only the slightest memento may stir the deepest emotions. That is now the function of the English country house. It is a mystic sign, and it is the nature of religious feeling to pass beyond mere specificity. If this is only suggested by Forster, it is the *leitmotif* of Cary's *To Be a Pilgrim*. Tolbrook, founded upon a monastic site, is an epitome of England, whose natural continuity is shown by immemorial oak, elm and ash. That old order is now, seemingly, in terminal decay. Tolbrook is like a Roman villa threatened by barbarians, or like a house of the *ancien régime* in an age of revolution. But this is more a religious than a social theme. The sensitive 'pilgrim', Wilcher, of the novel's title celebrates his mother's room as a 'blessed' and a 'holy place'; in the 'burning' lime tree in the garden he senses God's presence; and the house itself stirs in him 'a passionate love of home, of that peace, of that grace and order which alone can give beauty to the lives of men living together'. Here is Forster's 'only connect' again, made religious. The word 'grace' is indicative of divine mercy, and the peace of Tolbrook is close to that of God which passes all understanding. At the end the house (which is now a working farm, for a living must be made from the estate) passes from Wilcher to his nephew and is reconsecrated to England.

Robert has brought it back into the English stream and he himself has come with it; to the soft corn, good for home made bread; the mixed farm, so good for the men; to the old church religion which is so twined with English life that the very prayers seem to breathe of fields after rain and skies whose light is falling between clouds.   (146)

Virgil had written in his patriotic *Georgics* (in lines Pope recalled) how 'happy Ceres' reassumes the land as the fields crop again after civil war. The date – 1942 – of *To Be a Pilgrim*, written in the darkest days of war, explains this deeply sentimental and religious patriotism.

Cary is not an isolated example. The same religious love of country inspires Virginia Woolf's last novel, *Between the Acts* (1941). As the Luftwaffe gather in the skies, in the grounds of Poyntz Hall the village community act out a pageant of English history through the language of past generations of English literature in aid of the illumination of the village church. House and church and farm are built from the local stone, and in the garden the roots of a great tree reach down into the very soil beneath the Hall. The symbolism is clear. One might say of Poyntz that it is 'no alien fabrication, no startling stranger set between the beeches and the oaks. No other country but England could have produced it, and into no other country would it settle with such harmony and such quiet.' The words are not Woolf's but those of her friend Victoria Sackville-West describing 'Knole of the Sackvilles' (a house, she claimed, which seen from afar seems a veritable village community).[4] The sentiment is an exact gloss on the symbolic role of Poyntz where the community gather about the house to express their unity of being. 'What we need is a centre to bring us all together', Woolf writes. 'Only connect'.

The pageant is the closest the English novel comes to recreating the communal ending of *A Midsummer Night's Dream*. The trivial village entertainment at Poyntz Hall, like Theseus's hymeneal celebrations in his great hall, is a ritual act, and Woolf's art, like Shakespeare's, finely balances the sublime and the ridiculous. There is the singing of 'home, sweet home' and 'God save the King'; the gathering together of the villagers for a festive tea (the last sign of the symposia of the classic world or the feast in hall of Gothic times); and those moving moments when the delving peasantry are seen on the stage moving across the centuries, their words lost in the wind. However amateur the show and imperfect the audience, these are the kinds of acts appropriate for Poyntz Hall. The magic element of the rite is that it is these things which must be duly performed in order.

It seems natural as stone and tree, yet it is also deeply grounded in culture and memory. It is to the library that the inmates of the house gravitate, and it is in a series of parodies of the language of great English books that the villagers outside perform their roles on stage, here only becoming the great men and women of history conceived imaginatively through books. The medium of communication for this culture from library to village is the local school teacher, the writer of the pageant. The interpreter of the message is the local clergyman (hesitant and stumbling) at the end:

were we not given to understand – am I too presumptuous? Am I treading, like angels, where as a fool I should absent myself? To me at least it was indicated that we are members one of another. Each is part of the whole.   (World's Classics edn, 172)

It seems that he has got it right. This is what we are shown: through the unifying consciousness of Mrs Swithin, born in the house; in the gathering of the Dyces of Denton, the Wickhams of Owlswick, '*Adsum*; I'm here, in place of my grandfather or great grandfather'; and above all in the small girl who begins the pageant, 'Gentles and simples, I address you all. . . . England I am.' As 'England' she is infinitely old, yet as a girl child a sign of youth and fertility, the world waiting to be born. . . .

There is yet greater idealisation of the country house elsewhere in Woolf's fiction. In the long peroration of *Orlando* (1928) she had already created an imaginary dwelling, out of time, perfect in the imagination, which is forever England. It is understood by the consciousness of one special soul, the ambi-sexual hero/ine who like Tiresias has been a traveller in time, and who may speak for all English history. *Orlando*, in its conclusion, commits itself wholeheartedly. The hero/ine is vouchsafed a vision:

There was a village with a church tower among elm trees; a grey-domed manor house in a park; a spark of light burning on some glasshouse; a farmyard with yellow corn stacks. The fields were marked with black tree clumps, and beyond the fields stretched long woodlands, and there was the gleam of a river, and then hills again. In the far distance Snowdon's crags broke white among the clouds; she saw the far Scottish hills and the wild tides that swirl about the Hebrides.

All was still now. It was near midnight. The moon rose slowly over the weald. Its light raised a phantom castle upon earth. There stood the great house with all its windows robed in silver. Of wall or substance there was none. All was phantom. All was still. All was lit as for the coming of a dead Queen. Gazing below her, Orlando saw the dark plumes tossing in the courtyard, and torches flickering and shadows kneeling. A Queen once more stepped from her chariot.   (Penguin edn, 230–1)

This house is Knole, and *Orlando* is dedicated to Victoria Sackville-West. That great house, said to possess seven courts and fifty-two stairways and three hundred and sixty-five rooms (so Woolf and Sackville-West tell), had been, for Jonson, a House of Pride, an antithesis of Penshurst. But now, detached from all social significance, it is the navel of a vision of the whole of Britain. The very house itself has dissolved into the imagination: 'of wall or substance there was none'. The pattern of numbers, 7:52:365, makes it emblematic of the years; its setting in its park beside the village and the church unites the agricultural order with the structures of Church and State. This place had been the still centre of Orlando's literary pilgrimage across history from Shakespeare's age to contemporary Bloomsbury. The house, like Poyntz Hall, is thus perceived through literature, and that cultural process is naturalised. It is fitting that he/she has been carrying in her pocket through the centuries a poem called 'The Oak Tree' and that it is her wish to bury the text in the soil of the park beneath an oak planted in 1588. Literature is thus naturalised, Nature made literary. The major ceremonial act in the vision, however, is to welcome the monarch to the house (so it was at Penshurst long before). It is now a dead queen who comes and the 'dark plumes' toss in the courtyard as if this were a funeral cortège. There is no longer a living presence but an imagined icon. The perceiver of all this (and the creator) is a woman. Orlando began life as a man, but is now a lady of letters. The fertility of a great family is now the fertility of the mind and the power of a sensitive spirit to create. English literature, once the prerogative of men, is now in the keeping of the women of the race.

Earlier in this visionary sequence Orlando had wandered, like a familiar ghost, through the rooms of Knole where once she had lived. It is now no more than a show house. 'Everywhere were little lavender bags to keep the moth out and printed notices, "Please do not touch," and ropes to keep back the curious visitor.' This is no longer her home. 'It belonged to time now; to history; was past the touch and control of the living' – and

24 Stowe, the Temple of Liberty, from Benton Seeley, *Stowe, A Description* (1797)

25 Holkham Hall, the grand hall and ascent to the saloon

26 Osterley Park, the library

27 Kedleston, the saloon, classical urns as stoves for heating

28 Syon House, the hall

29   Newstead Abbey

30   Garendon Hall, A. W. Pugin's unexecuted design (1841)

31 Alton Towers, from Llewellyn Jewitt and S. C. Hall, *The Stately Homes of England* (1874)

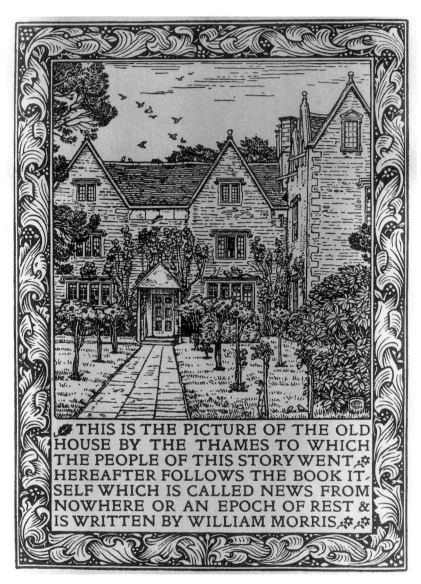

THIS IS THE PICTURE OF THE OLD
HOUSE BY THE THAMES TO WHICH
THE PEOPLE OF THIS STORY WENT
HEREAFTER FOLLOWS THE BOOK IT
SELF WHICH IS CALLED NEWS FROM
NOWHERE OR AN EPOCH OF REST &
IS WRITTEN BY WILLIAM MORRIS

32   Kelmscott, the frontispiece for *News from Nowhere* (1890), drawn by C. M. Gere, with
border designed by Morris, and cut by W. H. Hooper

33 Cardiff Castle

34 Cardiff Castle, the fireplace in the great hall

35 Clandon Park, the great hall fireplace

36 Castle Howard/Brideshead

as she sees it thus, the great figures of history rise before her, Dryden, Swift, Pope, Elizabeth herself, and 'beyond the Elizabethans and the Tudors, someone older, further, darker, a cowled figure, monastic, severe, a monk.'

No signification is attached to this litany of names. What matters is the sign of 'history' as the record of national time and being. There is no concern with the expropriation of the monastic lands, or the show house of Tudor pride, or the satiric vision of Pope or Swift of a society which has lost its ancient values. All that matters is the house itself as an historic icon. It speaks of immortality even to an unbeliever,

She, who believed in no immortality, could not help feeling that her soul would come and go for ever with the reds on the panels and the greens on the sofa. . . . Ah, but she knew where the heart of the house still beat. Gently opening a door, she stood on the threshold so that (she fancied) the room could not see her and watched the tapestry rising and falling on the eternal faint breeze which never failed to move it. Still the hunter rode, still Daphne flew. The heart still beat, she thought, however faintly, however far withdrawn; the frail indomitable heart of the immense building.   (224)

It is only one step from that to the peroration at the end of *Brideshead Revisited*. Millions now know a Catholic celebration of a great house, linked imaginatively (though not in historical truth) with a great palace once built by the Earl of Carlisle to celebrate his pride.[5]

The builders did not know the uses to which their work would descend; they made a new house with the stones of the old castle; year by year, generation after generation, they enriched and extended it; year by year the great harvest of timber in the park grew to ripeness. . . . Something quite remote from anything the builders intended, has come out of their work . . . a small red flame – a beaten-copper lamp of deplorable design relit before the beaten-copper doors of a tabernacle; the flame which the old knights saw before their tombs, which they saw put out; that flame burns again for other soldiers, far from home, farther in heart, than Acre or Jerusalem. It could not have been lit but for the builders and the tragedians, and there I found it this morning, burning anew among the old stones.

This is Brideshead (or Castle Howard) in the imagination of Charles Rider as he ends his story. It is a house separated from the Marchmains, who have little to recommend them. His own high snobbery separates it too from the army of 'the age of Hooper' – the vulgarians, barbarians camped in the park, new Goths and Vandals around the symbolic castle, built from the stones of a real fortress. A parallel with the fall of Rome comes to his mind. *Quomodo sedet sola civitas*, he reflects in Augustinian sentiment. The barbarians will not understand the words.[6] So much for any form of community. Rider is quite alone, except for the spirit in the place. It is, in one manifestation, the old monastic order reasserting its religious values – that monk whom Orlando glimpsed. It is also the religious sense of place Cary felt in *To Be a Pilgrim*. This religious feeling cannot be separated from the process of time that Brideshead embodies 'generation after generation', nor from the integration of the country house in the countryside, 'the great harvest of timber in the park' which grew to 'ripeness'. But this apprehension depends on the unique consciousness of the artist, Rider, who has entered into his cultural inheritance through the ancient university of Oxford, itself the preserver of the traditions of old households. Behind Rider is the intelligence and sensibility of Waugh himself who, as the shaper of the fiction, is speaking to others (not to Hooper) who can apprehend what he is saying, and with such success that now Castle Howard, floating like an exhalation in its green parkland, mirrored in the waters of a lake like a dream, seen to the accompaniment of plaintive, ancient music, is popularly linked to this moment of religious apprehension.[7] In Woolf, Knole is the sign of England; from Waugh, Castle Howard has become a shrine of pilgrimage, as much as Canterbury a place of visitation.

But, perhaps, no existing house can carry quite that weight of signification. It is in Eliot's 'Burnt Norton' and 'East Coker' (1936–43) that the mystic transformation of the English house reaches its apotheosis, a cultural transformation through deep reading and religious affirmation which ultimately dissolves a vanished civilisation into a country of the mind in which the spirit, through a sense of time and history and the divine order, seeks consolation, renewal and transformation.

In my beginning is my end.   In succession
Houses rise and fall, crumble, are extended,
Are removed, destroyed, restored, or in their place
Is an open field, or a factory, or a by-pass.
Old stone to new building, old timber to new fires,
Old fires to ashes, and ashes to the earth
Which is already flesh, fur and faeces,
Bone of man and beast, cornstalk and leaf.
Houses live and die: there is a time for building
And a time for living and for generation
And a time for the wind to break the loosened pane
And to shake the wainscot where the field-mouse trots
And to shake the tattered arras woven with a silent motto.   ('East Coker', 1–13)

The Biblical cadence, 'there is a time', links the religious sense of fitness and transience with the process of Nature itself where even a great house is 'ashes to the earth'. Houses, like humankind, both live and die. The wind that shakes the tattered arras is the same breath which stirs the tapestry of Daphne at Knole, but the death of a house, its very marriage to the earth, bone of its bone, flesh of its flesh, is part of a necessary cycle. In my beginning is my end. The 'end', or purpose of life, will be found in origins, here in the history of the succession of houses. The 'end', not termination but purpose, of these houses, is a new 'beginning'. Just as the lamp shone at Brideshead, so, out of the past, there comes the promise of a new faith for the future.

The imaginative eye, seeing no actual house, perceives in 'East Coker' the community of workers tilling the soil only in a vision of an invisible past, united in rustic community of marriage, the sacrament of fertility.

> Round and round the fire
> Leaping through the flames, or joined in circles,
> Rustically solemn or in rustic laughter
> Lifting heavy feet in clumsy shoes,
> Earth feet, loam feet, lifted in country mirth
> Mirth of those long since under earth
> Nourishing the corn.

These are the *Urvolk*, the sturdy peasant farmers of Roman tradition, the yeomanry of England, the unlettered, necessary originals of all. The circles in which they move are those of purgatorial fire, which lead closer to Paradise above. Closer to the house, in the garden (the work of cultured Nature) there still grow roses at Burnt Norton. There are clipped alley-ways, a circle of box, the old topiary work of the Jacobeans (or of Pliny) and the basin of a pool empty of water. The leaves are full of children, hidden excitedly, laughing, signs of future generations (as at Howards End). But this is Paradise Hall, for beyond them are Adam and Eve still in 'our first world':

> There they were, dignified, invisible,
> Moving without pressure, over the dead leaves,
> In the autumn heat, through the vibrant air.

But the house itself, beyond field and garden, is no longer to be seen, and from the air fall incendiary bombs like purgatorial fire. Barbarity is at the gate. *Quomodo sedet sola civitas.*

> The houses are all gone under the sea.

> The dancers are all gone under the hill.

Except in the poetic imagination.

Epilogue

THE LITERATURE OF the English country house has not been written by the owners of the houses. Theirs is another discourse. They speak the language of politics and electioneering, of rents and accounts, farming and industry, building and furnishing. Sometimes in the diaries and letters of the women of the house one comes near to the domesticity of the novel, but those who live in a place are too close to the daily texture of life there to seek to symbolise their role.[1]

The conservative idealisation of the great good place in England was created by outsiders: Jonson, invited to dinner at Penshurst; Marvell, the tutor in a great family; Pope, eager to show his familiarity with the aristocracy; a magistrate, a printer, a clergyman's daughter, an upwardly mobile Jew, a sybaritic American tourist. . . . The aspiration upwards is obvious. So, too, is the critical attitude. It is the necessary salt of scepticism.

That upward mobility of the imagination is matched by the remarkable penetration of the country house ethos downward into society. An engraving of Wilson's 'Cicero' multiplies images of Roman villa culture in the drawing rooms of the middle classes; cheap printing today enables the images of high art to permeate everywhere. The Palladian villa has become a normative style for suburban architecture; Lutyens is imitated by any petty builder. The literature which imaginatively both creates and reflects the country house ethos has become a staple of education, institutionalised in school examination and university department, paperbacked for wider consumption, popularised in film and television serial. Pemberley, Gatherum Castle or Brideshead are known to millions.

It is appropriate, therefore, to take leave of this story with an example from popular culture: an immensely successful novel. But the work is also well known as a film, and moving images are now the most widely diffused means of cultural communication. That film is available as a video. The leading actor was a figure who bridged the divide between high Shakespearian art and the matinee idol; the director the maker of popular thrillers who is now a cult figure for the intelligentsia. The writer of this remarkable work was a woman, for women, more and more, have been the carriers of literary culture, and her Norman name suggests aristocratic blood, as did her love of the country house on which her work is based. But she was not a member of the old order.[2]

Daphne du Maurier's *Rebecca* is resonant with the myths of the conservative tradition. It is the story of an outsider who marries into a great house expecting to find it a great good place. Manderley, the perfect and beautiful, is set, she tells, in a 'Happy Valley'. That had been Byron's choice of setting for Norman Abbey, and beyond Byron stands Paradise Hall, and then Eden itself. But this is a tale of paradise lost, though, as Milton had written, it is a fortunate fall. 'I believe there is a theory that men and women emerge finer and stronger after suffering, and that to advance in this or any world we must endure ordeal by fire', so the anonymous heroine writes, making of the burning of Manderley a symbol of purgatorial flame and of progressive pilgrimage.

Manderley is also a type of the Tudor prodigy house. The 'perfect symmetry' of the ancient mansion is an eminent architectural feature, and that symmetry is linked with the punctilios and luxurious ritual of the house. This we have seen before in Timon's villa or Northanger Abbey. So again we are shown the formal serving of coldly elaborate meals (whatever happens to the waste? our heroine asks, but does not discover – of old it was given to the poor, so Jonson wrote; now it just vanishes). At different times of the day fires are lit in different rooms according to a hollow ritual of circulation in the house, but our heroine is lost, following the fires rather than centring home about the hearth. Yet, cold though the ritual is, it makes of Manderley a place of 'culture and grace', beautiful in the perfection of its form and in the richness of its possessions, fine library and ancient pictures, and above all the formal garden whose flowers pour into the house.

The tension between the grace of this culture and the emptiness of its forms is centred upon Rebecca herself, the first Mrs de Winter, a woman of extraordinary beauty and grace and the creator of much of the loveliness of Manderley. She is also, we learn late and at a climactic moment, totally profligate, degenerate and selfish, a beautiful mask concealing the cancer of evil beneath. It is a Jamesian theme, but surpasses the master himself by the indirection of the viewpoint and the gradual steps of our heroine's discovery of the truth. For Rebecca has died before the story begins, but lives, like a ghost in the house, in constant memory. Her wing at Manderley, preserved in its visible perfection by the familiar spirit of the necrophiliac Mrs Danvers, is the popular novel's equivalent of a bower of Duessa or Acrasia, the spider's web of the evil but beautiful witch. Her commitment to the old hospitality (so much stressed by tradition) has degenerated to the pointless and debauched society parties for which she is both famous and infamous. It is fitting that the story comes to its crisis at the 'Fancy Dress Ball', an act of masquerade in which people pretend to be characters from a lost past, and our heroine is tricked into pretending to be what she is not, the image of Rebecca, the dead mistress of Manderley.

Our heroine is quite incapable of fulfilling that role. Hers is the usual longing of social aspiration upwards to the country house of dream. Then comes the awakening. She has no real part in such a world, nor was that world worthy of her aspiration. The burning of Manderley is a symbolic act, though it does not free her soul from purgatory. Maxim and she end the novel as displaced people wandering around the hotels of Europe, the modern equivalent of the country house at its utmost remove from community. Manderley, meantime, remains present. For there is no escape, after all, from the world the imagination has created. The novel is closed within a loop: 'in my beginning is my end.' The famous first chapter takes our nameless heroine (you, gentle reader) through the padlocked gate back up the drive again, and in the moonlight, like Knole in the imagination of Orlando, one sees the great house alive once more. 'Time could not wreck the perfect symmetry of those walls, nor the site itself, a jewel in the hollow of a hand.' Nature, for a moment, sustains a balance between the works of art and encroaching decay. We recognise those 'things of culture and of grace' which mark the site, though now 'nettles were everywhere, the vanguard of the army. They choked the terrace, they sprawled about the paths, they leant, vulgar and lanky, against the very windows of the house.' We see the signs of barbarity, the common vulgarity of the mob. *Quomodo sedet sola civitas?* The voice of the narrator, in whose mind our own is totally absorbed, provides the answer. The house exists in memory, and will ever do so. 'These things were permanent, they could not be dissolved.'

Last night I dreamt I went to Manderley again.

Notes

In the citation of literary texts I have modernised quotations before 1800. Original spelling and typography for early texts can be an impediment for the present day reader. On the same principle of accessibility I have provided references which may be used with any edition of the literary text. For novels, reference is to the chapter, or, where two figures are given, to section and chapter. Thus, *Tom Jones* I, 4 indicates Book I, Chapter 4. In Byron's long poem, *Don Juan*, I give Canto and stanza. Not every reader has access to standard scholarly editions in university libraries. In the few cases where it has not been possible to apply this general guide, I have used commonly available paperbacks.

CHAPTER ONE

1. See his *Experiment in Autobiography*, 1934.
2. Muthesius (1979), first published 1904/5.
3. Sackville-West (1922), 18.
4. Devonshire (1982), 15–16.
5. 17 February 1990. The quotations conflate the views of Susan Young and Jane Darbyshire.
6. The primitive hut is described by Vitruvius (*floreat* 40 BC) in the only surviving classical treatise on architecture, *De Architectura*. The second edition of M. A. Laugier's *Essai sur l'architecture* (1755) illustrates the hut as its frontispiece, stressing its natural origins by showing it constructed from four trees growing from the ground, above which a triangular wooden cruck forms the roof. See Rykwert (1972).
7. For the theoretical issues involved see Duckworth (1981) and (1989) with bibliographical references; Burke (1945) and (1950); Curtius (1953); Barthes (1970); Foucault (1970) and (1972). Ackerman (1990) appeared too late to be incorporated into the main body of the text. There is substantial agreement between us on the interpretation of the ideological tradition.

CHAPTER TWO

1. For Wilson and the country house tradition see Solkin (1982).
2. Roestvig (1954). The phrase *Beatus ille*, 'happy the man', opens Horace's *Epode* 2; the celebration of the country life, *o rus, quando ego te aspiciam?* is in *Satires* II.6.
3. For discussion of the idea of Arcadia see McClung (1989). For further information on the concepts Arcadia, Golden Age and Utopia see Mumford (1922); Levin (1969); Manuel and Fritzie (1979). Lemprière's *Classical Dictionary*, entry 'Arcadia', provides a list of prime classical sources. Virgil's *Eclogues* widely diffused the ideal of Arcadian existence.
4. I.50 and 56.
5. Juvenal X.356: *mens sana in corpore sano*: a healthy mind in a healthy body; Cicero, *Pro Sestio* XLV.98: *cum dignitate otium*: a peaceful life with honour.
6. Sekora (1977).
7. *Silvae*, I.3; I.6; II.2; for Pope and Timon see ch. 7 below.
8. Freeman (1975).

CHAPTER THREE

1. Gotch (1909), 2.
2. Chambers (1985), 54.
3. Girouard (1983), 19.
4. Cook (1974), 48. For the iconography of gateways generally see Mowl and Earnshaw (1985).
5. Girouard (1983), ch. 6. See n. 2 to the chapter for bibliographical guidance.
6. Girouard (1981).
7. *The Elements of Architecture*, 1624, 4.

CHAPTER FOUR

1. Hibbard (1956); McClung (1977); Wayne (1984); to whom I am heavily indebted. Among the substantial critical literature see also Cubeta (1963); Hart (1963); Maclean (1964); Molesworth (1968) and (1971); Fowler (1973), (1975) and (1986); Cain (1979); Dubrow (1979); McGuire (1979); Peterson (1981); Tolliver (1985); McClung (1989).
2. Tipping (1920), Period 1, vol. 1; Binney (1972).
3. It has often been observed that Penshurst is like the house of Kalender in Sidney's romance *Arcadia*.
4. The classic attack on the country house ethos is Williams (1973). The allusion to 'the dark side of the landscape' is to Barrell (1980). There are good discussions of the theoretical issues in the development of major Marxist critiques in Turner (1979) and Wayne (1984). My own concern is merely descriptive of the way a favourable interpretative community constructed literary *topoi*.
5. Sir Henry Wotton, *The Elements of Architecture*, 1624, refers to 'the natural hospitality of England' (71) as a commonplace, and therefore insists that the

buttery be given architectural prominence in the usefully designed house. Stone (1965a) has several examples of hospitality and charity (142–3, 172). McClung (1977) ch. 2, discusses the issue.

6. Bacon's *Praise of Queen Elizabeth*, 1608; William Harrison's *Description of England*, 1577. For the economics of building and running a great house see Smith (1990).

7. *Georgics* II.458 *f.*; see also Horace *Satires* II.6 cited above, ch. 2, n. 2.

8. Cook (1974), 84.

9. Friedman (1989).

10. Friedman (1989) argues that there is a shift in the Tudor and Stuart periods from the feudal household to a more domestic and modern environment. Formerly the lady of the house was an isolated figure among male retainers owing allegiance to her husband; then she becomes the mistress of the house in a society more equally divided between the sexes. See also Lewalski (1989).

CHAPTER FIVE

1. Rathmell (1971).

2. 'Wretched is the hall . . . each day in the week/ There the lord and the lady liketh not to sit./ Now have the rich a rule to eat by themselves/ In a privy parlour . . . for poor men's sake,/ Or in a chamber with a chimney, and leave the chief hall/ That was made for meals, for men to eat in.' *Piers Plowman*, Text B, Passus X, 97–101.

3. See Marcel Mauss, *The Gift: Forms and functions of exchange in archaic societies*, translated by Ian Cunnison, New York, Norton, 1967, and Wayne (1984), 75, for a materialistic reading of ritual.

4. For Smythson as architect see Girouard (1983); for the iconography of the plasterwork see Bostick (1990).

5. Hill and Cornforth (1966) and Tipping (1920–36), Period IV. For the change in the function of the hall see Pevsner (1960), and for the decline in the status of servants from retainers to menials see Chambers (1985), 94.

CHAPTER SIX

1. Legouis (1965); Wallace (1968); Hunt (1978).

2. McClung (1977), 157, reproduces the illustration from Clement Markham's *Life of the Great Lord Fairfax*. but the authority of the image is uncertain.

3. In 'Upon the Hill and Grove at Bill-borow', stanza 4.

4. *Aeneid* VIII. 362–7; for the *casa Romuli* see Ovid, *Fasti* III. 183–4; cf. also the entrance to the House of Holiness, *Faerie Queene*, I. x. 5.

5. Vitruvius at the beginning of the third book of *De Architectura* argued that sacred edifices should have the same proportions as a man. A correctly proportioned body, with arms and legs extended, fits the 'perfect' geometrical forms of the circle and the square. See Wittkower (1971).

6. See above, ch. 4, n. 10.

7. Pope 'Epistle to Bathurst', 299–306.

Notes

CHAPTER SEVEN

1. *Epistolary Description* (1747); Brownell (1980). See also Henry and Dixon (1970); Gibson (1971); Brownell (1978); Erskine-Hill (1979); Hunt (1984); Martin (1984); Ayres (1990).
2. Clark (1989) argues that Burlington's admiration for the Stuarts was political as well as cultural. I find the case not proven.
3. Mack (1969), to whom I am extremely indebted.
4. In Wallace (1968), 13.
5. Cotton writes of 'the great owner' of Chatsworth as one 'whose noble mind/ For such a fortune only designed./ Whose bounties as the ocean's bosom wide,/ Flow in a constant, unexhausted tide/ Of hospitality and free access,/ Liberal condescension, cheerfulness,/ Honour and Truth, as ev'ry of them strove/ At once to captivate Respect and Love.' *The Wonders of the Peak*, 1464–71. On the country house and the literature of economics, see Kenny (1984); on the more general issues of commerce and virtue, Pocock (1985); and on the actualities of estate management, Mingay (1963).
6. In MS (Chatsworth) the words addressed to Timon, 'what his hard heart denies,/ His charitable Vanity supplies', are ambiguously applicable to Burlington also.

CHAPTER EIGHT

1. Girouard (1978).
2. Pope's and Swift's contrasting country house ideologies are analysed by Fabricant (1982).

CHAPTER NINE

1. For the religious implications of architectural mathematics in Palladio see Witkower (1971); Ackerman (1966), ch. 5. The divine symbolism of three in one and one in three is suggested by the fenestration of Pope's Roman Catholic villa, but has no textual authority in his writing that I know to support it. The use of the Palladian façade to recall a temple is a religious motif, however, and Pope's construction of a mound in his garden known as 'paradiso' – in memory of his mother – and the incorporation of the Crown of Thorns and the Five Wounds of Christ in his grotto all indicate a religious symbolism for the villa. For the continuation of numerological ideas in Pope's lifetime see Robert Morris's *Defence of Ancient Architecture* (1728); *Lectures on Architecture* (1734); *Essay upon Harmony: As it relates chiefly to situation and building* (1739).
2. Summerson (1959); Wittkower (1974); Beaumont (1975); Brownell (1978); Harris (1981); Cruickshank (1985); Ackerman (1990). In addition to Leoni's translation of Palladio, cited below in the text, Palladio was translated again by Isaac Ware (1738). William Kent's *Designs of Inigo Jones* (1727) and Colen Campbell's *Vitruvius Britannicus*, 3 vols. (1715–25), are other important contemporary sources. Palladio was as much a symbol as a source. Richard Hewlings indicates in the Chiswick House guide (English Heritage, 1989) that the origins of the movement were extremely eclectic.

188

3. Rupprecht (1966), with good bibliographical guidance.
4. For the republican tradition see Pocock (1975); for its association with Palladian architecture specifically, Ackerman (1990), and the discussion of Stowe in ch. 10 below.
5. *Miscellaneous Reflections*, cited in Allen (1937), I.87. For the symbolism of Pope's grotto see Mack (1969), Hunt (1976), Brownell (1980); also Frederick Bracher, 'Pope's Grotto: the Maze of Fancy', *Huntington Library Quarterly* 12 (1949), 141–62, and Naomi Miller, *Heavenly Caves*, London, Allen and Unwin, 1982.
6. Parr's engraving of Twickenham, 1735, reproduced in Pl. 16, gives canonical status to the poet's hospitality, quoting from the *Imitations of Horace* (II.ii); 'To Hounslow-Heath I point, and Bansted Down,/ Thence comes your mutton, and these chicks my own;/ From yon old walnut tree a show'r shall fall/ And grapes long-ling'ring on my only wall.'
7. The first recorded appearance of gnomes in the English garden is at Lamport Hall in the 1890s. They represent the spirits of Nature; but some were used to symbolise striking miners in the wake of the miners' strike of 1894, thus providing a remote link with Disney's *Snow White*.

CHAPTER TEN

1. Lees-Milne (1962), 262.
2. Attributed to Pope on doubtful authority. I am indebted to Martin (1984).
3. Lees-Milne (1962).
4. Hussey (1967).
5. For bibliography see Desmond (1988).
6. Cited by Whistler *et al.* (1968), 19.
7. VI.847 *f.*
8. *Apollo* 97 (June 1973), 575, to which I am indebted throughout this chapter.
9. The Duke of Chandos's pretentious seat, Canons, at Edgware was reputedly a source for Pope's portrait of Timon's villa. Maynard Mack, *Alexander Pope: A Life*, New Haven and London, Yale University Press, 1985, provides an account of the controversy.
10. *Apollo* 97 (June 1973), 583.

CHAPTER ELEVEN

1. Aubin (1936). See also Brownell (1983); Radcliffe (1990).
2. *Tom Jones*, VIII, 1. Fielding praises, none the less, the 'beauties, elegances, and curiosities' of Esher, Stowe, Wilton, Eastbury, as well as Prior Park: IX, 9.
3. Duckworth (1989) discusses the motif of the old house with numerous examples.

CHAPTER TWELVE

1. I am indebted throughout this chapter, as in the last, to Duckworth (1971), (1981) and (1989).

2. Duckworth (1971) draws attention to the symbolic storms which threaten the house of innovative speculation in *Sanditon*, ch. 4.

3. Jane Austen's 'conservatism' is currently the subject of debate, but even a radical critique of *Mansfield Park* has granted that 'Fanny internalizes the best values of Mansfield Park – probity, propriety, delicacy – but there is equally no doubt that she "improves" them in the process' (Isobel Armstrong, *Mansfield Park*, Harmondsworth, Penguin Books, 1988). The rise of new, radical readings of the novel in terms of gender and politics, paradoxically, indicates the strength of that conservative appreciation of Jane Austen (through Henry James and Virginia Woolf) which is described here. The issue is well discussed in the revised edition (1987) of Marilyn Butler's *Jane Austen and the War of Ideas*, Oxford, Clarendon Press, and Armstrong, 95–104.

CHAPTER THIRTEEN

1. The cause of the poaching 'war' has been the focus of controversy. J. L. and Barbara Hammond in the classic *The Village Labourer 1760–1832* (London, Longmans, Green & Co. 1911) see its cause in the poverty and exploitation of the poor; Robinson (1988), writing on behalf of the National Trust, argues that the armed gangs were often urban criminals motivated by a desire for profit. A detailed account of the violence of the 'war' is given by Harry Hopkins, *The Long Affray*, London, Secker and Warburg, 1985.

2. The Young England movement originated about 1842. Its romantic Toryism idealised a chivalric past imaginatively conceived from reading works such as Clarendon's *History*, Bolingbroke's *Patriot King*, Kenelm Digby's *Broadstone of Honour* and Scott's novels. The movement aimed at reconciling differences between the classes. See the next chapter, and Robert Blake, *Disraeli*, London, Eyre and Spottiswoode, 1966, ch. 8.

CHAPTER FOURTEEN

1. For Disraeli's country house politics see Holloway (1953). See also Disraeli's *Vindication of the English Constitution* (1835) on the nation conceived 'as a family' and the whole country, buildings, parks and gardens, as a common 'landed inheritance'.

2. Malthus's *An Essay on the Principle of Population* was first published in 1798, revised 1803. His original claim that population would increase beyond the means of subsistence (unless restrained by poverty, disease and starvation) was subsequently modified by the argument that the regulation of greed and sexual activity would act as more acceptable checks on population.

3. Girouard (1981).

4. Girouard (1979); Robinson (1988); on the economics of the nineteenth-century estate and country house life see Spring (1963); Thompson (1963); Mingay (1977).

5. Chambers (1985).

6. Catullus 31: 'O! what greater blessing is there than to put away cares when the

mind unburdens itself, and, tired with the fatigues of travelling, we come to our own home. This alone is what is worth all our toil.' William Flavelle Monypenny and George Earle Buckle, *The Life of Benjamin Disraeli*, London, John Murray, 1929 edn, Bk. III, ch. 6, discusses life at Hughenden.
7. Horace, *Satires* II.6.60, cited above, ch. 2, n. 2.

CHAPTER FIFTEEN

1. Clark (1962); Macaulay (1975); McCarthy (1987).
2. Cf. Morris's *Manifesto of the Society for the Preservation of Ancient Buildings* (1877) and his seventh paper to the Society: 'the untouched surface of ancient architecture bears witness to the development of men's ideas, and to the continuity of history, and, so doing, affords never-ceasing instruction, nay education to the passing generations, not only telling us what were the aspirations of men passed away, but also what we may hope for in time to come.' The documents are reprinted in Volume I of May Morris, *William Morris, Artist, Writer and Socialist*, Oxford, Basil Blackwell, 1936. Paul Thomson draws attention to Morris's closeness to Ruskin's claim that 'we have no right whatever to touch' ancient buildings, for they 'belong, partly to those who built them, and partly to all the generations of mankind who follow us' (*The Work of William Morris*, London, Heinemann, 1967, 59). The statutory listing and protection of secular buildings developed from the work of the SPAB. Though Morris held (by 1877) that the contemporary revival of Gothic architecture was impossible before the material conditions of society were radically changed, some of his arguments for the reform of proletarian housing show the influence of country house ideals; for instance, his proposal that workers' apartment blocks should possess 'a great hall for dining in' (May Morris, II, 127). For Morris's place in architectural history generally see Nicholas Pevsner, *Pioneers of Modern Design*, rev. edn, Harmondsworth, Penguin, 1960.
3. A frame of tinted convex glass intended to cast a soft glow over the landscape after the manner of paintings of the French seventeenth-century artist Claude.
4. The voyage is described in J. W. Mackail, *The Life of William Morris*, 2 vols, London, Longmans, Green and Co., 1899, ch. xii. In the best account of Morris's socialism that I know. E. P. Thompson makes the same identification of Guest and Morris as this chapter, but seen from Thompson's perspective the actual house, Kelmscott, is merely a parenthesis in a process of political development and class struggle. I do not wish to question the 'reality' of Morris's socialism, but merely to emphasise the way in which the old house acquires for Morris a large measure of imaginative autonomy. See E. P. Thompson, *William Morris: Romantic to revolutionary*, London, Merlin Press, 1977 edn, 171–5 and 692–8.
5. *Aeneid* XI.14–15, untranslated and without source given, 1977: meaning, here, 'a great deal has been accomplished, workmen, but, I fear, there is still much to be done.'
6. The National Trust was founded in 1895, but was originally concerned with the preservation of vernacular architecture; the Trust's Country House Scheme was enacted by parliamentary bill in 1937.

7. Weaver (1913); the entire introductory discussion is pertinent.
8. See above, ch. 1, n. 6.
9. The famous 'red house', illustrated in Chambers (1985), 254.
10. Dunster (1986), with bibliography; I am indebted to the whole of Philip Inskip's formalist chapter, 'Lutyens' houses', which I cite.

CHAPTER SIXTEEN

1. Hussey (1955c); Joseph Nash's *Mansions of England in the Olden Time*, 1839–49, was immensely influential in creating a sentimental and nationalistic view of the Gothic country house.
2. Girouard (1981).
3. Cited in Thompson (1963), 291.
4. Wordsworth, 'Lowther'.
5. Genesis 18; Romans 4.19; 9.9; Hebrews 11.11.
6. 'Providence has ordained the different orders and gradations into which the human family is divided, and it is right and necessary that it should be maintained. . . . The position of a landed proprietor, be he squire or nobleman, is one of dignity. . . . He is the natural head of his parish or district – in which he should be looked up to as the bond of union between classes. To him the poor man should look up for protection; those in doubt and difficulty for advice; the ill disposed for reproof or punishment; the deserving of all classes, for consideration and hospitality; and *all* for a dignified, honourable and Christian example. . . . He has been placed by Providence, in a position of authority and dignity, and no false modesty should deter him from expressing this, quietly and gravely, in the character of his house.' Sir Gilbert Scott, *Secular and Domestic Architecture*, 1857, in Girouard (1979), 4–5.
7. Girouard (1979), 290; for Burges generally see Crook (1981).

CHAPTER SEVENTEEN

1. *The Sunday Times*, 'Comment', 8 April 1990, observed that of the 200 richest people in Britain, 54 are aristocrats, 25 served in the same regiment (Brigade of Guards) and 35 went to the same school (Eton).
2. Robinson (1984).
3. Cited by Gill (1972), 143, to whom I am indebted in this and the next chapter.
4. Goetsch (1983), 316–17, to whom I am indebted in this chapter.
5. Cited by Gill (1972), 154–5.
6. Cited by Goetsch (1983), 300; the subsequent Gissing quote is from p. 295.

CHAPTER EIGHTEEN

1. Ed. F. O. Mathiessen and Kenneth B. Murdock, New York, Oxford University Press, 1955, 34–5.

2. The idea of the organic community is a leading theme in Gill's (1972) account of the modern country house novel, but has a different contextual emphasis.
3. For the house as a conservative political symbol see above, ch. 11, n. 3.
4. Discussed above, in ch. 1.
5. Smith (1990).
6. *Lamentations* 1.1: 'How doth the city sit solitary.' Again, it is a sign of the culture we have lost that Waugh does not think it is necessary to translate the Latin, nor to cite the source. The sentiment recalls St Augustine's *The City of God* for it compares the falling earthly 'city' (Rome/the country house) with the divine city (Jerusalem/Heaven).
7. The television serialisation of *Brideshead Revisited* is now used to promote visits to Castle Howard in the advertising literature for the estate.

EPILOGUE

1. See, for instance, Lucy (1987) and Ketton-Cremer (1962).
2. Daphne du Maurier, granddaughter of George du Maurier. The film of *Rebecca* stars Laurence Olivier, matinee idol and future director of the National Theatre, and was directed by Alfred Hitchcock.

Selected Bibliography

Abrams, M. H. (1985), 'Art as such: a sociology of modern aesthetics', *Bulletin of the American Academy of Arts and Sciences* 38, 8–37

Ackerman, James S. (1966), *Palladio*, Hardmonsworth, Penguin Books

Ackerman, James S. (1990), *The Villa: Form and ideology of country houses*, London, Thames and Hudson

Airs, Malcolm (1975), *The Making of the English Country House 1500–1640*, London Architectural Press

Allen, B. Sprague (1937), *Tides in English Taste (1619–1800): A Background for the study of literature*, Cambridge, Mass., Harvard University Press

Allen, Don Cameron (1960), *Image and Meaning: Metaphoric traditions in Renaissance poetry*, Baltimore, Johns Hopkins Press

Apollo 97 (June 1973), special issue on Stowe House: George Clarke, 'The gardens of Stowe' and 'Grecian taste and Gothic virtue'; Desmond Fitz-Gerald, 'A history of the interior of Stowe'; Michael Gibbon, 'Stowe House, 1660–1779'

Aslet, Clive (1982), *The Last Country Houses*, New Haven and London, Yale University Press

Aslet, Clive and Alan Powers (1986), *The National Trust Book of the English House*, Harmondsworth, Penguin Books (first published 1985)

Aubin, Robert Arnold (1936), *Topographical Poetry in XVIII-Century England*, New York, Modern Language Association of America

Ayres, Philip (1990), 'Pope's *Epistle to Burlington*: The Vitruvian analogies', *Studies in English Literature* 30, 429–44

Baillie, Hugh Murray (1967), 'Etiquette and planning of the state apartments in baroque palaces', *Archaeologia* 101, 161–99

Baridon, Michel (1989), 'History, myth, and the English garden', in Jackson-Stops (1989), 373–92

Barrell, John (1972), *The Idea of Landscape and the Sense of Place, 1730–1840: An approach to the poetry of John Clare*, Cambridge, Cambridge University Press

Barrell, John (1980), *The Dark Side of the Landscape: The rural poor in English painting, 1730–1840*, Cambridge, Cambridge University Press

Barrell, John (1983), *English Literature in History 1730–80: An equal, wide survey*, London, Hutchinson

Barthes, Roland (1970), L'ancienne rhétorique', *Communications* 16, 172–227

Batsford, Harry and Charles Fry (1932), *Homes and Gardens of England*, London, Batsford

Beaumont, Charles (1975), 'Pope and Palladians', *Texas Studies in Literature* 17, 461–79

Beckett, J. V. (1986), *The Aristocracy in England 1660–1914*, Oxford, Blackwell

Bentmann, R. and M. Müller (1970), *Die Villa als Herrschaftsstruktur: Versuch einer Kunstgeschictlichen Analyse*, Frankfurt a. M., Suhrkamp Verlag

Bermingham, Ann (1986), *Landscape and Ideology: The English rustic tradition 1740–1860*, Berkeley and Los Angeles, University of California Press

Binney, Marcus (1972), 'Penshurst Place, Kent: The seat of Viscount De L'Isle, V.C.K.G.', *Country Life*, 151, 9 March–4 May, 554–8; 618–21; 994–8; 1090–3

Bostick, David (1990), 'Plaster to puzzle over' and 'Plaster puzzle decoded', *Country Life*, 184, 12 July, 90–3; 26 July, 76–9

Bourdieu, Pierre (1984), *Distinction: A social critique of the judgement of taste*, London, Routledge and Kegan Paul, translated by Richard Nice

Braudel, Fernand (1973), *Capitalism and Material Life, 1400–1800*, London, Weidenfeld and Nicolson, translated by Miriam Kochan

Brownell, Morris R. (1978), *Alexander Pope and the Arts of Georgian England*, Oxford, Clarendon Press

Brownell, Morris R. (1980), *Alexander Pope's Villa*, London, Greater London Council

Brownell, Morris R. (1983), 'Poetical villas: English verse satire of the country house, 1700–1750', in J. D. Browning (ed.), *Satire in the 18th Century*, New York and London, Garland, 9–52

Burgevin, Leslie Gale, *et al.* (1936), *Horace: Three phases of his influence*, Chicago, Chicago University Press

Burke, Joseph (1976), *English Art 1714–1800*, Oxford, Clarendon Press

Burke, Kenneth (1945), *A Grammar of Motives*, New York, Prentice Hall

Burke, Kenneth (1950), *A Rhetoric of Motives*, New York, Prentice Hall

Cain, William E. (1979), 'The place of the poet in Jonson's "To Penhurst" and "To My Muse"', *Criticism* 21, 34–48

Castell, Robert (1728), *The Villas of the Ancients Illustrated* (reprinted by Garland, New York, 1982)

Chambers, James (1985), *The English House*, London, Methuen

Chandler, Alice (1970), *A Dream of Order: The medieval ideal in nineteenth-century English Literature*, Lincoln, Nebraska, University of Nebraska Press

Clark, J. C. D. (1985), *English Society 1688–1832: Ideology, social structure and political practice during the ancien régime*, Cambridge, Cambridge University Press

Clark, Jane (1989), 'The mysterious Mr. Buck: Patronage and politics, 1688–1745', *Apollo* 129 (May), 317–22

Clark, Kenneth (1962), *The Gothic Revival*, London, John Murray (first published 1928)

Cohen, Ralph (ed.) (1985), *Studies in Eighteenth-Century British Art and Aesthetics*, Berkeley and London, University of California Press

Colie, Rosalie L. (1970), *My Echoing Song: Andrew Marvell's poetry of criticism*, Princeton, Princeton University Press

Selected bibliography

Colie, Rosalie L. (1973), *The Resources of Kind: Genre-theory in the Renaissance*, Berkeley, University of California Press

Colvin, Howard and John Harris (eds) (1970), *The Country Seat*, London, Allen Lane

Comito, Terry (1978), *The Idea of the Garden in the Renaissance*, New Brunswick, Rutgers University Press

Cook, Olive (1974), *The English Country House*, London, Thames and Hudson

Cook, Olive (1984), *The English House through Seven Centuries*, Harmondsworth, Penguin Books (first published 1968)

Cosgrove, Denis and Stephen Daniels (eds) (1988), *The Iconography of Landscape*, Cambridge, Cambridge University Press

Crook, J. Mordaunt (1981), *William Burges and the High Victorian Dream*, London, John Murray

Cruickshank, Dan (1985), *A Guide to the Georgian Buildings of Britain and Ireland*, London, Weidenfeld and Nicolson

Csikszentmihalyi, Mihaly and Eugene Rochberg-Halton (1981), *The Meaning of Things*, Cambridge, Cambridge University Press

Cubeta, Paul M. (1963), 'A Jonsonian ideal: "To Penshurst" ', *Philological Quarterly* 42, 14–24

Curtius, Ernst Robert (1953), *European Literature and the Latin Middle Ages*, Princeton, Princeton University Press

Delbaere-Grant, J. (1969), 'Who shall inherit England?', *English Studies* 50, 101–5

Desmond, Ray (1988), *Bibliography of British Gardens*, Winchester, St Paul's Bibliographies

Devonshire, Duchess of (1982), *The House: Living at Chatsworth*, London, Macmillan

Douglas, Mary and Baron Isherwood (1979), *The World of Goods: Towards an anthropology of consumption*, London, Allen Lane

Dubrow, Heather (1979), 'The country house poem: a study in generic development', *Genre* 12, 153–79

Duckworth, Alistair M. (1971), *The Improvement of the Estate: A study of Jane Austen's novels*, Baltimore, Johns Hopkins Press

Duckworth, Alistair M. (1975), 'Raymond Williams and literary history', *Papers in Language and Literature* 11, 420–41

Duckworth, Alistair M. (1981), 'Fiction and some uses of the country house setting from Richardson to Scott', in David C. Streatfield and Alistair Duckworth (eds), *Landscape in the Gardens and the Literature of Eighteenth-Century England*, Los Angeles, William Andrews Clark Memorial Library, 91–128

Duckworth, Alistair M. (1989), 'Gardens, houses, and the rhetoric of description in the English novel', in Jackson-Stops (1989), 395–413

Dunster, David (ed.) (1986), *Edwin Lutyens*, London, St Martins Press

Dutton, Ralph (1935), *The English Country House*, London, Batsford

Eagleton, Terry (1990), *The Ideology of the Aesthetic*, Oxford, Basil Blackwell

'Epistolary Description of the Late Mr Pope's House and Gardens at Twickenham, An,' (1747), reprinted in John Dixon Hunt and Peter Willis, eds, *The Genius of the Place: The English landscape garden 1620–1820*, London, Paul Elek, 1975, 247–53

Erskine-Hill, Howard (1975), *The Social Milieu of Alexander Pope*, New Haven, Yale University Press

Erskine-Hill, Howard (1979), 'Heirs of Vitruvius: Pope and the idea of architecture', in Howard Erskine-Hill and Anne Smith (eds), *The Art of Alexander Pope*, London, Vision Press, 144–56

Fabricant, Carole (1982), *Swift's Landscape*, Baltimore, Johns Hopkins University Press

Fabricant, Carole (1985), 'The aesthetics and politics of landscape in the eighteenth century', in Cohen (1985), 49–81

Foster, John Wilson (1970), 'A redefinition of topographical poetry', *Journal of English and Germanic Philology* 69, 394–406

Foucault, Michel (1970), *The Order of Things*, London, Tavistock (first published 1966)

Foucault, Michel (1972), *The Archaeology of Knowledge*, London, Tavistock (first published 1969), translated by A. M. Sheridan Smith

Fowler, Alastair (1973), 'The "better marks" of Jonson's "To Penshurst" ', *Review of English Studies* n.s. 24, 266–82

Fowler, Alastair (1975), *Conceitful Thought: The interpretation of English Renaissance poems*, Edinburgh, Edinburgh University Press

Fowler, Alastair (1986), 'Country house poems: the politics of a genre', *The Seventeenth Century* 1, 1–14

Frankl, Paul (1960), *The Gothic: Literary sources and interpretations through eight centuries*, Princeton, Princeton University Press, translated by Priscilla Silz

Franklin, Jill (1981), *The Gentleman's Country House and Its Plan 1835–1914*, London, Routledge and Kegan Paul

Freeman, James A. (1975), 'The roof was fretted gold', *Comparative Literature* 27, 254–66

Friedman, Alice T. (1989), *House and Household in Elizabethan England: Wollaton Hall and the Willoughby family*, Chicago, University of Chicago Press

Friedman, Donald M. (1970), *Marvell's Pastoral Art*, London, Routledge and Kegan Paul

Gibson, William A. (1971), 'Three principles of Renaissance architectural theory in Pope's *Epistle to Burlington*', *Studies in English Literature* 11, 487–505

Gill, Richard (1972), *Happy Rural Seat: The English country house and the literary imagination*, New Haven, Yale University Press

Girouard, Mark (1978), *Life in the English Country House*, New Haven, Yale University Press

Girouard, Mark (1979), *The Victorian Country House*, New Haven, Yale University Press (first published 1971)

Girouard, Mark (1981), *The Return to Camelot*, New Haven, Yale University Press

Girouard, Mark (1983), *Robert Smythson and the Elizabethan Country House*, New Haven, Yale University Press (first published 1967)

Goetsch, Paul (1983), 'Der Landsitz im Spätviktorianischen Roman', in Paul Geotsch (ed.), *Engliche Literatur zwischen Viktorianismus und Moderne*, Darmstadt, Wissenschaftliche Buchgesellschaft, 293–320

Goode, John (1971), 'William Morris and the dream of revolution', in Lucas (1971), 221–80

Gotch, J. A. (1909), *The Growth of the English House*, London, Batsford

Gradidge, Roderick (1980), *Dream Houses: The Edwardian ideal*, London, Constable

Green, David (1951), *Blenheim Palace*, London, Country Life

Greene, Thomas M. (1982), *The Light of Troy: Imitation and discovery in Renaissance poetry*, New Haven, Yale University Press

Guillen, Claudio (1971), *Literature as System*, Princeton, Princeton University Press

Harris, John (1979a), *The Artist and the Country House*, London, Sotheby's

Harris, John (1979b), *A Country House Index*, Isle of Wight, Pinhorns

Harris, John (1981), *The Palladians*, London, Trefoil Books

Harris, John (1985), *The Design of the English Country House 1620–1920*, London, Trefoil Books

Hart, Jeffrey (1963), 'Ben Jonson's good society', *Modern Age* 7, 61–68

Henry, Avril and Peter Dixon (1970), 'Pope and the architects: a note on the *Epistle to Burlington*, *English Studies* 51, 437–41

Hibbard, G. R. (1956), 'The country house poem of the seventeenth century', *Journal of the Warburg and Courtauld Institutes* 19, 159–74

Hill, Oliver and John Cornforth (1966), *English Country Houses: Caroline*, London, Country Life

Holloway, John (1953), *The Victorian Sage*, London, Macmillan

Holmes, Michael (1986), *The Country House Described*, Winchester, St Paul's Bibliographies

Howard, Maurice (1987), *The Early Tudor Country House: Architecture and politics 1490–1550*, London, George Philip

Hunt, John Dixon (1976), *The Figure in the Landscape*, Baltimore, Johns Hopkins University Press

Hunt, John Dixon (1978), *Andrew Marvell: His life and writings*, London, Paul Elek

Hunt, John Dixon (1984), 'Pope's Twickenham revisited', *Eighteenth Century Life* 8, 26–35

Hunt, John Dixon (1986), *Garden and Grove*, London, Dent

Hussey, Christopher (1955a), *English Country Houses: Early Georgian*, London, Country Life

Hussey, Christopher (1955b), *English Country Houses: Mid Georgian*, London Country Life

Hussey Christopher (1955c), *English Country Houses: Late Georgian*, London, Country Life

Hussey, Christopher (1967), *English Gardens and Landscapes 1700–1750*, London, Country Life

Jackson-Stops, Gervase (ed.) (1985), *The Treasure Houses of Britain*, Washington, DC, National Gallery of Art

Jackson-Stops, Gervase (ed.) (1989), *The Fashioning and Functioning of the British Country House*, Washington, DC, National Gallery of Art

Kelso, Ruth (1929), *The Doctrine of the English Gentleman in the Sixteenth Century*, Urbana, University of Illinois Press

Kenny, Virginia C. (1984), *The Country House Ethos in English Literature 1688–1750*, Hemel Hempstead, Harvester Wheatsheaf

Kerr, Robert (1864), *The Gentleman's House*, London, John Murray

Ketton-Cremer R. W. (1962), *Felbrigg: The story of a house*, London, The Boydell Press

Knights, L. C. (1937), *Drama and Society in the Age of Jonson*, London, Chatto and Windus

Lees-Milne, James (1962), *Earls of Creation*, London, Hamish Hamilton

Lees-Milne, James (1970), *English Country Houses: Baroque*, London, Country Life

Legouis, Pierre (1965), *Andrew Marvell: Poet, puritan, patriot*, Oxford, Clarendon Press

Levin, Harry (1969), *The Myth of the Golden Age in the Renaissance*, Bloomington, Indiana University Press

Lewalski, Barbara K. (1989), 'The lady of the country-house poem', in Jackson-Stops (1989), 261–74

Lloyd, Nathaniel (1975), *A History of the English House*, London, Architectural Press (first published 1931)

Lodge, David (1966), '*Tono-Bungay* and the condition of England', in *The Language of Fiction*, London, Routledge and Kegan Paul, 214–42

Lucas, John (ed.) (1971), *Literature and Politics in the Nineteenth Century*, London, Methuen

Lucy, Mary Elizabeth (1987), *Mistress of Charlecote: The Memoirs of Mary Elizabeth Lucy*, edited by Alice Fairfax-Lucy, London, Victor Gollancz

Macaulay, James (1975), *The Gothic Revival 1745–1845*, Glasgow, Blackie

McCarthy, Michael (1987), *The Origins of the Gothic Revival*, New Haven, Yale University Press

McClung, William Alexander (1977), *The Country House in English Renaissance Poetry*, Berkeley, University of California Press

McClung, William Alexander (1983), *The Architecture of Paradise: Survivals of Eden and Jerusalem*, Berkeley, University of California Press

McClung, William Alexander (1989), 'The country-house arcadia', in Jackson-Stops (1989), 277–87

McGuire, Mary Ann C. (1979), 'The cavalier country-house poem: mutations on a Jonsonian tradition', *Studies in English Literature* 19, 93–108

Mack, Maynard (1969), *The Garden and the City: Retirement and politics in the later poetry of Alexander Pope 1731–1743*, London, Oxford University Press

Maclean, Hugh (1964), 'Ben Jonson's poems: Notes on the ordered society', in Millar MacLure and F. W. Watt (eds) *Essays in English Literature from the Renaissance to the Victorian Age Presented to A. S. P. Woodhouse*, Toronto, University of Toronto Press, 43–68

McMaster, Juliet (1982), 'Trollope's country estates', in John Halperin (ed.), *Trollope Centenary Essays*, London, Macmillan, 70–85

Malins, Edward (1966), *English Landscaping and Literature 1660–1840*. London, Oxford University Press

Manuel, Frank E. and Fritzie P. (1979), *Utopian Thought in the Western World*, Oxford, Basil Blackwell

Martin, Peter (1984), *Pursuing Innocent Pleasures: The gardening world of Alexander Pope*, Hamden, Connecticut, Archon Books

Mercer, Eric (1954), 'The houses of the gentry', *Past and Present 5*, 11–32

Mercer, Eric (1962), *English Art, 1553–1625*, Oxford, Clarendon Press

Mingay, G. E. (1963), *English Landed Society in the Eighteenth Century*, London, Routledge and Kegan Paul

Mingay, G. E. (1976), *The Gentry: The rise and fall of a ruling class*, London, Longman

Mingay, G. E. (1977), *Rural Life in Victorian England*, London, Heinemann

Molesworth, Charles (1968), 'Property and virtue: the genre of the country-house poem in the seventeenth century', *Genre* 1, 141–57

Molesworth, Charles (1971), ' "To Penshurst" and Jonson's Historical Imagination', *Clio* 1, 5–13

Molesworth, Charles (1973), 'Marvell's "Upon Appleton House": the persona as historian, philosopher, and priest', *Studies in English Literature* 13, 149–62

Mowl, Tim and Brian Earnshaw (1985), *Trumpet at a Distant Gate: The Lodge as prelude to the country house*, London, Waterstone

Mumford, Lewis (1922), *The Story of Utopias*, New York, Boni and Liveright

Muthesius, Hermann (1979), *The English House*, translated by Janet Seligman, London, Crosby Lockwood Staples (first published 1904/5)

Norbrook, David (1984), *Poetry and Politics in the English Renaissance*, London, Routledge and Kegan Paul

Palladio, Andrea (1738), *The Four Books of Architecture*, translated by Isaac Ware, London (first published 1570)

Paulson, Ronald (1975), *Emblem and Expression: Meaning in English art of the eighteenth century*, London, Thames and Hudson

Peterson, Richard S. (1981), *Imitation and Praise in the Poems of Ben Jonson*, New Haven, Yale University Press

Pevsner, Nikolaus (1951–), *The Buildings of England*, Harmondsworth, Penguin Books

Pevsner, Nikolaus (1960), *The Planning of the Elizabethan Country House*, London, Birkbeck College

Pevsner, Nikolaus (1968), 'The architectural setting of Jane Austen's novels', *Journal of the Warburg and Courtauld Institutes* 31, 404–22

Pinto, John (1980), 'The landscape of allusion: literary theory in the gardens of classical Rome and Augustan England', *Smith College Studies in History* 48, 97–113

Pocock, J. G. A. (1975), *The Machiavellian Moment: Florentine political thought and the Atlantic republican tradition*, Princeton, Princeton University Press

Pocock, J. G. A. (1985), *Virtue, Commerce, and History*, Cambridge, Cambridge University Press

Pugh, Simon (1988) *Garden–Nature–Language*, Manchester, Manchester University Press

Radcliffe, David Hill (1990), 'Genre and social order in country house poems of the eighteenth century: four views of Percy Lodge', *Studies in English Literature* 30, 445–65

Rathmell, J. C. A. (1971), 'Jonson, Lord Lisle, and Penhurst', *English Literary Renaissance* 1, 250–60

Rivers, Isabel (1973), *The Poetry of Conservatism, 1600–1745*, Cambridge, Rivers Press

Robinson, John Martin (1984), *The Latest Country Houses*, London, The Bodley Head

Robinson, John Martin (1988), *The English Country Estate*, London, Century

Roestvig, Maren Sofie (1954), *The Happy Man*, Oslo, Akademisk forlag

Rupprecht, Bernhard (1966), 'Villa: Zur Geschichte eines Ideals', in *Wandlungen des Paradiesischen und Utopischen: Studien zum Bild Eines Ideals*, Berlin, Walter de Gruyter, 210–50

Rykwert, Joseph (1972), *On Adam's House in Paradise: The idea of the primitive hut in architectural history*, New York, Museum of Modern Art

Sackville-West, Victoria (1922), *Knole and the Sackvilles*, London, Heinemann

Sackville-West, Victoria (1941), *English Country Houses*, London, Collins

Sambrook, A. J. (1967), 'The English lord and the happy husbandman', *Studies in Voltaire and the 18th Century* 57, 1357–75

Sambrook, A. J. (1972), 'Pope and the visual arts', in Peter Dixon (ed.), *Alexander Pope*, London, Bell, 143–71

Sekora, John (1977), *Luxury: The concept in western thought, Eden to Smollett*, Baltimore, Johns Hopkins University Press

Smith, Charles Saumarez (1990), *The Building of Castle Howard*, London, Faber and Faber

Smith, Warren Hunting (1934), *Architecture in English Fiction*, New Haven, Yale University Press

Solkin, David H. (1982), *Richard Wilson: The landscape of reaction*, London, The Tate Gallery

Sombart, Werner (1967), *Luxury and Capitalism*, Ann Arbor, Michigan University Press, translated by W. R. Dittmar (originally published 1912)

Southall, Raymond (1973), *Literature and the Rise of Capitalism: Critical essays mainly on the sixteenth and sevententh centuries*, London, Lawrence and Wishart

Spring, David (1963), *The English Landed Estate in the Nineteenth century*, Baltimore, Johns Hopkins University Press

Spring, David (1962/3), 'Aristocracy, social structure, and religion in the early Victorian period', *Victorian Studies* 6, 263–80

Spring, David (1983), 'Interpreters of Jane Austen's social world: literary critics and historians', in Janet Todd (ed.) *Jane Austen: New Perspectives*, New York, Holmes and Meier, 53–72

Stone, Lawrence (1965a), *Social Change and Revolution in England 1540–1640*, London, Longman

Stone, Lawrence (1965b), *The Crisis of the Aristocracy, 1558–1641*, Oxford, Clarendon Press

Stone Lawrence (1973), *Family and Fortune: Studies in aristocratic finance in the sixteenth and seventeenth centuries*, Oxford, Clarendon Press

Stone, Lawrence (1977), *The Family, Sex and Marriage in England 1500–1800*, London, Weidenfeld and Nicolson

Stone, Lawrence and J. C. F. Stone (1984), *An Open Elite? England 1540–1880*, Oxford, Clarendon Press

Summerson, Sir John (1948), 'The London surburban villa', *Architectural Review* 104, 63–72

Summerson, Sir John (1959), 'The classical country house in 18th–century England', *Journal of the Royal Society of Arts* 107, 539–87

Summerson, Sir John (1965), *Architecture in Britain 1530–1830*, Harmondsworth, Penguin Books (first published 1953)

Summerson, Sir John (1966), *Inigo Jones*, Harmondsworth, Penguin Books

Thomas, Keith (1983), *Man and the Natural World: Changing attitudes in England 1500–1800*, London, Allen Lane

Thomas P. W. (1973), 'Two cultures? Court and country under Charles ɪ', in Conrad Russell (ed.) *The Origins of the English Civil War*, London, Macmillan, 168–93

Thompson, F. M. L. (1963), *English Landed Society in the Nineteenth Century*, London, Routledge and Kegan Paul

Thompson, Francis William (1949), *A History of Chatsworth*, London, Country Life

Tipping, H. Avray (1920–36), *English Homes*, London, Country Life

Tolliver, Harold (1985), ' "Householding and the poet's vocation": Jonson and after', *English Studies* 66, 113–22

Turner, James (1979), *The Politics of Landscape: Rural scenery and society in English poetry 1630–1660*, Oxford, Basil Blackwell

Veblen, Thorstein Bunde (1899), *The Theory of the Leisure Class*, New York, Macmillan

Wallace, John M. (1968), *Destiny His Choice: The loyalism of Andrew Marvell*, Cambridge, Cambridge University Press

Watkin, David (1982), *The English Vision: The picturesque in architecture, landscape and garden design*, London, John Murray

Wayne, Don E. (1984), *Penshurst: The semiotics of place and the poetics of history*, Wisconsin, Wisconsin University Press/London, Methuen

Weaver, Lawrence (1913), *Houses and Gardens by E. L. Lutyens*, London, Country Life

Whinney, Margaret and Oliver Millar (1957), *English Art 1625–1714*, Oxford, Clarendon Press

Whistler, Lawrence, *et al.* (1968), *Stowe: A guide to the gardens*, Buckingham, printed by E. N. Hillier and Sons

Wiebenson, Dora (1985), 'Documents of social change: publications about the small house', in Cohen (1985), 82–127

Williams, Raymond (1973), *The Country and the City*, London, Chatto and Windus

Wilson Knight, G. (1945), *The Dynasty of Stowe*, London, The Fortune Press

Wittkower, Rudolf (1971), *Architectural Principles in the Age of Humanism*, New York, Norton (first published 1949)

Wittkower, Rudolf (1974), *Palladio and English Palladianism*, London, Thames and Hudson

Index